LIVABLE COMMUNITIES FOR AGING POPULATIONS

LIVABLE COMMUNITIES FOR AGING POPULATIONS

Urban Design for Longevity

M. Scott Ball

WILEY

JOHN WILEY & SONS, INC.

This book is dedicated to Milner Shivers Ball, June McCoy Ball, Jill Marie Lawler, and William Thomas Lawler and to the strength, grace, and dignity with which they have led their lives.

This book is printed on acid-free paper.♾

Copyright © 2012 by M. Scott Ball. All rights reserved.

Unless otherwise noted all images are Copyright © 2012 by Milner Scott Ball and Duany Plater-Zyberk & Company

Published by John Wiley & Sons, Inc., Hoboken, New Jersey.

Published simultaneously in Canada.

No part of this publication may be reproduced, stored in a retrieval system, or transmitted in any form or by any means, electronic, mechanical, photocopying, recording, scanning, or otherwise, except as permitted under Section 107 or 108 of the 1976 United States Copyright Act, without either the prior written permission of the Publisher, or authorization through payment of the appropriate per-copy fee to the Copyright Clearance Center, 222 Rosewood Drive, Danvers, MA 01923, (978) 750-8400, fax (978) 646-8600, or on the web at www.copyright.com. Requests to the Publisher for permission should be addressed to the Permissions Department, John Wiley & Sons, Inc., 111 River Street, Hoboken, NJ 07030, (201) 748-6011, fax (201) 748-6008, or online at www.wiley.com/go/permissions.

Limit of Liability/Disclaimer of Warranty: While the publisher and author have used their best efforts in preparing this book, they make no representations or warranties with the respect to the accuracy or completeness of the contents of this book and specifically disclaim any implied warranties of merchantability or fitness for a particular purpose. No warranty may be created or extended by sales representatives or written sales materials. The advice and strategies contained herein may not be suitable for your situation. You should consult with a professional where appropriate. Neither the publisher nor the author shall be liable for damages arising herefrom.

For general information about our other products and services, please contact our Customer Care Department within the United States at (800) 762-2974, outside the United States at (317) 572-3993 or fax (317) 572-4002.

Wiley publishes in a variety of print and electronic formats and by print-on-demand. Some material included with standard print versions of this book may not be included in e-books or in print-on-demand. If this book refers to media such as a CD or DVD that is not included in the version you purchased, you may download this material at http://booksupport.wiley.com. For more information about Wiley products, visit www.wiley.com.

Library of Congress Cataloging-in-Publication Data:

Ball, M. Scott.
   Livable communities for aging populations: urban design for longevity / M. Scott Ball.
      p.   cm.
   Includes index.
   ISBN 978-0-470-64192-7 (cloth); ISBN 978-1-118-19726-4 (ebk); ISBN 978-1-118-19727-1 (ebk); ISBN 978-1-118-19728-8 (ebk); ISBN 978-1-118-18104-1 (ebk); ISBN 978-1-118-18176-8 (ebk)
      1. Retirement communities.   2. Older people—Housing.   3. Older people—Dwellings. 4. City planning.   5. Community development.   I. Title.
   HQ1063.B34 2012
   307.3'370846—dc23
                                                                                      2011033590

Printed in the United States of America

10 9 8 7 6 5 4 3 2 1

CONTENTS

PART III

SENIORS HOUSING   125

FOREWORD

Urbanism is a uniquely sympathetic framework for addressing needs that will arise over the horizon. In this, urbanism is often misunderstood. Because cities are large, it is commonly thought that urbanism is like architecture, only bigger. This is not so. What makes urbanism a completely different field of activity from architecture is the element of *time*. An architect must complete a building within, say, two to five years; the design is constrained by the realities of the near future. Urbanism, on the other hand, operates over the very long term. To give an illustration: our firm is completing its very first new town—and it is thirty years since it was designed. Indeed, what makes urbanism so challenging, but also so promising, to those who practice it is that we must think into the future as in no other endeavor. Most businesses must deliver the goods within a week or a fortnight. Most businesses work within the time frame of the next payroll, or the quarterly or yearly report. Scott and his colleagues are usually thinking ten, twenty, and thirty years out, making plans now that will prepare us for the future. And so when he writes a book about the aging of America the reader must undergo a translation into the fourth dimension—that of time. It is not about now—it is about things to come, both good and bad, and the preparations we need to make today.

This book is timely because it is just now possible to discern the outlines of the twenty-first century. The centuries don't really turn over at the double zero. The twentieth century, for example, did not begin until the First World War, which is to say, its second decade. The first decade of that century was an extension of the nineteenth century. The nineteenth century itself did not begin until Napoleon had been defeated at Waterloo and the new and more peaceful order had been set up by the Congress of Vienna. Few before 1815 could have predicted whether Europe would consist of many nations or just a French empire.

Take our current situation. The first eight or so years of this century were a seamless extension of the twentieth and then on or about 2008 everything changed. There came a series of overlaid crises that unsettled certainties and awoke us to a scenario very unlike that which we had known. The crises consisted of (1) the real estate bubble; (2) the increases in the cost of petroleum; and (3) the consciousness of climate change. Their convergence has convinced us that we are not the nation of infinite wealth that we thought we were. And so here we are in 2012, a nation that is publicly and privately less confident about its future than we were one hundred years ago.

Now, for the good news: the twentieth century has endowed humans with more life than we have ever enjoyed before. We live nearly twice as long now on average than we did at the turn of the twentieth century. The effects of increased longevity will peak when the baby boom generation is fully in its retirement years, from 2015 to 2045. But it is not just a boomer phenomenon: the graying of the population is a permanent new reality that will be with us for as long as we continue to provide modern healthcare. This book offers opportunities to improve our standard of living as we age while simultaneously mitigating the challenges that confront us. It points to the easiest and perhaps most effective avenue for social, environmental, and economic activism ever offered to a generation. All of these crises insofar as they affect the American people can be ameliorated by what John Norquist calls "the convenient solution to the inconvenient truth." The kinds of communities that are described in this book—the ones that are walkable, compact, complete, and convivial—mitigate all of these crises while supporting us better as we age. By walking to satisfy their ordinary daily needs, residents use less petroleum and produce less carbon. They live more affordably without incurring the cost of automobile dependency. They will also be healthier and more able to sustain a social life in their community, and they will forestall or entirely avoid the extraordinary costs associated with specialized "seniors" housing.

Society will be returning to an earlier time when we were poorer but, perhaps because of that, smarter. The good, old-time, diverse, walkable community will allow an aging population to thrive, offering more dignity, mobility, and independence at lower cost for housing, with less need for petroleum, and with less environmental impact, as compared with the socially isolating development patterns of suburban sprawl. These communities will be attractive enough that our children and our children's children will be happy to visit and indeed to live among us.

The ultimate result of the intersection of increased longevity with these three major crises is that we are actually returning to the times and places in which life was simpler but more pleasurable, where things made more sense. I am personally looking forward to the great rearrangement that began in 2008—I think it will have brought us to our senses. This book offers the opportunity to prepare for our successful aging in a manner that creatively and ethically engages the major challenges that confront us.

Andrés Duany

INTRODUCTION

We know that Americans 65 and over like where they live, with nine out of ten saying they want to stay in their current home as long as possible. This is good. It means that people have invested heavily in the communities in which they live. Remaining at home continues to be the preference of eight out of ten people 65 and older even if they believe they will need help caring for themselves. And there is a good chance they will need help. Despite declining disability rates, 68 percent of people past the age of 65 will need assistance with two or more activities of daily living or a cognitive impairment at some time.

This need for assistance can either be minimized or amplified by the communities in which we live. Simple things such as unsafe or unwelcoming sidewalks, traffic problems, and lack of accessible public transportation can unintentionally double the risk of functional loss for older people. And doubling this risk increases the likelihood that they will not be able to remain in the community or that their quality of life will be degraded. In fact, the loss of mobility and related independence is what older people say they fear most.

Unfortunately, many of the predominant planning principles of the past half century are now widely acknowledged to have created unintentional barriers to people remaining in their home or community as they age. These barriers limit pedestrian and vechicular mobility for older people, prohibit needed housing and care options, and complicate service delivery and public transportation due to enforced low-densities. These barriers lead to significant induced disability and substantial personal and governmental costs as we try to overcome them with additional programs.

The good news is that through the thoughtful observation and creativity of planners, services providers, advocates for the aging, researchers, and policy makers over the last twenty years, there are new approaches and best practices that can help new and existing communities evolve to support the needs and preferences of their aging residents. While successful approaches will require time and a myriad of planning and physical modifications, elements can be implemented incrementally that will have impact immediately.

So with the population age 65 and older on track to increase from 40.2 million in 2010 to 72.1 in 2030, Scott Ball's *Livable Communities for Aging Populations* could not come at a better time. Scott's work offers a compendium of lessons drawn from our collective successes and failures as well as his and many others' creative solutions. Its significant contribution is to assemble these lessons and insights into a coherent framework for communities and leaders to use in analyzing their needs, selecting successful approaches, setting priorities, and beginning the work.

Robert Jenkens
Director, The Green House Project
Managing Director, NCB Capital Impact

PREFACE

West Hagert Street in Philadelphia is gifted with urbanism. The street is lined with old row houses—two stories high and pulled up close to the broad sidewalks and street. Stoops and porches present attractive spots for passing time. Still living in these row houses is a group of women who have worked for decades building the West Hagert Street community. The women have, without exception, outlived their husbands. Some have outlived a series of husbands. All are now over eighty and they occupy these homes alone. Every morning after the women awake they go downstairs, open their front doors with storm doors still closed, and leave them open for most of the morning. The open doors are a way of signaling that the women have made it through another night and everything is okay. Each watches for these signals from the others.

The open doors are a small gesture that reflects the uncommon strength of the community on West Hagert Street. Through years of worshiping, singing in the choir, working on each other's gardens, cooking for the needy, organizing, and running voter registration drives, the women of West Hagert Street have developed a collective identity and sense of interconnection. They have also developed a sense of defiance. The doors issue a challenge: Bring on old age, deteriorating health, economic fluctuations, disinvestment, ailing spouses, good times, bad times, whatever—the door is open and they are ready for it.

Many characteristics of the four-block long West Hagert Street community make the open door gesture possible. The street is safe enough to leave a door open. People are around and close enough see the signal. People care enough to look for the signal. Help is near enough to respond if the signal doesn't come. The houses are not falling down. There are parks and stores nearby enough to create foot traffic and populate a street life. Transit connects the neighborhood to the larger surrounding city so that it does not feel isolated. The space of the street is intimate and well defined. Three-car garages do not obscure the front doors. The homes are not divided by large tracks of front yard. The street is open and airy enough to make one want to leave the door open in the first place. A very simple gesture reveals much about the quality of urbanism available on West Hagert Street and the dignity with which aging can be supported there.

Livable Communities for Aging Populations takes cues from places like West Hagert Street and begins with the premise that neighborhood places can provide a wealth and diversity of supports for the entire life cycle. This book provides a lens through which aging concerns can be reinvented as integral aspects of urbanism. It is for policy makers, developers, planners, health professionals, and advocates for the aging who seek to expand health and wellness opportunities for older adults across the common spaces of traditional urban neighborhoods. Livable Communities for an Aging Population:

- covers how healthcare can be repositioned as a lifelong, continuous function of urban environments that integrated into daily life and provide services along a seamless continuum, ranging from wellness to acute care;

- builds the argument that many lifelong services can be delivered in neighborhood environments more effectively and cost efficiently than those delivered in clinical settings;

- details critical political and economic leverage points where these types of changes can be best affected;

- provides innovative tools and references some of the best practices in lifelong neighborhood development; and

- details how the best practice achievements can be replicated along a contextual range of urban to rural to provide healthy neighborhoods of choice.

Organization of This Book

Part I lays out the challenge that increased longevity poses for the built environment. Chapter 1 introduces the challenge, the most strategic scale of response, and the role that planners and seniors housing developers can play in responding. Chapters 2, 3, and 4 touch on some emerging policy and implementation leverage points at which broad changes might be effected in the way we relate healthcare to the built environment. Chapter 2 reviews the positioning of accessibility in regulatory structures. With increased longevity, the majority of Americans will experience an extended period of disability at some point in their lives. Disability has become a majority concern and it now makes sense to base accessibility regulation on general consumer protection, which is focused on the entire population, rather than the protection of a minority class's civil rights. Chapter 2 lays out a framework for approaching disability as a population-wide, urban, lifelong concern rather than an individual, minority condition.

Chapter 3 reviews the positioning of health in regulatory structures. Public health professionals have introduced the "ecologic framework" as a collaborative, multifaceted mode of inquiry and operation, and this framework could also be utilized to structure interdisciplinary coordination between health and planning professions. Coordination and cooperation between real estate developers and community service agencies could be an effective implementation strategy capable of cross leveraging efforts and making the most efficient use of limited resources. In order to pursue these types of interdisciplinary strategies, challenges will first need to be overcome on multiple fronts: from differences in institutional culture to the ways in which these professions are positioned in government and industry organizational structures. The goal of creating lifelong neighborhoods can serve as a coordinating theme that helps us overcome these differences in institutional culture and separation in governmental structures.

Chapter 4 reviews market trends in the health and wellness industry. Americans have sought in recent decades to integrate health supports, fitness opportunities, and wellness routines into our daily lives, and we have most frequently done so through regionally scaled, big box, and campus opportunities. The neighborhood gym has been displaced by the regional fitness and recreation campus facility, the retirement home has morphed into the retirement community, and the nursing home has swelled to near-hospital proportions. Medical attention is primarily provided on sprawling hospital campuses or in nearby satellite clinics. As healthy environments result from a careful balance of regional and neighborhood concerns, the wholesale movement of health and wellness industries to regional models of service delivery has had the effect of divorcing health concerns from environmental considerations and even contributing to the further degradation of our environment.

Part II examines some of the street and building relationships that must be in place in order for lifelong neighborhoods to gain footings and flourish. While the main focus of this book concerns healthy environments at neighborhood scales (half- and quarter-mile distances that can be easily covered in five- or ten-minute walks), many transportation and land-use policies need to align at the regional scale in order for healthy urbanism to emerge at this local scale. Chapter 5 reviews connectivity and access as prerequisite conditions for lifelong neighborhoods to emerge. Good connectivity and access ensure that a neighborhood can tap into critical regional forces without being overwhelmed by them. Chapter 6 reviews building diversity within the neighborhood as another prerequisite issue. Lifelong neighborhoods must accommodate a wide variety of building types and uses in order to make daily needs and routines more accessible and more socially integrated. The ideal urban structure for a lifelong neighborhood is locally complete but regionally connected.

Part III examines the role of senior housing in supporting lifelong neighborhoods. Chapter 7 reviews the evolution of seniors housing to help provide a context for its building types and culture and to reframe them as community-based medical institutions rather than institutionally based residential communities. Chapter 8 reviews the complex financing structures of seniors housing that integrate healthcare, support services, and real estate industries. Both the complexity and value of these financing systems should not be underestimated. Even so, seniors-housing financing cannot simply rest on the predictable economies of mass industrial repetition of single use, single demographic, and single trend building types. Though the market for these repetitious forms is predictable, it is becoming predictably weaker as the resulting urban fabric fails to provide the complex urbanism that the market is now demanding. Market analysis has evolved over the past few decades, and whereas once it was used solely to judge the feasibility of a proposed project, today it is often used to proactively gauge markets and shape a project to reach them. Chapter 8 reviews market-study techniques that can help nudge the industry toward applying the existing seniors housing financing, development, and service systems in a manner that does not lead to specialized and segregated development responses. The end goal is not to dismantle the seniors housing industry, but rather to open it up and expand it. The integrated systems and expertise maintained by the seniors housing industry are too valuable and too hard won to ever replace or abandon wholesale. Chapter 9 goes on to lay out the individual building types and building components typical of seniors housing developments. The types are laid out as modular elements that can be integrated into a neighborhood rather than drawn together into a complete, autonomous facility. Along with these modules, a suite of policies and services typically utilized by community service agencies to support older adults in the community is provided. The integration of community services and housing development components can be an effective means of opening up and extending the seniors housing model to whole communities.

Part IV surveys some of the most progressive examples of lifelong care integrated into the built environment. The first two examples, the dense urban neighborhoods of Penn South in New York City and Beacon Hill in Boston, are reviewed because of the notoriety they have gained for advancing cooperative living models: the Naturally Occurring Retirement Community (NORC) and Villages models, respectively. Both of these best practices have been the subject of large-scale replication efforts, but in each case the efforts have attempted to replicate only the organizational models without much consideration for the role of the built environment context from which they arose. Part IV reviews some of the organizing principles and achievements alongside a discussion of their urban contexts. Older adult led community efforts in Mableton and Indiana are reviewed as prospective efforts to influence both urban form and service delivery in a combined manner. These are both community-planning efforts and are just beginning to generate results. All four best practices reviewed will cover issues of built forms, business models, and policy frameworks that have enabled achievements.

Longevity concerns and opportunities manifest themselves differently in various urban contexts. The best practices are selected to cover a range of urban-to-rural contexts. The longevity possibilities inherent to these different contexts primarily result from the different market catchments each context provides: Urban centers have sufficient density and consolidated purchasing power to demand a wide range of home- and community-based support options based on the immediately surrounding market alone; town centers can often serve the immediate community better by drawing from the larger region; and neighborhood centers can incrementally and organically "grow" their own services through cooperative organizations and satellite facilities developed in partnership with their regional service providers.

ACKNOWLEDGMENTS

I must thank first my wife Kathryn Lawler, in appreciation of our lifelong collaboration on this topic, as well as our children Eleanor and Milner in appreciation for their good humor and long-suffering in the face of my time at the computer preparing the manuscript for the book.

This book has been a group effort with significant contributions from Glen Tipton, Duncan Walker, Jessica Wolfe, Susan Brecht, and Kathryn Lawler—all of whom have been uncommonly generous with their time and support. The Congress of New Urbanism (CNU) and Heather Smith in particular have provided many opportunities for members of the book team to make presentations on the subjects covered in this book, test our ideas, and get feedback. Thank you also to Robert Jenkens, John Sanford, and Edward Steinfeld, who have provided thoughtful advice, and Dodd Kattman and Zachary Benedict for their chapter and example of the Elder-Centric Villages work.

Anyone who writes about urbanism is indebted to the work of many others. I am particularly indebted to three groups of colleagues that have helped form my understanding of the subject: members of the Community Housing Resource Center, especially Kate Grace and Mtamanika Youngblood, for their leadership on issues of aging in community; the Atlanta Regional Commission's Division on Aging, especially Cheryl Schramm and Cathie Berger, for involving me in Aging Atlanta and other pursuits; and Duany Plater-Zyberk & Company, particularly Elizabeth Plater-Zyberk and Andrés Duany for providing many learning experiences, professional space, encouragement, and the example of their constant daring.

While many more deserve to be thanked for their contributions, I would like to specifically mention: Paul Knight, Saji Girvan, Sarah Ball-Damberg, Phillip Stafford, Larry Frank, David Goldberg, Jeff Rader, Ellen Dunham Jones, Jane Hickie, Henry Cisneros, Nancy McPherson, William "Buck" Baker, Paul Wisner and Eve Byrd for helping to formulate ideas, images, and sentences. And last but not least, thank you to the team at John Wiley & Sons, particularly to John Czarnecki, for pushing me to take on this project and then to see it to completion.

PART I

CHALLENGES AND OPPORTUNITIES

THE CHALLENGES PRESENTED BY INCREASED LONGEVITY AND INCREASED percentages of older adults did not spring up all at once—they are issues we have chosen to neglect as they have steadily crept up over decades. Though the issues had been framed many times before, Jerome L. Kaufman's 1961 report "Planning and an Aging Population" is a particularly eloquent and direct assessment of these challenges. In the introduction of his report, Kaufman states:

> Planning for all age groups is an inviolable principle; in practice, however, planners have been unduly preoccupied with certain age groups. Like the post-war housing boom, the approach to community development and planning has been child- or family-centered. Most significant advances in school and recreation planning, in subdivision design, and even in neighborhood planning, sprang originally from a conception of the needs of the young family with children. . . .
>
> The impact of this pronounced shift in age composition on community services, on urban form and on economic activity is beginning to be realized. For the community planner, sooner or later, it will necessitate some reshuffling—discarding some outmoded theories, recasting some tenuous theories, and originating some new theories.[1]

Sun City Peachtree, a 1,726-acre senior community, currently under construction 35 miles south of Atlanta, Georgia.

Kaufman goes on to call out some of the specific issues that will need to "sooner or later" be reconsidered:

> Traditionally, planners relegated older persons to a few cursory sentences in the comprehensive plan report; the number and possibly percent of older persons was mentioned, but rarely did subsequent proposals and plans reflect this analysis. Only now is there evidence that the elderly are coming in for more searching appraisal.
>
> Many questions are being asked—some simple, some complex—to which planners can help find answers. What qualities of a community make it more livable for

---

[1] J. L. Kaufman, "Planning and an Aging Population," *Information Report No. 148* (Chicago, IL: American Society of Planning Officials, July 1961).

older persons? Should a dispersal or concentration of older citizens be encouraged? Given their diverse backgrounds and characteristics, what kinds of housing and community service accommodations do older people need? Where should housing for the elderly be located? To what extent should urban renewal account for older persons? Should zoning and subdivision control regulations be modified to accommodate housing developments for the elderly? Should local policy encourage the building of special housing units for the elderly or increase their economic capacity to compete for housing in the open market? What impact will an increasing number of older persons have on the local economy, the transportation system?[2]

In the fifty years since Kaufman asked these questions, seniors have achieved little advancement in comprehensive development planning, and most efforts at environmental planning for older adults have focused on specialized age-segregated retirement and care communities. Over the next fifty years and beyond, these measures will not be sufficient to accommodate older adults without enormous expense and/or neglect; hence, Kaufman's questions must be raised again.

Part I reviews some of the critical contexts in which answers to these questions will need to be formulated. Accessibility laws did not exist in 1961, but today the basic regulatory structure for accessibility is in place and if repositioned strategically, it could provide a means of addressing critical upgrades to the general built environment. The healthcare system has grown exponentially since 1961, but it has done so with little relationship to the neighborhoods in which most of us will age. A robust wellness and fitness industry has grown since 1961 and has branched out into niche services, including many valuable supports for older adults. Accessibility regulations, healthcare systems, and wellness industries have provided new opportunities to once again raise Kaufman's questions. Part I provides frameworks for structuring responses with these relatively recent opportunities.

---

[2] Kaufman, "Planning," 1.

THE LONGEVITY CHALLENGE TO URBANISM

CHAPTER 1

With contributions from Susan Brecht,
Kathryn M. Lawler, and Glen A. Tipton

The Challenge

Longevity was the great gift of the twentieth century. Learning what to do with this gift is the great challenge of the twenty-first century.

Americans born in 1900 would not have been able to drive a car, ride in an airplane, see a motion picture, work a crossword puzzle, use a washing machine, or talk on the phone. But they could do all of this and more by the time they were 30. Within the next forty years, they would have witnessed the construction of the interstate highway system, experienced the great suburban expansion, and even watched the first man walk, and then drive, on the moon. Cross-country and international travel, unheard of at the turn of the century, would have become a regular and frequent experience for thousands by the end of the century.

The tremendous creativity and innovation of the twentieth century changed the lives of individuals and families, radically redefining how we live in our neighborhoods, cities, and counties and how we carve out a role in an increasingly international economy and culture. Consider that Americans born before 1900 were far more likely to live just like those living in the two or three prior centuries—heating their homes by fire, growing almost all of their own food, walking or riding a horse for transportation, and communicating via postal mail at best. The incredible advancements of the twentieth century were not only numerous, they occurred at an almost incomprehensible pace. What is remarkable is that one of the most significant advances—longevity—went largely unnoticed and unaccounted for.

As with generations that came before them, most Americans born in 1900 would have lived on the same street as their parents and maybe even their entire extended families. But it's also just as likely that their children and grandchildren would live hundreds of miles away. Twentieth-century progress spread families and neighborhoods across much larger geographic areas than had ever been previously feasible. As homes dispersed across the landscape, public transit disappeared and the interstate highway system facilitated suburban sprawl, with its relatively uniform housing stock, reduced walkability, and lack of transportation choices, families and communities changed to fit their new environments. The attenuation of settlement patterns and social networks challenged urbanism: the spatial and cultural phenomena of place.

Now that the first suburbanites are aging, it's becoming quite clear that the twentieth-century progress that allowed us to spread out, live in larger homes with larger yards, and drive our cars to work, shop, and play cannot accommodate the brand new, and without precedent, experience of living much longer. Suddenly, communities that were sold as a healthy refuge for families from the polluted and congested neighborhoods of the city are unable to support anyone who can't take care of their home and yard and drive their own car. Without sidewalks, trails, and, most importantly, destinations, these suburban neighborhoods make it difficult to maintain health and remain free of chronic disease. It's now very clear that suburbia was built while science and medicine were making it possible to live longer. But the designers, planners, architects, and financiers who made suburban living possible, along with the suburbanites themselves, invested billions of dollars without ever considering that the residents would grow and stay old much longer than ever before.

The gift of longevity very well may be the catalyst that returns Americans to a full appreciation of the urbanism we once had and can have again. We grow more reliant on close proximities in both physical and social relationships as we advance in age. "Urbanism" refers to close relationships in both respects: the compactly built environment and the collective sense of identity that such an environment fosters. Closeness is the operative condition of both the physical and social structures of urbanism. Until a movement is launched to shorten the lifespan or to halt the scientific and medical progress that is almost exclusively focused on extending life even further, communities will be forced to look back at how we used to live together—in urban environments—to ensure that longevity is a gift we are truly equipped to receive.

Demographic Revolution

For the first time ever, the older adult population will match in size the youngest populations on the planet. The traditional population pyramid will morph to a population rectangle (fig. 1.1). In the entire time human beings have populated the

Figure 1.1

Expanding Aging US Population. Information from "Aging and Cancer Research: Workshop Report"; National Institute of Health and National Institute of Aging, June 2001.[1]

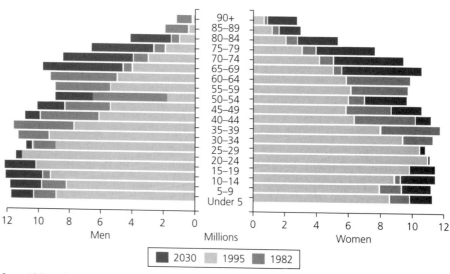

Source: US Census Bureau, Population Projections of the United States by Age, Race, and Hispanic Origin 1993–2050, P25-1104, 1993

[1]National Institute of Health and National Institute of Aging (NIH/NIA), *Aging and Cancer Research: Workshop Report* (June 2001).

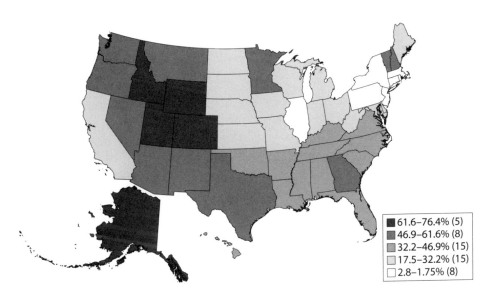

Figure 1.2
Percentage growth in elderly populations, 2000–2015.

61.6–76.4% (5)
46.9–61.6% (8)
32.2–46.9% (15)
17.5–32.2% (15)
2.8–1.75% (8)

earth, this has never before happened. Communities have always been organized around a very young population, with the highest percentage of individuals being between zero and five years of age. Even as life expectancy grew, and people were more likely to survive childhood illnesses and live into adulthood, the relationship between the young and the old remained almost the same as it had always been. It was only when the increase in the older adult population began to outpace the growth in the youngest populations that the transformation began. With decreasing birth rates and increased longevity, this trend will continue well into the twenty-first century. While most people have become increasingly aware of this unprecedented demographic shift, the basic statistics are worth a review (fig. 1.2).

■ By 2030, the United States will be home to approximately 71 million people over the age of 65, making one out of every five US residents an older adult.[2]

■ The growth in the older adult population is driven by both the aging of the baby boomer generation and increased life expectancy. As a result, there will be a larger number of both older adults and old-older adults (those over the age of 85) than ever before.

■ Of the approximately 71 million people over the age of 65 in 2030, 5 million will be over the age of 85, and still only a small number will be over the age of 100. In ten years (by 2040) however, it's estimated that 12 million people will be between the ages of 85 and 99, and 1 million people will be over the age of 100 (fig. 1.3).[3]

■ The dependency ratio—the proportion of working-age populations (ages 15 to 64) compared to nonworking-age populations (ages 0 to 15 and ages greater

[2]Centers for Disease Control, *The State of Aging and Health in America* (2007).

[3]www.cenus.gov

Figure 1.3

US Population Aging 65 Years and Older: 1990 to 2050. Information from "Aging and Cancer Research: Workshop Report"; National Institute of Health and National Institute of Aging, June 2001.[4]

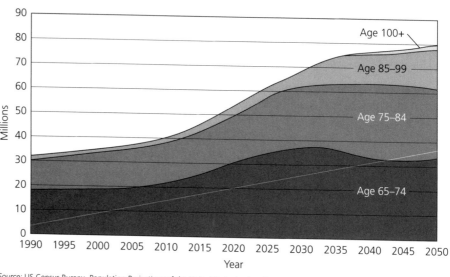

Source: US Census Bureau, Population Projections of the United States by Age, Race, and Hispanic Origin 1993–2050, P25-1104, 1993

than 64)—will also experience a record high, as fewer working people are available to support those who do not work. This means that there will be more people demanding services and less people available to deliver these services. Companies across the globe are working to understand and prepare for how this will impact their labor force. For example, 60 percent of all nonseasonal federal employees will be eligible for retirement by 2016.[5]

■ Current debates about deficit reduction highlight how the magnitude of this population dramatically affects both revenues and spending in the United States. Social Security was created when there were twelve workers for every one beneficiary and when average life expectancy was about 62. But by 2050, there will be two workers supporting each beneficiary. This program wasn't designed to support a population of people likely to live well into their 80s and 90s; therefore, we will continue to debate how to restructure it to meet the broad and growing needs coupled with a decreasing pool of workers contributing to the system.

■ Aging is also occurring for the first time on a large scale in the post–World War II suburbs. In 2000, 70 percent of baby boomers lived in the suburbs and accounted for roughly 31 percent of the total suburban population in 2000.[6]

■ Older men are far more likely to be married than older women. In 2008, 74 percent of older men were married but only 51 percent of older women were married. Even among the 85-plus population, 55 percent of men were married,

---

[4]NIH/NIA, *Aging and Cancer Research: Workshop Report* (June 2001).

[5]US Office of Personnel Management, *An Analysis of Federal Retirement Data* (March 2008).

[6]W. Frey, "Boomers and Seniors in the Suburbs: Aging Patterns in US Census 2000" (Washington, DC: Brookings Institute, 2003).

but only 15 percent of 85-plus women were married.[7] An increasing number of older adults live alone. With a comparatively higher divorce rate among baby boomers, the trend is expected to grow. In 2008, 40 percent of women over the age of 65 lived alone, while almost 20 percent of men lived alone.[8]

■ In 1959, the poverty rate among older adults was roughly 35 percent, compared to 11 percent today. But savings do not go as far today, and we are likely to see the poverty rate increase as boomers age.

It's clear that the aging population can no longer be simply considered as one of many subsets or specialized population groups. The rapid and expansive growth in the older adult population will reshape all parts of society and the more quickly we can understand and anticipate how and when these impacts will occur, the better prepared and more cost effective our response will be. This book makes the argument that with some design, as well as policy and regulatory changes, many of the solutions to the challenges of an aginng population lay within the neighborhood—the place where people lived when they were young and the place they want to live when they grow old.

The Scale of Response: Pedestrian Sheds and Neighborhoods

Older adults do not generally define their challenges as those of aging. In fact, aging is so relative that it can seem as if no one is doing it. Ask 65-year-olds at what age they become senior, and they are likely to answer 85. Ask 85-year-olds the same question and they are likely to say 92. So despite all the statistics showing an aging nation, it is very hard to find an aging American. But there are plenty of people living their lives, enjoying retirement or part-time employment, and wanting to stay in the homes and communities they have loved and invested in, sometimes for decades. Neighborhoods and the places people call home are the spaces in which they will age. To address the challenges of longevity, then, we must address the challenges of place. In his book *Elderburbia, Aging with a Sense of Place in America,* Philip Stafford makes a compelling argument that "Aging in Place" has been erroneously equated with aging in one's home. Stafford draws on sources as wide as Martin Heidegger, John Berger, and the geographer Yi-fu Tuan to detach the meaning of "place" from a home, and realign it with dwelling in a larger spatial, social, and spiritual sense. Stafford proposes that place is defined through a process of answering these questions:

> Can we fill our spaces with meaning and memory? Can we attain a sense of agency, where what we do makes a difference? Can we dwell in the other? Can we transform space into a place that reflects who we imagine ourselves to be?[9]

[7] US Census Bureau, Current Population Survey, *Annual Social and Economic Supplement* (2008).

[8] Ibid.

[9] P. B. Stafford, *Elderburbia: Aging with a Sense of Place in America* (Santa Barbara: ABC-CLIO, 2009), 14.

In examining the neighborhood and urbanism that is fostered at the neighborhood level, this book attempts to create physical and social environments beyond the home that assist in creating positive answers to Stafford's questions.

What Is a Neighborhood?

The neighborhood is a complex organizational structure that is both physical and social—a district that may overlap with others, shift over time, or tighten down, depending on the context in which it is being defined. There are however, basic physical building blocks that can be empirically determined that structure and support neighborhoods (fig. 1.4). Comfortable walking distances of quarter- to half-miles, known as pedestrian sheds, are these basic building blocks of the neighborhood. The pedestrian shed should gather the residents within walking distances of many daily needs, including transit, which is ideally placed at a central node next to shops. Other daily needs that are ideally balanced and mixed within the five-minute walking distance are shopping, work, school, recreation, and dwellings of all types. Neighborhoods continually come back to the quality of the pedestrian environment within the shed, not only as a value in itself, but also as an indicator of a variety of larger environmental, social, and health considerations.

Figure 1.4

The Prototypical Traditional Neighborhood Development is designed to support a variety of housing types, commercial and civic enterprises, recreation, and pedestrian activity all within a quarter mile radius. This neighborhood type is particularly well suited to support the needs of older adult residents. Daily needs are met by shops that are a short walk from homes. Opportunities for social engagement are supported by the pedestrian-oriented streets and strategically positioned community spaces.

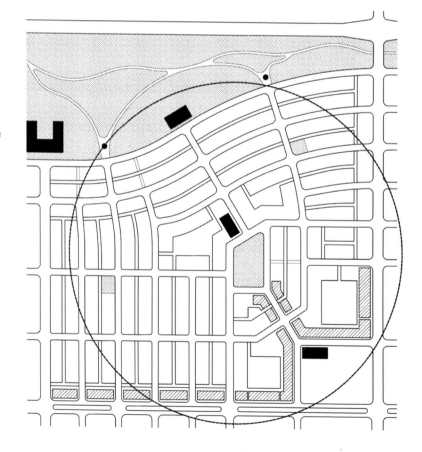

Multiple pedestrian sheds may combine and interact across an identified neighborhood district. Pedestrian-oriented urban form has some clear physical characteristics at the pedestrian shed scale, as well as more complex and subjective cultural characteristics across the whole neighborhood. The edges of neighborhoods should be porous and continue the surrounding street, path, and green space networks to the greatest extent possible. Age-segregated, senior living developments have tended to be constructed as secured compounds rather than connected neighborhoods, and this is not a trend that should be continued, if for no other reason than the over-supply of gated retirement communities. A neighborhood edge should be defined by perceptual boundaries that define a neighborhood without segmenting and separating it from the larger community via hard barriers like gates. The mix of clearly demarcated and more loosely adjoining passages of neighborhood boundaries are animated by the interplay of the walking limits of our bodies and the extensibility of our cultures projected over topography.

The neighborhood environment is at the core of urbanism. If neighborhoods hold solutions for an aging population, then aging and urbanism must also be explored. In their book *The Urban Web: Politics, Policy, and Theory*, Lawrence Henderson and John Bolland delve into the spatial/social complexities contained within the word "urban":

> Urban comes from the Latin, Urbs. The word derives from the palings or palisades that were once used to surround and protect a settled place from intruders. From the earliest of times, those who lived in settled, protected places developed a characteristic way of life associated with a nonagricultural, non-nomadic existence. Our English word *urbane* came into the language about 1500 AD, and with it came a sense of the qualities of life and mind that are traditionally associated with lives lived in an urban setting.
>
> The word *city* is also of Latin in its derivation. *Civitas,* to the Romans, carried in its meaning the idea of citizenship and the rights and privileges of those who were citizens.
>
> The meanings that attach to the word *city* have mostly to do with its legal and governmental status, while the meanings that attach to the word *urban* have to do with what is commonly called the culture of cities: their architecture, lifestyle, sociology, and economics.[10]

Urbanism is a set of spatial/cultural relationships that emerge when a place is sufficiently defined and sufficiently close to engender group identity and collective behavior. The word "urban" is not synonymous with the word "city." Hamlets are urban settlements in rural communities, neighborhood centers are urban areas in suburban communities, town centers form urban nodes around metropolitan areas, and cities are closely packed clusters of distinct urban neighborhoods whose interactions can take on the larger order of collective behavior know as cosmopolitanism. Urbanism exists in all of these environments. *Livable Communities for Aging Populations* advocates for a return to urbanism, but this does not imply a Stalin-like effort to move the population into mass-produced, Soviet-style high-rises. Rather, it is a way of incrementally nudging our existing communities, in whatever rural or city context, over time into a more centered, better structured, and more compact settlement pattern, one better

---

[10]L. J. R. Henserson and J. M. Bolland, *The Urban Web: Politics, Policy, and Theory* (Chicago: Nelson-Hall Publishers, 1990), 5.

suited to an aging population with changing mental, physical, occupational, social, and emotional needs. A return to urbanism is a process of evolving a range of environments, not a migration of the population to a single city-like environment.

The connection between health and planning is not new. There is a long history of debate in the planning profession over whether the social determinants of health (S-DOH in professional parlance) or the physical determinants of health (P-DOH) should be the primary focus of healthy planning initiatives. Positing these two determinants as exclusive or oppositional requires a type of theoretical construct that is neither based in the realities of developing, maintaining, or residing in neighborhoods nor particularly helpful to advancing either cause. Even so, the dichotomy between S-DOH and P-DOH is alive and well today in planning profession dialogue and was recently raised again by Jason Corburn.[11]

As Corburn reminds us, the S-DOH/P-DOH debate reached a crescendo at the first "National Conference on City Planning" in 1909. At that conference, Fredric Law Olmsted, Jr., presented observations on emerging planning practices in Europe, stressing the artful ways in which planning issues were coordinated. As a rebuttal to the Olmstead presentation, Benjamin Marsh and Robert Anderson Pope advocated for institutionalized and technically oriented planning efforts that would focus on correcting the significant social disparities reinforced by the built environment. Thus the battle lines were drawn: physical determinists versus equity advocates. In the end, this debate and the internal struggles it precipitated served mostly to help dismantle both the City Beautiful movement led by Olmstead and the social equity movement led by Marsh. The planning profession that emerged in its wake is often oriented toward neither beauty nor equity, but instead toward narrowly framed, formulaic institutional considerations. Looking back on developments over the past fifty years, it is hard to argue that the shaping and maintenance of the built environment has been guided by any larger vision of either harmony or mutuality. The S-DOH and P-DOH advocates have ended up on the same side of the table, or, more accurately, share a common exile from decision-making tables.

Meanwhile, the prestige of the planning professions has fallen. Recall that the keynote speaker at the 1909 conference was House Speaker Joseph Cannon, and that both Marsh and Olmstead had to hurry out of the conference to testify before various congressional committees on hotly debated planning issues widely perceive to be of national importance. Imagine planners testifying today. What would they say? What would Congress ask? Enhancing the quality of all places, working to ensure that social diversity is supported in codes and regulations, improving the processes through which residents are included in decision making, and elevating the position of neighborhoods in the metrics and policies that shape our regional, state, and interstate transportation systems—these are timely, appropriate topics, commensurate with the planning profession's current challenges and spheres of influence.

The value this book places on physically distinct and identifiable neighborhoods makes it easy to associate it with the City Beautiful movement of Olmstead, rather than with the social justice movement of Marsh. However, we now have too much empirical evidence on the influence of urban form on social behavior and community

[11]J. Corburn, "Toward the Healthy City: People, Places and the Politics of Urban Planning."

health for distinction between S-DOH and P-DOH to be of value as independent measures. The compartmentalization of the two subjects is counter to the very premise of approaching healthcare from a holistic, environmental perspective. We know that residents receive many tangible well-being benefits from living in beautiful, high-quality, and well-appointed neighborhood settings, and that both individual and collective health is harder to maintain in unattractive, low-quality neighborhoods without adequate public spaces or amenities. We also know that community organizing can powerfully transform and revitalize even the most blighted of communities, and the act of participating in neighborhood stewardship can improve an individual's mental and physical health in any community. Lastly, we know that development or redevelopment efforts that are heavy handed, and purely top-down will be hard to initially lease or sell and harder to sustain over time in today's economic climate. All planners should hold these truths as self-evident. Perhaps planners should again be testifying before Congress. Given changing demographics, they might be invited by a House committee on Medicaid and Medicare, and make the case for the health benefits of aging in an urban environment, or by a Senate housing committee, where they might advocate for integrating supportive housing models into vibrant urban communities with flexible transit and modern, café-style senior centers.

Seniors Housing Communities as Change Agents

Neighborhoods are a good scale for action: physically defined, culturally defined, or in the true meaning of urban, defined by both culture and form. The nation now has decades of history with community development organizations, neighborhood planning units, housing associations, and informal civic associations that demonstrate that the neighborhood is an effective scale of operation for organization and mobilization. Many types of development financing structures have emerged over these same decades that also work well at the neighborhood scale: everything from new subdivisions to urban redevelopment initiatives to continuing care retirement communities have been regularly carried out at the 100- to 200-acre scale that is the basic building block of neighborhoods.

Continuing Care Retirement Communities (CCRCs) offer a complicated example both of how senior housing can form a supportive neighborhood and how regulation can undermine the effectiveness of a model and its desirability for older adults. CCRCs are single communities that provide smaller scale, no-maintenance housing for older adults and offer a variety of housing types to meet different needs, most often including assisted-living facilities and nursing howes. In effect, CCRC developers have been designing and building neighborhoods, even if the end product does not always reflect a neighborhood aesthetic or the diversity that would normally be associated with a neighborhood environment. The CCRC industry has a market perception problem: The vast majority of the population does not want to move to a segregated seniors-housing development. This poor public perception is largely due to the fact that senior housing is viewed as providing care in settings that force the customers to leave their homes and communities.

In part, the for-profit Medicaid-dependent wing of the industry has earned this perception by mounting powerful lobbying campaigns to steer an array of public funds and insurance reimbursement policies toward their developments and away from home-based care models. To receive support, an individual must move to an instituation, most often a nursing home. The fact that Medicaid defaults to institutional care provision and requires a "Medicaid Waiver" to fund home-based care is a powerful testament to the success of these lobbying campaigns. Though 95 percent of the public never accesses a seniors housing facility of any type, Medicaid, the country's largest payer of long-term care services, considers nursing homes to be the normative environment for publicly funded care.

On the other hand, the negative public perception is not a fair assessment. The evolution of seniors housing over the past half century is a record of institutional care models moving progressively closer to more neighborhood or neighborhood-like settings. Early nursing homes (in the mid-twentieth century) grew out of the medical model and looked like hospital buildings both inside and outside (see Chapter 3). Over the past three decades, alternatives to highly institutional skilled nursing facilities have evolved, each moving progressively closer to more familiar neighborhood forms and styles. Compared to someone's home of three decades, a seniors housing development may seem institutional, but compared to the hospital system from which they have sprung, these developments are as close as the medical model has come to providing care in a neighborhood environment.

For the past fifty years, seniors housing developments have been approached as specialized suburban forms that are usually organized around recreation facilities, medical supports, or both. The developments have been age-segregated, often regulating the amount of non-senior residents and the duration of stays of non-senior visitors. Most constitute some form of internally oriented compound that contains common spaces for dining, recreation, and some type of medical support or daily assistance. Like Sun City, Arizona (fig. 1.5) these developments clearly meet a need and address a market, but do so in a highly specialized, age homogenous, autonomous urban form set apart from the surrounding community.

Figure 1.5
Sun City, which began development in the 1960s, is the prototype for thousands of active living retirement communities that followed. Circular neighborhood pods are oriented toward their centers where specialized recreation amenities and care services are provided. The plan's radial geometries are reminiscent of crop circles. The plan reflects its era, a time when heroic urban redevelopment efforts were proposed as the solution to a wide range of social problems. Sun City is designed to address, at an urban scale, the lack of social and economic roles for retired, healthy older adults by creating an expansive community tailored to their specific needs.

Seniors housing has evolved separate from its larger urban context, not out of any specific needs of the aging, but because communities have prevented it from growing organically in the neighborhoods where older adults live. The nation's built environment is in many ways not capable of supporting an individual's needs across a lifespan. In some areas, seniors housing is the only appropriately sized alternative to large lot, detached single-family homes. Local zoning boards are often only willing to allow more dense multifamily arrangements when they are restricted to the elderly and not made available as low income housing for the general population. As mobility functions decline, seniors housing communities may be the only places to find the appropriate accessibility features incorporated throughout the entire environment. Accessible and appropriately structured spaces for social interaction and community engagement are not widely available outside of seniors' facilities in many areas. Older adults are more susceptible to illness, and seniors housing serves as an alternative arrangement to our current hospital-oriented medical system: an alternative to either checking into a hospital for a long stay or remaining at home and foregoing adequate care. With communities and families alike becoming ever more attenuated, senior housing may be the only place an older adult could reliably expect to be able to get help in a crisis event.

However, the real differences between housing for the elderly and housing for the rest of the population are relative rather than categorical. Older persons on the whole require more emphasis on certain aspects of living arrangements than the rest of the community, but the differences are of degree rather than kind. There are benefits to supporting aging in the general built environment. Most of our communities would benefit from increased housing diversity, increased attention to continuous, accessible, walking routes, intentional social spaces, convenient access to daily needs, and easier access to both health care and crisis assistance. These are all qualities that provide value for all in any community. Seniors housing incorporates design features that are necessary for older adults but beneficial for the rest of the population, and a community that works well for older adults will provide benefits to all across their life spans. The housing challenges of older adults may be better approached, for the most part, as a general upgrading of the entire built environment rather than perfection of specialized and age-segregated urban forms. The seniors housing industry is beginning to shape a role in this general upgrading process.

Culture Change is a national movement led by a small group of practitioners that have organized as the Pioneer Network, which advocates for the transformation of older adult services in both facility and community-based settings. This movement seeks to re-center health systems on the needs of individuals receiving care, as well as the individuals who provide that care, rather than on the needs of the institutions and structures of care delivery. The goals of the Culture Change movement are to provide a more familiar, empowering, and hospitable care environment for individuals giving and receiving care. In "Culture Change in Nursing Homes: How Far Have We Come?" authors Michelle Doty, Mary Jane Koren, and Elizabeth L. Sturla observe:

> In the culture change model, which has gained momentum over the past decade, seniors enjoy much of the privacy and choice they would experience if they were still living in their own homes. Residents' needs and preferences come first; facilities

operations are shaped by this awareness. To this end, nursing home residents are given greater control over their daily lives—for instance, in terms of meal times or bed times—and frontline workers—the nursing aides responsible for day-to-day care— are given greater autonomy to care for residents. In addition, the physical and organizational structure of facilities is made less institutional. Large, hospital-like units with long, wide corridors are transformed into smaller facilities where small groups of residents are cared for by a consistent team.[12]

Toward the Development of Lifelong Neighborhoods

Spurred on in part by the Culture Change movement, Continuing Care Retirement Communities (CCRCs) have become the cutting edge of community-based medical care provision, representing a significant extension of the medical model into the daily life carried out in neighborhood settings. If this evolution toward community-like forms continues, senior housing developments could begin to blur distinctions between institutional and home-based care, perhaps even becoming so ubiquitous as to be considered an extension of community-based aging in place rather than an alternative to it. The nation's most innovative CCRCs are leading examples of what may eventually become Lifelong Neighborhoods. CCRCs have a substantial track record of accomplishment in the fields of environmental health, geriatric care, inter-industry coordination, complex financing, and creative lease, purchase, and fee structures. They have provided spaces and services that make up for deficiencies in our environmental, social, and economic systems. Both market demand and societal needs would be better served if these resources were better deployed to contribute to and draw on the wider community. Seniors housing has an opportunity to become a major civic contributor and would benefit from this engagement in terms of bottom line, public perception, market penetration, and social relevance.

Simultaneous to the built environment trends in seniors housing, there has been a trend to interact more with the surrounding community through service programming. In a 2009 article published in *Seniors Housing & Care Journal*, the authors presented the results of a survey of Midwestern CCRCs representing responses covering nearly 350 properties. Half or more (depending on community size) indicated they expect to be offering services to those not living on the campus (defined as homebound) by 2013, and 17 to 30 percent are already doing so.[13]

Providers who have traditionally served the market-rate elderly population through facility-based models are also increasingly offering home- and community-based services. This deepens and extends their reach. Life Care at Home Health, Inc., an outfit that provides home health, hospice, and private duty services in nine states across the nation, represents an early example of bringing services into the

---

[12]M. M. Doty, M. J. Koren, and E. L. Sturla, "Culture Change."

[13]S. B. Brecht, S. Fein, L. Hollinger-Smith, "Preparing for the Future: Trends in Continuing Care Retirement Communities," *Seniors Housing & Care Journal* 17 (2009): 84.

community while connecting community-integrated residents to a system that might eventually serve them in the facility-based campus environment. In other cases, outpatient services (such as rehabilitative therapy) are provided out of a facility embedded in the housing development that serves the development's residents and surrounding community alike. The effect of these outpatient and home-based care services is a flow of people into and out of the development that helps break down the strict delineation between life inside the property boundary and life outside. Services delivery and urban form are increasingly blurring the distinction between a seniors housing development and its surrounding community.

In efforts to better reach a broader community, some seniors housing developers have begun to move toward Traditional Neighborhood Development (TND) types that blend more easily with neighborhoods. This effort is beginning to despecialize the form of seniors housing as well as create a more engaged and reciprocating relationship with the surrounding community. The Summit in Lynchburg, Virginia, is an existing example of the driving force that older adult development could play in coming years (fig. 1.6). A co-venture of the Disciples of Christ and Central

Figure 1.6

Area plan showing the Summit seniors housing campus (ingrat) prominently featured in the Wyndemere master plan.

Health System, it is a modestly sized retirement community with approximately 100 independent living apartments and town homes, a 120-bed skilled nursing facility, a health center, a rehabilitation center, 43 assisted living apartments, and a relatively small commons building. Located eight miles outside of Lynchburg's center city, the seniors housing development was planned from the very start as an integral part of Wyndemere, Lynchburg's first traditional neighborhood development effort. A striking feature of the town is the prominent position occupied by the Summit along the central axis of the through corridor. Summit holds a position in the community that reflects the founding role Disciples of Christ and Central Health System played in developing the entire community.

The Summit began in 1988 as a mission of the Reverend Ken Burger, who had visited nursing homes to visit members of his congregation and felt called to find a better environment for older adults. Over the next decade, Reverend Burger rallied his congregation at Disciples of Christ around the mission. In 1997, the church had developed enough momentum to start investing in land and met with the city of Lynchburg's Office of Economic Development to make the city aware of their intention to develop a CCRC. The city had been considering the acquisition of right of way to establish a new connection between highways 221 and 460, two major arterials that radiated out from Lynchburg. The disconnected highways had been overrun by strip retail development, and the city wanted to work in coordination with landowners abutting the proposed new road to ensure that better development would occur when the road went in. Interestingly, the city withheld purchase of the right of way until development plans were prepared for the new corridor, and it used the construction of the new road as leverage in negotiating how development would take place alongside it. The 400 acres on which the Wyndemere community now resides, then comprised two tracts held by different investment companies who were both interested in selling. The city, interested in the vision Reverend Burger presented of a state of the art seniors development, helped broker the discussion between Burger and the landowners. Unable to afford the entire property or to move fast enough to secure them on his own, Reverend Burger brought a prominent local developer into the conversation, Bill Jamerson of J.E. Jamerson & Sons. Jamerson, Burger, and the city worked together with the local planning firm Sympoetica to plan Wyndemere as Lynchburg's first Traditional Neighborhood Development (TND) and to create the city's first TND zoning ordinance. As part of the effort, Jamerson underwrote and built a YMCA into the community early in the development process.[14]

Now a decade has passed since ground breaking, and the community has grown to a full neighborhood with nearly 2,000 residents, a variety of housing types, retail shops, restaurants, and a regional YMCA that offers an array of lifelong services, including those specialized for older adults. While the Summit has its own

---

[14]Interview with Reverend Ken Burger, May 17, 2011.

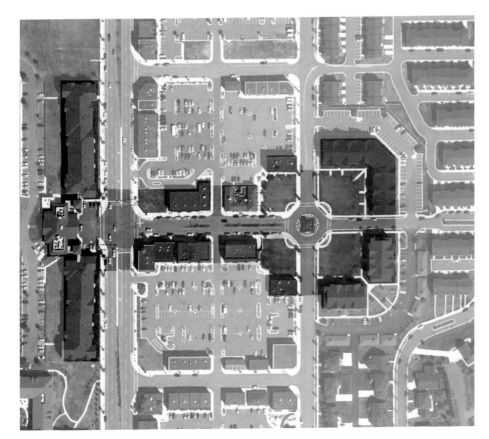

Figure 1.7
Detail shows the relationship of the Summit to the town square.

self-contained facilities, it is located off of the main arterial, directly across the street from the Wyndemere town center (fig. 1.7) and only a short three-block walk to the YMCA.

Wyndemere, the Summit, and the YMCA would not exist but for the cooperative efforts of stakeholders, the for-profit developer of Wyndemere, the nonprofit sponsors of the Summit and the YMCA, and, equally important, the jurisdictional planning and zoning officials of Lynchburg—all working together with the goal of creating a livable, walkable, sustainable, mixed income, and intergenerational community (fig. 1.8). As evidence of its success, Wyndemere was conceived as a ten-year-long development project, but it achieved completion in five years. The YMCA doubled its membership projections immediately upon opening and is currently undergoing its third expansion. While the basic forms of seniors housing are still recognizable, and while the Summit does not offer services outside of the facility, the role that this seniors housing development played in instigating a pedestrian-oriented neighborhood serves as an early example of the prominent role the seniors housing industry could play in upgrading the built environment.

The Summit development and Wyndemere are harbingers of things to come. The evolution of America's residential fabric can be seen as a physical record of the

Figure 1.8
The Summit terminates the vista of Wyndemere's main street.

Photo by Ken Burger

maturation of a single generation. This nation first built housing on a mass scale to accommodate returning World War II GIs and their new families. As their children became young adults, production switched to starter homes that sheltered the young "baby boomers" who were striking out on their own. As the boomer generation has progressed to its peak earning years, the market has continued to cater to their needs, supplying the suburban developments and larger estates that the boomers can now afford.

The next stage in the maturity of the boomer generation—that of retirement and aging—will require more than just the increased supply of a specific housing type; it will require developing new relationships between facility-based care, neighborhood, and community-based supports. Housing and supports will not easily be pushed to the edges of town as the baby boomers may demand them, but rather they will occupy increasingly prominent roles in developing and detailing our city, town, and neighborhood centers.

Conclusions

Aging affects the entire community, young and old. Everyone grows older each day. In geriatric circles, the standing joke is that while aging isn't fun, it's better than the alternative. You will have gotten older while reading this book. There are different opinions about wrinkles versus botox, gray hair versus color treatment, and individuals make their own choices about these matters. But there are a few elements of aging that most people share and fear and, which, by their nature, require community solutions, not just individual choice. Whether it's their knees or their mind that goes first, whether they seek out plastic surgery or complete a daily crossword puzzle to ward off Alzheimer's, everyone wants and attempts to maintain the highest quality of life. Independence and choice are shared values among the very diverse current and future older adult populations. While they can be impacted by genetics, the opportunity to save, and availability of family support, a person's quality of life, independence, and choice can be largely determined by the physical community: the housing stock, the transportation network, and the available services. Unfortunately, the last century has done nothing to prepare communities for an aging population. In fact, policies, programs, financing, and regulations have actually made it more difficult to age in the community, despite the fact that it is the stated preference of almost every older adult. Given the scale of the aging population, these are not and cannot just be the concerns of a specialized subset of the population. *How* and *where* to age well is a community issue that affects families and places almost as much the older persons themselves.

There is a short window of time to address these issues cost-effectively, and they will require a transformation of multiple systems, all of which have stakeholders and vested interests. Housing and transportation must be delivered, funded, and regulated differently if communities are going to be able to address the needs of their aging residents. Services, most importantly health services, must be located and administered differently if they are going to keep people active and healthy thereby decreasing costs to the medical system. Policy is important and incentives must be realigned if change is going to happen on any reasonable scale. But real success will come when professionals work across lines to foster innovative and interdisciplinary solutions. It was professional planners, architects, bankers, builders, and designers who constructed the communities of the last fifty years. These same professionals will now need to reach out to doctors, hospital administrators, and public health, aging, and mental health providers in order to invent and in many cases rediscover how communities can support people of all ages and abilities.

ACCESS AND URBANISM CHAPTER 2

Introduction

The Americans with Disabilities Act (ADA) is a powerful exertion of federal influence on the local built environment. ADA compliance measures have become ubiquitous across the urban landscape, but because they are implemented at architectural scales and applied one property at a time, the results are often incohesive and discontinuous at the urban scale. An increasingly older population will create more need for access accommodations, and this is a reality the nation should be considering now. The demographic shift will be registered in the disability community, which will be increasingly composed of older adults with age-related disabilities, as well as increasingly older developmentally disabled adults who will also experience more age-related disabilities. Aging brings with it universality: It is a universal experience, and as we live longer, disability will become a universal experience as well. The older adults who will represent an increasing percentage of the disabled population present a reason to revisit the framework in which we define, regulate, and enforce accessibility in the built environment.

The increasing universality of access concerns warrants shifting to regulatory frameworks that are more focused on the health, safety, and welfare of the entire population and less focused on the public accommodation of individual rights and liberties. This shift is warranted by the makeup of the disability class, but also by the need for access regulation that is further reaching. Protection of health, safety, and welfare is a familiar principle to planners and these factors are the enabling justification for governments to plan and zone. Approached in this way, accessibility assumes the DNA of all other built environment regulations and allows for easier integration of buildings into the general design of our communities.

Public accommodation of individual rights is a much less familiar concept to planning and zoning practices, and framed as such, accessibility tends to get positioned poorly in the process through which the built environment is designed. As a civil rights issue, ADA is worked into the built environment only as a minimal compliance afterthought, as site and architecture plans move from schematic into construction document phases. More could be accomplished if accessibility blended easily into the earlier health, safety, and welfare focused, population-wide concerns of planning rather than the later-stage measures taken at the architectural scale to ensure the public accommodation of individual rights. The framework of access regulation greatly impacts the stage at which access is integrated into design, and earlier integration would be better enabled if access were pursued as a health, safety, and welfare issue rather than a civil right issue.

As disability becomes a more universal experience, urban planning rather than architectural design may prove to be the more effective framework for implementation. Zoning ordinances can include architectural design requirements, so the shift to zoning would not require abandoning the American National Standards Institute (ANSI) 117.1 standards that currently guide construction detailing. However, introduced first in a zoning framework, ANSI 117.1 standards may be scoped more effectively and in order to respond to urban context they may be modulated, prioritized, and coordinated in a cohesive manner across the built environment. Architectural standards alone, applied without regard for urban context cannot be deployed strategically in this manner. As a population-wide concern raised early and broadly in the design of the built environment, accessibility goals could shift from the ubiquitous but piecemeal application of a few standardized, disparately applied measures to a more integrated and comprehensively applied strategy. Critical to this transformation will be the repositioning of access as a population protection, like nearly every other built environment regulation, rather than a stand-alone public accommodation concern of a protected class of individuals.

As covered further on in this chapter in more depth, the demographic makeup of the protected class as defined by the ADA today warrants more of a population protection approach than a civil rights protection approach. The disability class, as defined now, will include the majority of us for some period in our lives. Because we are a majority class, our vulnerabilities are more often related to generally indiscriminant application of accommodations than to specific acts of discrimination or willful neglect. The greater enemy of accessibility is thoughtlessness, not malice, and though both may result in exclusion, the two are remedied differently. Thoughtlessness is corrected by more thoughtful processes, and malice is countered through the enforcement of minimum acceptable standards. Shedding the protected class approach to regulation should be viewed as an opportunity to advance the cause of access. In practical application, we can get more access from an environment that supports our health, safety, and welfare than an environment that protects us from discrimination.

Go Forth Boldly

The ADA legislation of 1990 provides broad powers for regulation and invokes the commerce clause as well as the Fourteenth Amendment as justifications for this influence. The act could not be more clear that the intensions of the ADA are "to provide a clear and comprehensive national mandate . . . to provide clear, strong, consistent, enforceable standards . . . to ensure that the Federal Government plays a central role in enforcing the standards," and to do so in a manner that invokes "the sweep of congressional authority" (Title 42, Chapter 126, Sec. 12101 [b]). The congressional act does not mince words, nor does it hold back in expressing dissatisfaction with the judicial branch of government for decisions that scale back and narrow the Rehabilitation Act of 1973. It goes on to specifically call out, chide, and override each of these narrowing decisions. The ADA clearly declares that the nation is to move boldly to further the goals of access and reverse the historic tendency of society to "isolate and segregate individuals with disabilities." The language of the ADA is nothing short of bravado and is quite clear that the intent of Congress is to legislate broad actions and resist attempts to narrow the scope or force of the act through tempering interpretation.

Given the invocation of Congress's "sweep of authority," the architectural guidelines that have emerged as the primary built environment initiative seem rather timid. Access is as much or more an issue of urban configuration as it is an issue of architectural detailing. Because the ADA has been carried out without access guidelines or regulations to address the urban scale, enforcement focuses narrowly on small details at architectural scales and has no influence on the development patterns that have been shown to isolate and strand large segments of the population ten miles at a time.

Though legislation and case precedent have so far established that privately financed single-family homes are outside the realm of public accommodation mandates, the common public practice of zoning out all forms of housing from many suburban neighborhoods other than large lot, family-sized homes is an effective and thinly veiled public means of intentionally not accommodating several classes of people, notably including those who are impaired and thus unable to manage such large homes. It may not be the intention of the ADA to subject private homeowners to public accommodation requirements, but it would seem well within the intention of the act to scrutinize public zoning practices for excluding housing type diversity sufficient to support residents with diverse physical, mental, and social abilities.

The narrow focus on the civil rights of protected individuals also seems odd. Given that the commerce clause is invoked by the act, why hasn't access been pursued as a consumer protection in addition to a civil right? As defined by the act, the disability class will include the majority of us at some point in our lives, and thus the intent of the act would be more effectively pursued on many fronts as a consumer protection or general population protection rather than individual right protection. Though counter to the language of the act, the civil rights platform for enforcing the ADA requires that we ignore the near universal reach of disability status and instead identify, isolate, and segregate a specific class of people from the general population so that we can provide them with special protections. The heavy emphasis on protected civil rights doesn't make sense when juxtaposed with the act's broadly inclusive definition of disability that encourages widely inclusive interpretations of the protected class.

A more universal regulatory framework geared toward consumer protection might also prove to be more strategically effective in implementation. The protected right to access, though a powerful legal force, is probably not sufficient cause on its own to challenge the way urban growth is managed or the way urban redevelopment is planned. The politics of these kinds of urban development processes are too great, even for the full sweep of congressional authority, if approached solely as an access issue. Congressionally backed access mandates are, however, significant contributing considerations and when compiled with the financial, environmental, and social costs associated with sprawling development, they may someday soon add up to a compelling justification for land use reform. In its current packaging as the protected rights of a discriminated class of people, access is harder to coalesce with other advocacy issues. It must be defined as the special interest of a minority class rather than the universal concern of the majority of citizens. The broadly enabling clauses of the ADA provide potential for realizing access as a universal, coalition building issue, but developing this potential would require fundamentally reimagining what environmental access is and for whom it should be provided. The aging of the baby boomers provides impetus to begin this process of repositioning access as a more universal concern.

Nothing in the legislation limits the implementation of the ADA to minimum standards for architecture or discourages a more urban approach. Disability is defined by the ADA as a complex condition affected significantly by social, economic, and spatial factors across the community: a physical or mental impairment lasting more than six months that substantially limits one or more major life activities, a record of such impairment, or even being regarded by others as having such an impairment whether or not the impairment actually exists. Notice the weight that the ADA places on perception above and beyond actual physical condition in this definition. By comparison, the UN Convention on Civil Rights for People with Disabilities also alludes to the complexities of social perception in its preamble statement "that disability is an evolving concept and that disability results from the interaction between persons with impairments and attitudinal and environmental barriers that hinders their full and effective participation in society on an equal basis with others." Individual mobility rights alone cannot address the social complexities associated with attitudinal barriers and other complex social dynamics. Access is also about place: the complex spaces we individually allocate for each other and the spaces that gather us all. As defined, access is more a function of urbanity—the blend of social and spatial factors that make up place—than architecture.

On Whose Behalf We Regulate

Universal design broadly defines the user. It's a consumer market–driven issue. Its focus is not specifically on people with disabilities, but all people. It actually assumes the idea, that everybody has a disability and I feel strongly that that's the case. We all become disabled as we age and lose ability, whether we want to admit it or not.[1]

—Ronald L. Mace, FAIA, founder of the
Universal Design movement

Universal Desires and Individual Rights

True to its name, the Universal Design (UD) movement has always reflected a broad view of access issues and a fundamental commitment to a consumer-driven strategy. The movement has been enormously successful in impacting the design

[1]R. L. Mace, "A Perspective on Universal Design," Paper presented at the Designing for the 21st Century An International Conference on Universal Design, Curitiba, Brazil, June 19, 1998.

of buildings, fixtures, and all manner of implements. Everything—from carrot peelers to kitchen appliances to entire buildings—has benefited from the intensely ergonomic design approach. Universal Design has had substantial success as a purely market-driven effort applied on a voluntary basis beyond the minimal requirements enforced by regulation. The relationship between UD and federal access regulation professionals is interesting to chart over the years, with both efforts initially springing from many of the same founding advocates. The two movements have helped define each other: divvying up that which is minimally required and thus regulated from that which is driven more by aspirations to better serve a market force.

However, the divide-and-conquer strategy that has separated and defined ADA's regulatory efforts apart from UD's market-driven efforts underrepresents the role and potential power of law. Planning and zoning ordinances are adopted as laws that regularly move far beyond minimum requirements to orchestrate development so that it reflects larger visions and aspirations of a community. The separation of market-driven UD efforts from regulation-driven ADA efforts serves to bypass most of the legal terrain in which planners work: that of translating a community's aspirations and needs into an urban plan that is implemented through a cohesive set of guiding urban and architectural design standards. In access advocacy, the law is utilized primarily as a bulwark that protects the rights of vulnerable or marginalized individuals from willful exclusion or neglect. For planners, the law is utilized primarily as a means of coordinating collective action. In many ways the strict division of access into fields focused on market-driven appeal and the legal enforcement of minimum standard provisions has positioned the issue exactly where it is least effective: focused entirely on individual people (either those with protected rights or those with consumer desires) and on individual architectural details. As a planning concern, access has the potential to be more of an urban than architectural issue, more of a community than individual issue, and more informed by universally derived habitation patterns than isolated individual behaviors.

In 1960, seven years before the initial adoption of the first federal access legislation (the Architectural Barriers Act), the Douglas Fir Plywood Association, a trade association that represented the concerns of much of the building industry of the day, formed a task force known as the House of Freedom Advisory Committee. In 1961, the Advisory Committee released an industry-drafted report recommending that homebuilders incorporate a list of access provisions that would make homes more universally marketable. Though released with significant fanfare, the report was largely ignored by the industry. The House of Freedom report called for the following provisions to be incorporated as marketing amenities in all newly constructed homes:

1. No step at entry

2. Master light switches at three points

3. Nonskid floors throughout

4. All doors and hallways at least 3 feet wide

5. All light switches and doorknobs 36 inches above floor level

6. All electrical outlets 18 inches above floor level

7. Dressing seat next to bathtub

8. Strategically located grab bars in bathroom for safety

9. Lower cabinets in kitchen raised off floor, upper cabinets within easy arm's reach

10. Low sink permits sit-down dishwashing

11. Pull-down lighting fixtures make bulb replacement easy

12. Perimeter heat for warm floors

13. Extra storage space in garage

14. Hobby/workshop area in garage

15. All outdoor water faucets at least 24 inches above ground

16. Wide roof overhang protects walkways

Protecting the Civil Rights of Individuals

For the past fifty years, accessibility has been framed only as a civil rights issue and, therefore, as a protection offered to a minority class of people. As the population skews increasingly toward older adults, and as advances in both medicine and occupational therapy increase the number of people who live full lives with a disability, accessibility is better framed as a consumer protection issue. The basic civil rights premise has been that physical impairments define a distinct class of people who have historically been the victims of discrimination. Through various laws and regulations, the legal system has been empowered to protect this class of people from direct discrimination in the form of mistreatment, or indirect discrimination in the form of insufficient consideration of their access needs in the built environment and communications media.

The US Civil Rights Movement and Civil Rights Act (CRA) of 1964 served as the model for the Architectural Barriers Act (ABA) of 1968. Like the CRA, the ABA initially sought to end unequal access to public accommodations and first covered only building projects constructed with federal funds. Access to federally funded buildings was viewed as a civil right that affected an individual's ability to participate equally in civil society. Later legislation expanded coverage to any facility that housed programs funded by the government—again reinforcing that participation in the public realm rather than the shape of the public realm was the primary focus of the legislation. Over time, accessibility legislation began to branch out into more and more of the built environment. Later coverage was expanded beyond facilities that housed public functions to privately owned places of public accommodation. Multifamily housing consisting entirely of private domiciles without any public functions were covered. Initially focused only on new construction, coverage was later, in part, extended to existing buildings. Coverage was extended beyond individual buildings to the rights of way that connected them: Municipalities that own and maintain the rights of way throughout communities have responsibilities to improve the connections over time to provide accessibility. Furthermore, public transportation must provide accessibility to people with disabilities.

As a civil rights issue, disability faces two awkward tests: defining the class of discriminated persons and establishing what constitutes an act of discrimination. While these tests might work well for judging violations of an individual's rights in a civil trial, the tests provide a clumsy basis for regulating the built environment. By way of comparison, the Civil Rights Act of 1964 established that classes protected by the act could be defined by race, color, religion, or national origin. An individual's race, color, and national origin are fixed conditions that can be established comparatively easily. Unlike race, color, and national origin, disability is not a condition associated with a distinct group of people; levels of ability fluctuate over any individual's lifetime, so disability status may come and go.

The definition of the disability class by federal authorities is complicated by lack of agreement on basic theories or methods for identifying disability. A variety of medical models (physical conditions) and social models (performance conditions) are employed differently by different authorities. For the purposes of the Social Security Administration, disability is defined as "the inability to engage in any

Table 2.1

2002 US CENSUS BUREAU DISABILITY STATISTICS
19% of the total US population is disabled. Of the disabled population:
30% have limitations in cognitive functioning or a mental or emotional illness that interfere with activities of daily living
21% need personal assistance with one or more activities of daily living
18% use an ambulatory aid such as a cane, crutches, or a walker
5% use a wheelchair
5% have difficulty speaking
4% have difficulty seeing
2% have difficulty hearing

substantial gainful activity (SGA) by reason of any medically determinable physical or mental impairment(s) which can be expected to result in death or which has lasted or can be expected to last for a continuous period of not less than 12 months." Because life itself is a condition that can be expected to result in death, the definition might at initial reading seem wholly inclusive of the entire population. However, from that initial inclusive definition springs a prolific and evolving case history, as the Social Security Administration has been charged with narrowing the field case by case, by developing criteria for segregating those of us who qualify from those of us who do not.

The fact that 19 percent of the total population is disabled at any given time does not mean that the same people continuously constitute that 19 percent. Rather, the percentage represents a minority designation that is time-shared among a majority of the population. Seventy one percent of the population will have developed a disability by the time they reach the age of eighty, an age increasingly common to reach.[2]

Once an individual's condition dips to a level of disability for a period, we are reminded (table 2.1) that this status represents an extremely heterogeneous and complex category of conditions, 95 percent of which do not require a wheelchair. Regulations directed primarily at wheelchair access do very little to address the access barriers experienced by the 30 percent of disabled citizens who have mental impairments, the 21 percent who have assistance needs and lack autonomy, or the 5 percent who have difficulty speaking. In total, 56 percent—the majority—of the disabled population is underserved by accessibility regulation. Thus the current approach to accessibility regulation awkwardly casts the right to access as a disproportionately defended right of 5 percent of the individuals within the protected class (wheelchair users) while largely ignoring the rights of another 56 percent of the protected class. In large part, the uneven provision of protections to various members of the protected class is a function of the reliance on litigation to define

[2]US Census Bureau, "65+ in the United States: 2005" (2005).

the protections. Either some rights are easier to assert or some categories of disabled individuals are more prone to litigation: Something is causing this imbalance of redress. The complications of defining a protected class based on heterogeneous and often transient physical conditions that require different manners of redress, all of which are experienced at some point in the life cycles of the majority of the population, raise the question of whether civil rights actions are the right venue for addressing the needs of access.

After the difficult test of establishing the disabled class such that it can be protected, accessibility regulations framed as civil rights protections are developed from the vantage point of an autonomous individual moving through individual isolated property types. Framed from this perspective, the regulatory structure cannot adequately address the whole chain of spatial and social relationships that affect accessibility across an entire community. Regulations cannot give attention to urban planning issues such as land use, urban design, zoning or housing, and transportation policy except insofar as they address the design issues covered in the federal regulations. Each property type is approached as a separate set of prescriptive specifications with the goal of providing autonomy of movement to the individual within the perimeter of the property. The single-building/single-individual nature of the regulations can be blind to the spatial and social aspects of community. In their current federal form, accessibility requirements are nonurban in approach and can be applied in ways that are antiurban. For example, the Fair Housing Act (FHA) does not require the construction of an accessible path of travel even between buildings covered by the law and on the same site. The urban relationship between housing units is missed. Even though the FHA has rigorous requirements for buildings that are covered by the act, and Uniform Federal Accessibility Standard (UFAS) has rigorous requirements for transportation systems, none of which requires a path from an FHA building to a bus stop covered by UFAS, unless the stop is within the immediate property boundary of the federally funded site.[3] Regulations cover aspects of sidewalk design and confer liability for noncompliance if a sidewalk is installed, but they do not require sidewalks in the first place. The result in many cases is to discourage the installation of sidewalks altogether.

Given the focus on individual, autonomous movement through isolated components of the built environment, it should be no surprise that urban relationships extending beyond a specific development are not considered. As accessibility law was expanded to cover an increasing percentage of the built environment, neither the initial premise of the law nor the manner of redress was ever revisited: The format remained focused on individual access to public accommodations assured by unimpeded autonomous mobility and enforced by civil litigation. Also during this same period, the built environment expanded rapidly—primarily in a sprawling development pattern that brought with it many new access challenges. The framework for accessibility regulation did not evolve sufficiently to address the challenges brought on by sprawl. When entire neighborhoods provide only a single housing type that

---

[3]US Department of Housing and Urban Development, "Fair Housing Accessibility Design Manual," http://www.huduser.org/portal/publications/destech/fairhousing.html (April 1998).

is appropriate for only a limited range of the lifespan, it is difficult or impossible for families to live in the same neighborhood as they age, or when their physical or mental abilities change (see Chapter 6). When daily needs are only provided at locations miles away from homes or there aren't any sidewalks, an automobile is required for basic daily routines. With automobile dependence access becomes an issue, even with relatively small declines in eyesight. Given the degree of dialogue and debate about the small construction details of accessibility, it is odd how little this rather significant assumption is questioned. Individuals with disabilities who are unable to drive or without a car are left to depend on friends and family, or on any paratransit services available in the area. Though a three-quarter-inch-high threshold on a public agency's front door has been firmly established as a violation of the right to access, the decision to locate that agency seven miles outside of downtown in an area not served by transit is both acceptable and commonplace. The full acceptance of motor vehicles as the single solution to accessibility at the urban scale also seems to have thwarted natural advocacy alliances among those unable to drive as a result of impairment, age limitation, or poverty.

The methods and means of regulating access were not sufficiently revisited as the definition of disability expanded to cover the majority of the population at some period in their lives and sprawling development patterns made access more difficult for all. Increased longevity will bring this issue to the forefront. In response, we will need to rethink how we address the issue of access. Increasingly we will need to regulate on behalf of the health, safety, and welfare of the whole population rather than the civil rights of a minority class within the population (fig. 2.1).

Figure 2.1
The successes of the 1964 civil rights movement led by Dr. Martin Luther King form the primary model for accessibility rights.

Consumer Protection and the National Traffic and Motor Safety Act

Enacted two years after the Civil Rights Act of 1964 and two years before the Architectural Barriers Act of 1968, the National Traffic and Motor Vehicle Safety Act of 1966 (NTMVSA) provided an alternative model for accessibility legislation that could potentially address accessibility more holistically. NTMVSA was an early demonstration of how consumer protection goals can be effectively pursued through federal legislation. The act was an early victory of the consumer protection movement led by Ralph Nader (fig. 2.2) and was heavily influenced by Nader's 1965 publication "Unsafe at Any Speed." This book took a critical perspective on the automobile industry and demonstrated that industry trends had increasingly focused on selling automobiles by highlighting lifestyle features like style, speed, power, luxury, and status symbols. From a health, safety, and welfare perspective, automobile performance was not monitored and reported in a manner that could guide regulation or even inform consumer choice, nor were thoroughfares being designed with sufficient concern for safety.

Figure 2.2

The successes of the 1966 consumer rights movement led by Ralph Nader have not been a model for accessibility regulation.

The effects of the legislation were quickly apparent. Safety features were required for all new vehicles, including head rests, energy absorbing steering wheels, shatter-resistant windshields, and safety belts.[4] Roads were adjusted and fitted with safety features. Public education campaigns were carried out to encourage safer driver behavior, and additional traffic safety laws were enacted. By 1970, only four years after the adoption of the act, motor vehicle–related death rates were significantly decreasing across the entire population as a result of initiatives spurred by the NTMVSA.[5]

A critical strategy of the consumer protection movement was to address market issues and combat the trend to market only to lifestyle. Instead, the new law required that factors related to safety and basic performance were brought to the consumer's attention, thereby addressing behavior as well as the physical environment. Automobile design prior to the act focused on increasingly exotic fantasies (cars with wing-like fins, rocket hood ornaments, and aerospace styling) rather than life safety realities. Traffic fatalities increased rapidly during this period. This market trend was closely paralleled in the built environment as well, with advertisements selling houses and communities on the basis of lifestyle possibilities, rather than the more prosaic but far more important realities of daily life (fig. 2.3). Community and housing advertisements portrayed fantasized worlds where appliances did all of the labor, men regularly got promotions at work, women reveled in elegant leisure, and children roamed happily through green grassy park-like neighborhoods. Almost completely absent from the marketing was any mention of energy efficiency, disability access, pedestrian accessibility, air and water quality, resistance to natural cycles of drought or extreme natural events, or the social consequences of pushing houses far apart from each other and from service and work destinations. Now, half

[4]Transportation Research Board, "Safety Research for a Changing Highway Environment," *Special Report No. 229* (Washington, DC: National Research Council Transportation Research Board, 1990).

[5]National Safety Council, *Accident Facts* (Itasca, Illinois: National Safety Council, 1998).

Figure 2.3
The house, like the automobile, was marketed for decades as a lifestyle fantasy.

of a century later, automobiles are marketed based on safety features, many of which go above and beyond the regulated standards. The housing market, on the other hand, continues to market almost exclusively to lifestyle and has only just begun to be influenced by comparable health, safety, and welfare considerations like resource efficiency and accessibility.

There are many parallels between the American dream marketed by the automobile industry and that of the housing development industry, and there are many examples of the parallel consequences of this market emphasis. In many ways, requiring measures that prevent a vehicle from ejecting its occupants during accidents is a good precedent for requiring measures that prevent a community from ejecting residents during periods of disability.

On a basic conceptual level, consumer protection integrates well with zoning, as they have shared legal underpinnings; protection of health, safety, and welfare forms the enabling concepts for both. As a result of their shared legal basis, both zoning and consumer protection are similarly able to look at well-being inclusively from a whole-community and whole-population vantage point, without having to focus on specific victims or specific instances of victimization.

Advancing Accessibility Aspirations Beyond Minimum Standards

One example I use to explain the difference between Universal Design and ADA is a hotel I visited that was ADA-compliant. The ADA requires that a certain number of rooms have accessible features that make them more universally usable for wheelchair users. In this hotel, there were accessible rooms on each floor, and, interestingly, they were the same room (e.g., 503, 603, 703) all the way up through the tower. Because of this, all accessible rooms provided only for left-handed transfers onto the toilet. The ADA does not require availability of left-handed *and* right-handed rooms, so this hotel was in compliance. It was not, however, universally usable. I couldn't stay in this hotel because I make a right-handed transfer and can't use a left-handed room. It's these kinds of subtleties that Universal Design has the ability to address.[6]

Community visioning and planning processes can provide effective forums to advance accessibility objectives well beyond the minimum standards required by ADA. Zoning codes and design standards can provide effective means of cross-community coordination to ensure that accessibility accommodations do not start and stop at each property line but instead weave together into an entire network.

With the aging of the baby boomers and the first widespread recognition that increased longevity is resulting in an older population, environmental accessibility is gaining market attention. Housing for older adults, particularly independent living housing arrangements, is a growing market. As covered in Chapter 8, even in market areas that are already saturated with supportive housing facilities of some kind, more community-integrated senior housing models are seen as a means to greater market penetration. This trend to reenvision neighborhoods and even whole municipalities as places attractive to older adults constitutes a new opportunity to portray access as an inherent function of a beautiful urban environment. Times have changed since 1968 when the first accessibility laws were passed, and progress in accessibility may now be more a matter of learning to elaborate and provide for market demand for enhanced levels of access than a matter of upholding very basic minimum rights of access.

Visioning

Visioning processes draw out and clarify a community's goals and ideal future. They enable a community to explore resolutions for existing problems, identify existing assets, and proactively address emerging needs and opportunities. Effective community access visions acknowledge that removing barriers is not enough. Even if all legally defined barriers to wheelchair access are removed from the built environment, without a guiding vision to pull together all the essential elements of a vibrant public realm, a community may continue to be inaccessible simply because there is no meaningful place to go—no destinations or environments within pedestrian range conducive to socialization, recreation, or leisure activity. The perception of safety is heavily affected by the design of the environment and is one of the most significant factors in access. In a neighborhood preferences survey of 2,001 Americans over the age of 45, 97 percent reported that safety was a critical factor in neighborhood life (Greenwald and Associates, Inc., 2003). The perceived or real threat of crime can be a significant barrier to access, particularly for those experiencing a degree of frailty or impairment. A guiding vision is necessary to ensure

---

[6] Mace, "Universal Design."

that beyond ADA compliance, a community is vibrant enough to foster access. Visioning processes help a community reframe the issues of accessibility in these larger contexts.

To help guide the visioning processes, the Global Universal Design Committee has developed design process standards to help ensure that universal design will be given appropriate attention throughout planning efforts. These process standards require that a development team be formed that includes a representation of end users who will live or work in or near the community, and who have a range of abilities and disability expertise (ergonomics, anthropometrics, vision, hearing, cognition, accessibility codes, aging, healthcare, and design). The process standards also stress the need to integrate Universal Design efforts with other aspects of the development project so that they are addressed simultaneously with other key goals such as contextual issues, sustainability, constructability, and cost effectiveness. Key design team decision-makers are required to participate in Universal Design training before design processes begin, and a confidential survey is sent to residents and other likely end users to identify existing problems they might have with usability and accessibility of the current or similar spaces in the community. Public meetings are also organized to solicit additional input and discuss how to address the problems identified in the survey. Communication goals and strategies are established to ensure that findings of the planning process are conveyed to stakeholders, that marketing materials explaining the universal design goals of the project will be created, and that universal design attributes are promoted in the general marketing of the planned projects to advance the public awareness of Universal Design.

Planning

It is nearly impossible to generate a continuously accessible, cohesive environment from a series of written specifications supplemented with a few illustrative diagrams. For example, an entry walk to a house may meet all accessibility standards and still not provide access. On one end of the walk, the house could be completely inaccessible and the other end may feed into an inaccessible streetscape. The whole set of relationships between house, walk, and streetscape must be considered within the framework of a larger vision and approach to accessibility where continuity is the foremost goal. The basic standards that inform most accessibility requirements (ANSI 117.1) form a valuable basis for beginning to address access, however the standards result in a disjointed community when applied at the architectural level, project by project, without an overarching master plan to guide them.

On the other hand, it must be remembered that master plans are not construction documents and they need to remain at a general level. Construction documents carry a greater degree of professional liability than master plans, and even more so when the governing codes are ultimately enforced by the US Department of Justice rather than the local building department. The relationships among master plan, site plan, architectural plan, and landscape plan are complex in any project, as are the individual roles of planner, engineer, architect, and landscape architect. Community-wide access must be constantly understood at both the scale of half-inch details and the scale of half-mile details, and care must be taken to include ample notation at each level of design so that the goal of access continuity will be upheld at each successive hand off between professions.

Graphic master plans are particularly useful in developing whole community accessibility strategies. Unlike a generic set of written code requirements abstractly applied as a blanket condition to the entire built environment, a graphic plan allows a community to quickly identify challenging conditions like dramatic topography or important seams and interfaces between properties. In this way, they can ascertain where extra attention is needed and call this out to the architects, engineers, and building department officials who will ultimately be responsible for implementation of the plan (fig. 2.4).

Rather than rely on written minimum slope specifications in the ADA to reveal where topography will present challenges, master planners can utilize topographic intensity maps (fig. 2.5) to identify critical zones, navigate them as effectively as possible with the street layout, and then provide general guidance on how accessible routes might best be provided in those areas. This reduces the need for unique solutions to be developed from scratch at each individual property and helps ensure that the solutions are compatible and create a cohesive frontage. Urban planning

Figure 2.4
This accessible path falters as it rounds a corner, collides with a fire hydrant, and then altogether peters out, 300 feet from a neighborhood retail district. Instances of non-coordination of the public realm like this one are common.

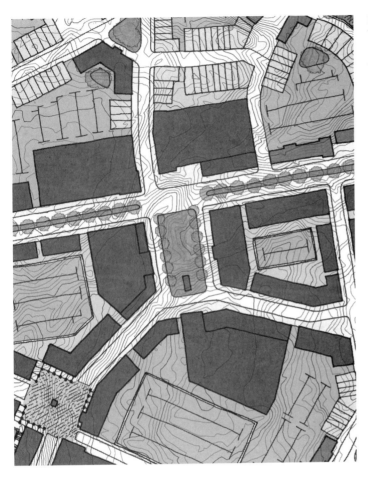

Figure 2.5
The accessibility
impacts of topography
can be studied and
mitigated at the master
planning stage.

can ensure that buildings define a cohesive and accessible public realm that is easily navigated, inviting, and well populated.

Most importantly, urban planning reinforces the principle that accessibility is as much about creating places that people want to be in as it is about ensuring that they can be there. Accessibility codes do not provide an avenue to gauge or respond to urban context in the way that master plans can.

An urban planning approach to accessibility can help to ensure that accessibility will

- be integrated and continuous across the entire community;

- include public, semipublic, and private spaces;

- consider the influence of design on the safety and vibrancy of public spaces;

- consider urban context;

- be calibrated to local conditions; and

- be phased in a manner that produces complete environments at each stage.

Zoning Codes and Design Standards

Construction code accessibility standards can be effectively supplemented with Zoning Codes and Design Standards, which also ensure that the resulting accommodations are integrated and coordinated across the built environment. Design standards for the public and private zones of a street frontage are particularly important in ensuring cohesive, accessible pathways from the work of multiple contractors and property owners of those spaces (fig. 2.6). Existing ADA design standards have proven themselves to be particularly ineffective at coordinating contractors to install storm water inlets, utility poles, fire hydrants, or other utility features so that sidewalk routes are not interrupted. Design standards help coordinate these multiple efforts across multiple parties over time by setting standards for the entire assemblage of the frontage rather than just the individual elements.

Zoning and design codes can also be utilized effectively to cover large swaths of the built environment that are not covered by ADA's architectural guidelines. Since the laws only apply to multifamily housing and a limited number of single family units, most of the residential environment remains largely inaccessible to people who have disabilities. Zoning is also an effective means of modulating accessibility requirements for housing based on urban context. Apartments close to the center of town and to transit stops should provide a higher level of access than those on the outskirts of town where frailty and physical impairments are harder to sustain without institutional support.

Zoning can also provide more opportunity for the local government to participate in reaching accessibility goals through the entitlement negotiation process. Developers agreeing to provide greater levels of accessibility can be rewarded by the

Figure 2.6

Access is a function of pedestrian vibrancy. Studies document factors that will contribute to or detract from vibrancy.

EXCELLENT FRONTAGE

DOORYARD

SHOPFRONT

ARCADE

STOOP

PORCH & FENCE

GALLERY

REGRETTABLE FRONTAGE

BLANK WALL

UNBUFFERED PARKING

UNBUFFERED LOT

local government with reduced on-site parking requirements, density bonuses, opportunities to mix uses on the property, fee waivers, or other benefits. An accessibility tax credit, modeled on historic preservation and affordable housing tax credits could be developed. Density bonuses are particularly beneficial because they forward access goals in two ways: by incentivizing developers to provide additional accessibility features and by making the community more compact and more able to support mixed uses. These are the kinds of negotiations and deliberations essential to achieving a more consumer-centric approach and to bringing additional resources to the table.

When an accessibility requirement is enacted in building code, however, it is rare for such negotiations and deliberations to take place; the developer must work within the constraints of the code unless there are some unusual circumstances. Moreover, it is to their advantage, in terms of reduced time for permit approval, to avoid negotiations. In most cases the property will not be made more valuable by the access measures, and any additional costs associated with its accommodation or installation will come out of the developer's profit alone. The dialogue between much of the development industry and accessibility advocates thus becomes confrontational and galvanizing in such a way as to prevent the exploration of nuanced and multifaceted solutions. The negotiated and cost shared processes described above would further more exploration.

Beyond the base requirements already in place, performance measures offer opportunities to advance the cause through a more comprehensive approach.

A zoning framework for accessibility regulation can

- include entitlement incentives to offset developer costs for exceeding minimums, while further contributing to whole-community accessibility;

- help communities to focus a vision for the future on desirable accessibility goals that improve livability for all;

- be the foundation for continuous improvement in environment standards as opposed to the limited goal of meeting legal requirements; and

- ensure optimum levels of accessibility through integration with pedestrian and transit accessibility.

Accessibility issues not addressed in American Disability Act Architectural Guidelines that can be addressed with zoning:

- Quality of pedestrian experience
  - Connectivity
  - Street width
  - Traffic density and speed
  - Intersection design
  - Setbacks
  - Curb height

- Personal safety
  - Lighting
  - Eyes on the street
  - Crosswalk signal timing
- Travel distances to daily needs
- Accessible housing options
- Available transportation modes

Stewardship

Seniors housing communities have pioneered many valuable approaches to environmental access through stewardship over time. In some ways the sole focus of a seniors housing development can be understood as access: to the whole environment, to services, to recreation, to entertainment, and to social experiences. Seniors housing managers have a stake in maintaining the health of their residents, both to maintain the reputation necessary in order to attract additional residents and to ensure that their current residents can remain active and healthy for as long as possible. Seniors housing management agencies deliver this full range of access by acting as ombudsmen for all spatial and social aspects of the community. They are called on regularly to resolve issues that could very broadly be defined as access problems. Obstacles needing attention may emerge anywhere—private residences, sidewalks, surrounding grounds, or central common areas. It could be any type of obstacle that they are asked to address—marauding teenagers, too much exposure to the elements, insects, dumpster odors, or cracked sidewalk. The management agency also has a range of means to mitigate an obstacle: providing staff assistance, organizing volunteer efforts, physically removing the obstacle, or reprogramming the space. In this sense, privately managed senior housing communities are testing grounds for accessibility defined as any item that impacts access rather than a specific list of architectural standards. The contrast between the level of accessibility in these communities and in the surrounding, often suburban, context, is dramatic even to the visitor (figs. 2.7, 2.8).

Well-managed retirement communities thus offer a good example of how thoughtful environmental access can be when developed over time to address user needs.

Figure 2.7
This handrail, designed by Perkins+Will, is worked into the hallway trim and is an example of the thought and consideration that goes into the detailing of higher-end senior housing facilities.

Photo by Cameron Triggs, Cowan Triggs

Photo by Cameron Triggs, Cowan Triggs

Figure 2.8
The handrail can be seen from another angle in this photo. This facility is for Alzheimer's patients and reminiscence cabinets are provided at each unit entry for residents to place photos and keepsakes that help trigger an identity with the room.

When sufficient resources and neighborhood organization are available to support them, some aspects of access are better left to this type of ombudsman process than the singular fixes that are detailed in construction documents, drawn up in plans, or specified in zoning documents. The means of developing access solutions with the involvement of a wide range of stakeholders may also produce as many benefits as the end solution itself. When accessibility is viewed only as the elimination of a few architectural barriers or a few fixed solutions, it becomes detached from the complex spatial and social community relationships that define disability.

When planning and regulating, it is important to have a good sense of the limits of what can and should be addressed as a fixed relationship that can be drawn up and implemented as a permanent solution. If the end goal is a community that supports continuous accessibility to things that are needed, inviting, and worth having access to, then prescriptive construction details alone can attempt to solve the problem too easily, finalize the solution too quickly, let critical issues go unaddressed, and miss the opportunity to bring many valuable community resources to bear in design and development. Good seniors housing developments are essentially very advanced accessible environments internally—the Ferraris of the accessible environment world. Stewardship is what ultimately works best.

The Beacon Hill Village's concierge service, discussed in depth in Chapter 11, is a good example of a management service common in seniors development exported to a general urban environment. Seniors housing developments are also rich in the detailing of physical access accommodations in the environment, some built in initially, others cobbled together over time to serve the unique needs of individual residents. The built environment is most accessible when it responds to the active stewardship of residents and proprietors. An engaged, ongoing relationship between people and place is the fullest expression of access, and the goal of access planning and design should not simply be permanently fixed, built-in assurance of the right to autonomous mobility.

The Medieval City

As an example of urban accessibility, this chapter concludes with the proposition that medieval cities offer ways of thinking about integrated accessibility at the urban scale. By contemporary standards, medieval cities are poster children for inaccessibility. Architectural barriers are everywhere to be found: cobblestones, steep grades, narrow passages, irregular steps, heavy doors, etc. Although lacking at the architectural scale, these cities provide access in abundance at the urban scale. The urban qualities do not make up for the architectural deficiencies, but the medieval example is useful in elucidating the distinction between architectural access detailing and urban access planning.

In his book *Medieval Cities,* Howard Saalman concludes that the medieval city was an instrument of commerce: "a tool for the production and exchange of goods and services."[7] The roads, squares, bridges, gates, buildings, and walls of western medieval cities were generated out of the interaction between two opposing commerce needs: passage and position. Consumer need pushed open space for passage access, while merchants encroached back upon the open space as they jockeyed for the best exposure to passing traffic. The interplay of counterpoised form and void that is unmistakably identifiable in a figure/ground map of a medieval city (fig. 2.9) evolved as an expression of commercial access dynamics.

Within the medieval city, the positioning of buildings in relation to access routes also establishes social and economic hierarchies: Civic and religious structures occupy primary positions, shops vie for attention in secondary positions, and residences retreat to the background. These hierarchal environments are visually legible—a church looks different than a house that can in turn be distinguished from a civic building, and each of these occupies a position appropriate to its role. In the competitive positioning of mass along access routes, open space was sufficiently enclosed and defined to be oriented by senses other than vision: light, sound, and breeze convey spatial qualities and directional orientation as they play across the close and varied site conditions (fig. 2.10). Access is provided on many levels and in many forms: Even a remote location in the square might generate access by roasting nuts and drawing traffic with the wafting scent.

Access is shaped by a very different dynamic in contemporary sprawling suburban development. Enormous open spaces that are cut through the urban fabric for vehicular passage and parking dominate the built environment. In all but the most local of streets, passage and parking spaces are too expansive and ill defined

---

[7]H. Saalman, *Medieval Cities* (New York: George Braziller, 1968).

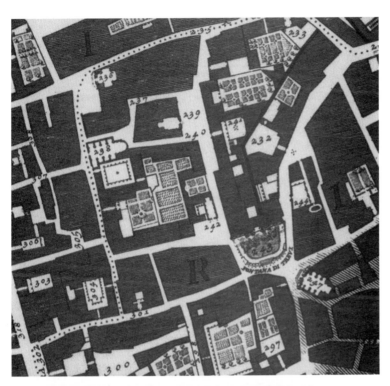

Figure 2.9
Detail from Giambattista Nolli's 1748 map of Rome portrays the interplay between passage voids and building mass.

Figure 2.10
Access for many impairments can be assisted by a well-defined, legible environment where sound, light, breeze, and smells can provide a rich array of orientating sensory cues.

Photo by Patrick Denker

Figure 2.11
Buildings in the upper section line up to shape public space, while those below do not.

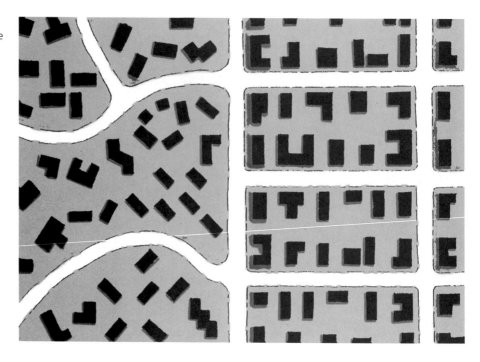

for the interplay of light and shade, shifts in breeze and sound quality, or any other environmental conditions that provide orienting cues (fig. 2.11). Billboards rather than buildings jockey for a position along these routes and navigation is mostly dependent on vision-oriented signage.

Accessibility regulation has only explored one side of these pitted forces of urban access dynamics—the carving of passages into urban mass, without regard to the access dynamics of massing around those passages. Tight massing around passages defines spaces sufficiently for haptic orientation that draws ambient conditions for sensory cues. Tight massing also has the obvious result of bringing multiple programs in a compact space, thus making them easier to access simply by providing proximity. Accessibility provisions, as they are now conceived, elevate mobility as the single determinant of an inclusive environment and ignore the complex role that proximity and spatial definition play in shaping and orienting an accessible environment. In taking this imbalanced prioritization to its extreme, brownstones (fig. 2.12) are viewed as a completely inaccessible space, and the Georgia Department of Driver Services (figs. 2.13, 2.14) is viewed as a completely accessible space. Both are deficient in terms of access: one at the architectural level and the other at the urban level.

What is lost in the extreme prioritization of a few architectural details as a means of accomplishing access is any sense of urban context, the many haptic experiences that urban form can provide, and any appreciation of the complex role urbanity can play in creating an inclusive community. Instead the auto-dependent sprawling condition is accepted by regulators as a given, and the focus is on increasing the ease of mobility through the environment no matter how sensorially parched, or extensively divided and compartmentalized it becomes. Way-finding by means other

Chris Ritter

Figure 2.12
Boston brownstones in a
compact community are
accessible at the urban scale,
but fail to provide access at the
architectural scale.

Figure 2.13
Georgia Department of Driver
Services in downtown Atlanta is
a celebration of ADA compliance,
while totally failing to provide
accessible urbanism.

Figure 2.14
Georgia Department of
Driver Services in exile
from the city it serves.

than sight is occasionally assisted by sensory cues that were designed in a laboratory, mass produced in factories, and installed to the letter of a generic construction specification. Factory-built sensory cues are usually designed to stand out and apart from the surrounding environment rather than work with it, and as a result they can be quite brash.

With increased longevity will come an increased need for accessibility. The more that access can be thought of as an integral part of the built environment, as a continuous part of the planning process, and as social as well as physical function of place, the more effectively it can be provided. The nation will be challenged to explore ways to move from our existing focus on mobility passages and architectural details to a more urban and environmental perspective on access that taps into the counter-dynamics of massing, program proximities, and ambient conditions. As accessibility is becoming a majority concern, consumer protection frameworks for implementation and enforcement of the ADA could prove to be effective in enabling this progress.

CHAPTER 3

HEALTH, HEALTHCARE, AND URBANISM

"Health" is not a simple or singular aspect of our lives and any effective approach to improving health must be multifaceted. The World Health Organization defines health as "a state of complete physical, mental, and social well-being and not merely the absence of disease or infirmity." Read carefully, the focus on complete well-being sets up health improvement and maintenance as a proactive enterprise, not "merely" a reaction to illness. The maintenance of well-being can, in fact, be the most cost-effective means of addressing disease and infirmity: by preventing both in the first place.[1] The increasingly chronic nature of the nation's morbidity provides a rationale to question the nearly total alignment we have established between healthcare and acute medical treatment. A greater emphasis on multifaceted approaches to well-being is warranted.

Environmental Health, Safety, and Welfare

Today, the most important environment for lifelong well-being is that of the neighborhood: front yards, sidewalks, parks, squares, and main streets that surround homes and work places.[2] People establish social relationships, behaviors, and daily routines in their neighborhoods and these have much more dramatic effects on their lifelong health than do visits to healthcare providers or admissions to hospitals. In spite of this, American healthcare systems over the past fifty years have grown increasingly focused on reactive treatment of acute illnesses and disease. This myopic focus on medical treatment is expensive and ineffective and needs to be addressed.

The Obama administration, building on the efforts of many prior administrations, has focused on the medical treatment system and its financing, once again demonstrating that major changes to the healthcare system are not made easily. Healthcare reform is the third rail of national politics, and the broad reinvention of systems is unlikely to originate from the top down. This chapter reviews collaborations that are beginning to affect changes one step at a time through professional working relationships: one community organizer, one doctor, one planner, and one developer at a time. Collaborations like these, which are increasingly common between public health and urban planning professionals, have already begun to reshape the goals and objectives of built-environment planning with more of a focus on creating healthy communities. On the implementation side, community service agencies and developers have begun to produce projects that coordinate

---

[1] American College of Preventive Medicine, *Four Truths About Prevention* (Washington, DC: ACPM, 2010).

[2] A. Kaczynski, L. Potawarka, and B. Saelens, "Association of Park Size, Distance, and Features With Physical Activity in Neighborhood Parks," *American Journal of Public Health* 98 (August 2008): 1451–6.

public and philanthropic resources with private investment capital to create places where acute care facilities and community-based services can be coordinated to create a multifaceted continuum of well-being support in neighborhood settings. Grassroots initiatives within the care, planning, and development professions are moving a broader agenda for change forward in small but steady steps.

Defining the Healthcare Paradigm

Public health professionals have long held that the healthcare system's singular emphasis on the treatment of illness is not an effective or efficient means of addressing the health of the population. In 2009, the Office of the Surgeon General released a report stating that the medical treatment model alone is especially ineffective in meeting the needs of an aging population, and that community-based self-management programs will be particularly important in helping older adults manage increasingly common chronic conditions. These self-management programs can help individuals gain self-confidence in their abilities to control symptoms and manage the progression of several long-term and chronic age-related illnesses.[3] Such programs can also help define the environments that facilitate the maintenance of healthy functioning.

The National Center for Healthy Aging has determined that at least 60 percent of primary health influences relate to an individual's behavior, social structures, and environmental conditions. In 2002, the top three causes of death for US adults aged 65 or older were heart disease (32 percent of all deaths), cancer (22 percent), and stroke (8 percent). These illnesses accounted for more than 60 percent of all deaths in this age group. Currently, at least 80 percent of older Americans are living with at least one chronic condition, and 50 percent of them have at least two conditions.[4] Many of these conditions, especially chronic ones, can be efficiently and effectively addressed in neighborhood settings by aligning resources with individuals' daily routines rather than the traditional reliance on stand-alone medical facilities. In spite of these opportunities, institutional acute care treatment, which accounts for no more than 10 percent of all health outcomes, commands a staggering 88 percent of all health expenditures (fig. 3.1). Factors related to the social and spatial quality of a neighborhood, on the other hand, receive at most 4 percent of our health dollars.[5]

Data reveal the value of placing a greater emphasis on environmental rather than medical approaches to health. Many preventable health risk factors such as tobacco use (including secondhand exposure), lack of adequate physical activity, and poor nutrition are strongly influenced by the physical and cultural contexts of neighborhoods. Heart disease, stroke, diabetes, cancer, obesity, asthma, and arthritis are all common examples of the chronic diseases that affect half of all Americans and account for seven of the ten leading causes of death in the United States.[6] These

---

[3]Surgeon General, "Self-Management Programs: One Way to Promote Healthy Aging," *Public Health Reports* 124 (July–Aug. 2009): 1.

[4]Centers for Disease Control and Prevention, *The State of Aging and Health in America 2007* (Whitehouse Station, NJ: The Merck Company Foundation, 2007).

[5]www.cms.hhs.gov/NationalHealthExpendData/

[6]American College of Preventive Medicine, *Four Truths*.

Factors influencing health

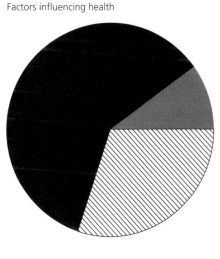

Figure 3.1
Health effects/health spending
chart.

National health expenditures

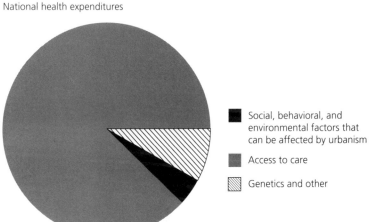

■ Social, behavioral, and
environmental factors that
can be affected by urbanism

■ Access to care

▨ Genetics and other

conditions cannot be effectively addressed by medical treatment alone, and they require broader approaches that should include planning and urban design strategies.

Exterior spaces are particularly important to neighborhood health, particularly those that incorporate natural features. In his 1984 book *Biophilia: The Human Bond with Other Species*, Edward O. Wilson hypothesized that humans have an innate sensitivity to and need for other living things. He defines *biophilia* as "the connections that human beings subconsciously seek with the rest of life" and presents the natural environment as a vital aesthetic and health resource that we are driven by biological needs to interact with. This work has become an important theoretical foundation for research on the relationship between natural environments and health, and in a 2001 article,[7] Dr. Howard Frumkin built on Wilson's hypothesis to lay out a broad agenda for environmental health research and outreach

---

[7]H. Frumkin, "Beyond Toxicity Human Health and the Natural Environment," *Journal of Health and Medicine* 20, no. 3 (April 2001): 234–40.

initiatives. Frumkin's agenda challenges the field of public health to look proactively at the multifaceted well-being benefits supplied by parks and other environmental amenities rather than only at ways to reactively control the outbreak of disease.

Frumkin's agenda has economic rationale as well. The places we currently associate with healthcare—medical offices and hospitals—reflect an exorbitantly expensive imbalance between health systems and health needs. Treatment facilities have evolved as highly specialized, structurally segregated facilities frequently accessed for a single treatment or unique medical procedure. For individuals with multiple health problems, healthcare reimbursement regulations structure in care discontinuities, and even the transitions between specialized facilities can be full of risk and trauma. According to a study in the New England Journal of Medicine, "almost one fifth (19.6 percent) of the 11,855,702 Medicare beneficiaries who had been discharged from a hospital were hospitalized again within thirty days."[8] This revolving door pattern that makes hospital discharge tantamount to ruptures in care, results in multiple admissions and is as expensive as it is traumatic and ineffective.

A stark contrast exists between the resources lavished on the medical system and the occasional afterthought given to sidewalks, parks, and civic spaces—tangible investments in the places where healthy routines can be reinforced in a continuous and passive manner. Neighborhood resources are unfortunately valued as amenities only, and though comparatively cheap across their useful existence, they are viewed as luxuries rather than long-term health investments. Healthcare facilities continue to improve and grow, even in a significant economic downturn, while public space amenities are the first programs to be cut when budgets tighten. On the one hand, this disparity highlights the lack of awareness of the ways in which the built environment is intrinsically tied to lifelong well-being. On the other hand, it highlights the lack of administrative systems capable of assigning value to the health benefit of environmental planning and decision-making.

Reestablishing a Healthy Land-Use Paradigm

Simplistic public health objectives have undergirded the practices through which communities regulate their built environments. In the 1926 landmark case of *Ambler Realty v. Village of Euclid, Ohio,* the justices declared that Euclid would promote "the health and safety of the community" by protecting residential areas from the "danger of fire, contagion and disorder, which attach . . . to the location of stores, shops or factories." Since the mid-twentieth century, government policies based on this paradigm have promoted the growth of suburbs divided into isolated residential, shopping, office, industrial, and institutional pods.

More recently, public health research has established as an empirical fact that it is precisely the division of urban components into segregated zones that contributes to some of our nation's most intractable health problems: declining rates of physical activity resulting from auto-dependent environments and widespread respiratory

---

[8]S. F. Jencks, M. V. Williams, and E. Coleman, "Re-hospitalizations Among Patients in the Medicare Fee-for-Service Program," *New England Journal of Medicine* 360 (2009): 1418–28.

problems associated with poor air quality. Mental health and quality of life issues are also profoundly affected by contextual factors that range from the stress and difficulties of lengthy work commutes to isolation-related depression for those retired or unable to maintain employment. Poor and minority communities are especially vulnerable, based on their disproportionate exposure to numerous environmental pollutants, crime, and poor access to healthcare.

A growing body of evidence, much of it sponsored by the Robert Wood Johnson Foundation's Active Living Research initiative, has established that compact neighborhoods with vibrant pedestrian environments positively correlate with decreases in a variety of serious health conditions such as obesity, diabetes, hypertension, and asthma. In addition, a number of "follow-on" effects associated with decreasing automobile dependence are emerging. These include

- improved regional air quality leading to decreases in asthma and other respiratory problems;

- improved community access for those unable to operate automobiles for economic or disability reasons;

- improved water quality through the reduction of point-sources of water pollutants like petroleum hydrocarbons;

- decreased vehicular and pedestrian injuries; and

- decreased commuter stress and the incidence of "road rage."

The Centers for Disease Control and Prevention's National Center for Environmental Health (NCEH) recognizes several broad health conditions that are improved by well-designed pedestrian-oriented neighborhoods. Walkable neighborhoods can

- make it easier for people with mobility impairments or other disabling conditions to move about their environments;

- improve children's school performance and overall health;

- improve the general well-being of older adults;

- reduce motor-vehicle injuries;

- improve mental health;

- reduce air pollution and related respiratory health problems;

- increase social capital; and

- improve water quality and related health issues.[9]

With a mounting body of evidence-based documentation regarding the relationships between sprawling development patterns and negative health outcomes, and the relationships between compact pedestrian-oriented patterns and positive health

---

[9]http://www.cdc.gov/healthyplaces/factsheets/Health_Issues_Related_to_Community_ Design_factsheet_Final.pdf

outcomes, it seems obvious that the next step would be to correct the planning and zoning regulations that create unhealthy sprawling urban conditions and prohibit healthy, compact, walkable communities.

There is an urgent need to update the basic premises through which health, safety, and welfare are protected through planning and zoning regulations. When the Euclid versus Amber decision was first handed down by the Supreme Court in 1926, basic sanitation was a much more pressing concern in urban areas than it is today. The vast majority of the cities in 1926 were not yet even treating raw sewage before releasing it into the environment. Epidemiology in America in 1926 was focused primarily on communicable diseases like malaria and tuberculosis, rather than on the chronic diseases that are now our challenge. In this context of very different environmental health concerns, zoning did provide protections through use segregation. However, the basic paradigm for how health and safety can be protected through zoning needs to be brought up-to-date with current environmental health knowledge and challenges.

Knowledge and Action: Finding an Institutional Basis for Public Health and Land-Use Planning Integration

The professions of planning and public health hold enough shared history and institutional genetics that ostensibly they should be able to integrate easily. Both professions grew in response to environmental degradation created by the unmanaged industrializing and urbanization of cities in the nineteenth century. The two professions share many of the same founding fathers and mothers.

While there are a number of effective methods for integrating health considerations into land-use and transportation planning processes, the decision to utilize these methods is almost always made at the discretion of local governing authorities, except in dire emergency cases of disaster or health crisis. Despite the similar histories, planning and public health have evolved on separate paths and now occupy positions in distantly separate branches of governmental structures. Final authority for ensuring health safety and welfare in the planning of the built environment is conferred upon local government officials without dedicated funding sources for related research and education. Dedicated funding for research and education on the built environment is provided to public health professionals through the National Center for Environmental Health, which has very little authority to plan or regulate the built environment. In the case of environmental health, knowledge and authority would be more effective in combination than in isolation from each other.

Even though the authority given to state and local governments to plan and zone is legally empowered by the need to protect health, safety, and welfare, a century of eminent domain case history has established nearly unlimited home rule powers for local governments to define those terms as they see fit, with or without empirical evidence. Virtually unlimited home rule powers make it unlikely that a legal challenge could be mounted to force the hand of local governments to give more weight to health factors in planning and zoning processes. Oddly, constitutional enabling of local-planning and zoning authorities to protect health was handed over without any standard of healthy practice or level of health performance. The power was conferred without contingencies or standards of accountability.

The Department of Health and Human Services (DHHS), which does have clear definitions of health and healthy practice, is unlikely to weigh in forcefully, even though it has mounting insights into impacts on health—often negative impacts of contemporary planning practices. What smaller educational campaigns are mounted will likely focus on positive encouragement of healthier land use policy rather than discouraging unhealthy land-use policy. While the nation has seen the surgeon general exercise significant powers in the past decade in efforts to reduce tobacco use, and while DHHS does have a powerful cavalry at hand, it will not likely be mobilized on issues outside of the department's regulatory scope. Assertive, large-scale health interventions like the anti-tobacco campaign are generally reserved for food and drugs or other fields in which DHHS has regulatory authority.

Environmental health findings on the health impacts of land use and transportation decisions gathered by the CDC are limited to advisory uses and can only influence regulation when local jurisdictions choose to adopt them on a voluntary basis. The structural separation of the nation's major environmental health and wellness expertise from the decision-making authorities responsible for upholding the health, safety, and welfare of the built environment places the onus for change on the respective individual professionals: The existing organization of institutional structures will not enable top-down, systemic means of reform.

Near-term efforts will be most effective when they focus on encouraging implementing authorities to utilize health factors in decision-making and encouraging environmental health professionals to utilize implementation considerations in their research pursuits. The two professional fields have strong incentives for diverging from the other. Implementing authorities must operate within a world that is heavily influenced by political and economic considerations, while environmental health researchers operate in a world that is heavily influenced by peer review of research integrity and evidence quality. The two incentives pull these two professions in opposite directions.

For local implementing officials, welfare protections in practice will often become the predominant factor in planning and zoning decision-making—usually translating to mean economic development. Economic development can provide a positive motivation for including evidence-based review of health impacts in comprehensive planning efforts. Local governments compete to lure businesses to their community, and places like Seattle and King County, Washington, have found that documenting the health benefits of the planning decisions they have made is a powerful tool in branding their quality of life. Seattle and King County is positioning itself as a healthy city with well-planned neighborhoods featuring connected street networks, nearby shopping, walking paths, and transit service through an initiative known as HealthScape. The county has worked closely with Larry Frank & Company, a leading firm specialized in analyzing the relationship between health and urban form, to carefully detail the data and methodology that inform their health and land-use review process.

The competition among cities to lure big employers is intense, and quality of life issues can play a significant role in encouraging initiatives like HealthScape. There are several map and data resources that can help broadcast quality environmental health results, including County Health Rankings (countyhealthrankings.org), which rates counties by health, although it does not yet include built environment factors; Gallup-Healthways Well-Being Index (well-beingindex.com), which ranks cities and congressional districts on well-being factors evaluated through ongoing surveys; and Walk Score (walkscore.com), which rates addresses and neighborhoods by their walkability. Though protection of health and safety constitute two thirds of the legal basis for planning, successful strategies for integrating health and planning will focus on the third enabling consideration, that of welfare. In practice, evidence-based findings on environmental health impacts will be more widely used when they are clearly translated into compelling and marketable quality of life benefits. Benefits can range from greater ability to attract large employers looking for communities with high-quality-of-life factors to greater ability to retain and attract older adult residents with disposable income.

Establishing Intent

Another leverage point for elevating the role of health in planning is in the way communities establish the intent of transportation and land-use ordinances. As stated earlier, home rule has defused intention by stating the enabling principles of protection of health, safety, and welfare, but then defining those terms so loosely as to render them meaningless. The resulting regulations predictably tend to be perfunctory setbacks and separations, and are divorced from common cause or any local visions for distinct places. Most communities have generic zoning codes purchased from national providers and applied with little to no local calibration.

In order for planning and zoning codes to be effective, they must enable collective action around common goals for the built environment. Few zoning ordinances today are based on a master plan or vision for what their communities are to look and feel like. Comprehensive development plans often stop at allocating various forms of development intensities across their jurisdictions only to the degree necessary to predict demand loads on infrastructure. Often there is little to no direction given to the kind or quality of community that will be shaped by those development allocations. Master plans are the best means of establishing a community's vision and intent, but in advance of plans, and with the input and assistance of public health professionals, intent statements can be effective tools for establishing a healthy planning context and clearly defining the health safety and welfare qualities that need to be forwarded and protected in zoning.

Local Intent   Codes usually contain a statement of intent in the initial sections of their ordinance. At a minimum, this statement should establish a preference for developing land within or contiguous to existing urbanized areas over land that is out at the edges of town or beyond. Locating near existing communities is more economically and environmentally sustainable for the end occupant of the housing, the businesses, and the local government that supplies the infrastructure and services. Development closer in is more capable of providing the building and use variety needed to support lifelong neighborhoods. The reciprocal complements to infill preference statements are statements that establish the intent for established communities to make room for new homes and businesses. It is not effective to discourage growth at city edges if densification inside the city is not encouraged. As cities and towns grow denser, the public realm plays an increasingly critical role in preserving neighborhood quality. Additional statements should also establish a preference for development that pays more attention to building and street form coordination so that the public realm is intentionally framed as a prominent asset to the community rather than a loose agglomeration of residual spaces left over after all individual, private property interests are satisfied and all motor-vehicles needs, no matter how excessive, are provided for. A well-defined public realm is essential to the creation or recovery of mixed-use, pedestrian friendly, mixed-income communities, and its production must be framed as a positive, instigating element and a primary intent of code rather than a hopeful by-product.

Intention statements can establish the comparative value weights placed on health, safety, and welfare, elevate health as an essential criterion in planning decisions, and even establish processes and benchmarks for calibrating progress. Simply stating an intent to consider the readily available base of environmental health evidence can begin to refocus zoning ordinances in the abstract on urban goals that are more sustainable and more healthy across lifetimes, doing so in advance of actual project proposals that must weigh a collection of local, proprietary interests.

Regional and Statewide Intent

Older adult issues can be particularly effective as a focal point for intention statements issued from the larger jurisdictional levels of regional and state planning processes that influence zoning practice but are outside of zoning codes. At the time of this writing, South Carolina's House and Senate have adopted and are reviewing, respectively, a sprawl repair act (2011–2012 House Bill 3604) that encourages local governments to adopt zoning ordinances that promote more hospitable, accessible, and sustainable human habitats. The "whereas" statements of the bill include lifelong considerations:

> *Whereas*, the Baby Boom Generation, the largest demographic group among South Carolina residents, will not be well served by being able to live only in automobile dependent suburban areas; and
>
> *Whereas*, the Millennial Generation, the second largest group and the most important to the future workforce of South Carolina, has shown a preference to urban areas.[10]

[10]South Carolina General Assembly, *House Bill 3604* (Columbia, 119th Session, 2011–2012): 1.

As described in more detail in Chapter 12, the Atlanta Regional Commission (ARC) has successfully used older adult issues as the focus of "lifelong communities" intention statements. Lifelong communities are particularly effective because they have a non-technocratic, kitchen table appeal to the general population and frame a performance goal as the animating intent of action—the ability to live in a community for a lifetime. The performance goals can be used to coordinate and orchestrate across many agencies and divisions: land use, transportation, social and government services and so on. Lifelong community goals also target an older adult constituency that usually votes and participates in civic affairs in greater numbers than other demographics. It is an effective rallying cry. The ARC's Lifelong Communities Initiative proved effective enough as a messaging and coordinating tool that the commission's board adopted a resolution in 2008 stating the following:

> Now therefore, be it resolved that the Atlanta Regional Commission Board as representatives of the communities that make up the ten county metropolitan area, *adopts as agency policy* its goal to transform the Atlanta Region into a Lifelong Community by: promoting housing and transportation options, encouraging healthy lifestyles, and expanding information and access services.[11]

Intent statements, like those of the South Carolina act and Atlanta Regional Commission resolution, help establish a context for local, legally enforceable action. Once established, these statements can be further backed by policies and programs at the state and regional levels—policies that set minimum standards for local comprehensive development plans or set criteria that guide the award of public construction funding of all types. Programs can provide education and technical assistance for local governments that want to pursue the regional and state intentions in their local policies. In this way, regional and state intention statements can help provide political reinforcement and cover for local officials who already want to do the right things, but face constituents who are resistant to change. Intention statements are not a silver-bullet end solution to the deficiencies of the built environment—they are underutilized tools for seeding the ground and creating base conditions that allow local solutions to take root. Today, the Achilles heel of planning is not the knowledge and expertise necessary to produce healthy communities, but rather is the rationale for doing so.

Beyond Intent and Toxicity: Establishing Frameworks for Planning Action
Ecologic Frameworks

In an effort to establish more prevention-focused care, public health professionals advocate the use of "ecologic" health frameworks that emphasize community-based health strategies. These frameworks incorporate a combination of built environment,

---

[11]Atlanta Regional Commission, *Lifelong Communities: A Regional Guide to Longevity* (Atlanta, 2009), 3.

social network, and public policy factors into health delivery approaches.[12] Ecologic frameworks have primarily been used by public health professionals in the very local settings of neighborhood to develop community-based solutions to specific epidemics within specific at-risk populations. These frameworks typically center on the welfare of participating individual "clients" and through investigation of their circumstances, lead to a broader understanding of how the local social, economic, and built environment contexts have influenced clients' health.

The Common Ground Initiative in Fulton County, Georgia, is a good example of an ecologic approach to public health focused on creating more collaborative approaches to service delivery among a wide array of governmental agencies, regional and community-based nonprofit organizations, faith-based organizations, universities, and school boards. The initial goal of the initiative was to optimize service delivery among departments within the Fulton County government, although it quickly evolved into a much larger strategic initiative to develop a system wide approach that would address the essential factors and resources in the social environment that contribute to or detract from the health of individuals and communities. Innovative programs that have grown out of the Common Ground Initiative include a "one-stop shop" resource in the Oak Hill Family include Center that addresses family health and wellness issues in a multifaceted, culturally competent manner, and the Neighborhood Union Primary Care Partnership, which integrates the once compartmentalized services—public health, mental health, human services, and primary care—so that they can together foster holistic strategies for improving the well-being of underserved individuals and communities.[13]

The patient centricity of the ecologic framework mirrors the way in which public health and community service agencies have developed an understanding of larger environmental influences through a focus on individual clients and their specific needs. A broader understanding of the larger community environment and the resources and challenges it presents to health is gained as a second layer of analysis through their impact on the client. The firsthand knowledge of the health impact of neighborhood form on actual residents of the neighborhood is an invaluable resource, one that planners and architects think of as "post-occupancy evaluation." However, if this knowledge is to be used proactively in shaping healthier environments, the information needs to be abstracted and projected forward in a manner so that it can be used in development or redevelopment planning.

Without this process of abstraction and projection, ecologic frameworks can only react to built environment conditions, either by spot-checking and correcting comparatively minor environmental deficiencies like missing curb cuts, poor lighting, and code enforcements on unsafe housing development or by developing service "patches" to address major deficiencies like transportation programs that fail to reach frail or impaired individuals who are isolated by auto-dependent development patterns. Ideally, ecologic frameworks could instead be applied proactively in

[12]J. Stein, T. Schettler, B. Rohrer, and M. Valenti, "Environmental Threats to Healthy Aging," in *Greater Boston Physicians for Social Responsibility and Science and Environmental Health Network*, ed. N. Myers (2008), 1–210.

[13]American College of Preventive Medicine, *Four Truths.*

Figure 3.2
Public-health professionals'
version of the ecologic
health diagram centers on
individuals.[14]

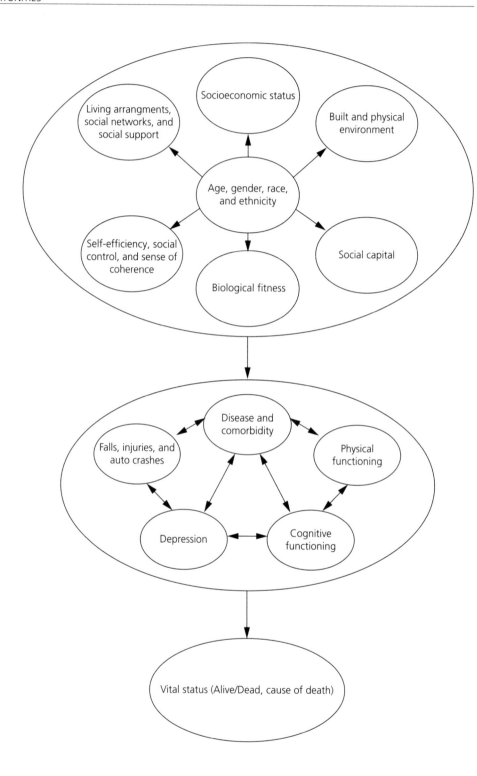

[14]W. A. Satariano, *Epidemiology of Aging: An Ecological Approach* (Berkeley: University of California, 2006), 61

making development decisions that will produce health benefits over time rather than only reacting to environmental health problems that occur after development has been completed.

In a proactive model, an ecologic approach to a lifelong neighborhood would initially look at the built environment and apply sound planning principles to its development or redevelopment. This proactive ecologic framework would relate the same array of influencing factors but would insert findings gleaned from prior investigations as a central focus rather than those gathered from work with a single client. The basic client-centric ecologic framework diagram (fig. 3.2) would be altered to the urban-centric framework (fig. 3.3).

Ideally, both frameworks would be applied over time: The proactive framework would be applied when development or redevelopment objectives are initially established and the reactive framework would be applied as health conditions of residents are monitored and maintained, thereby using the lessons learned as the community's development vision, plans, and codes are periodically updated and revised. The two diagrams would thus frame stages in a continuous feedback loop that tailors health strategies to community conditions and development plans and regulations to health strategies.

The July/August 2008 edition of the Journal of Environmental Health presents four case studies documenting successful collaborative efforts in which environmental health professionals became effective participants in the development of healthy local land use policy. These case studies review a health impact assessment tool developed for Inghram County, Michigan,[15] the involvement of a Colorado tri-county health department in development planning,[16] the work Seattle and King County have done to integrate health professionals and health criteria into planning processes,[17] and the smart-growth initiative led by environmental health professionals in Delaware County, Ohio.[18] Each case study describes the importance of interdisciplinary coordination as a first step to becoming engaged in planning discussions.

Health and Scenario Planning Frameworks

Scenario planning is a common means of integrating health, land use, and transportation planning processes. In recent years, many metropolitan areas in the United States have engaged in some form of scenario planning to quantitatively evaluate

---

[15]K. Roof, and R. Glandon, "Tool Created to Assess Health Impacts of Development Decision in Ingham County, Michigan," *Journal of Environmental Health* 71, no. 1 (2008): 35–38.

[16]K. Roof, and C. Maclennan, "Tri-County Health Department in Colorado Does More Than Just Review a Development Plan," *Journal of Environmental Health* 71, no. 1 (2008): 31–34.

[17]K. Roof, and N. Oleru. "Public Health: Seattle and King County's Push for the Built Environment," *Journal of Environmental Health* 71, no.1 (2008): 24–27.

[18]K. Roof, and S. Sutherland. "Smart Growth and Health for the Future: 'Our Course of Action' Delaware County, Ohio," *Journal of Environmental Health* 71, no. 1 (2008): 28–30.

Figure 3.3
Planners' version of the
ecologic health diagram centers
on the built environment.

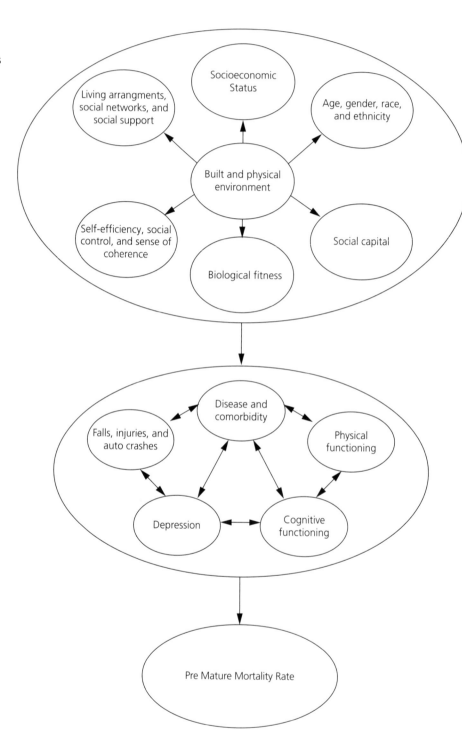

several alternative development patterns and analyze their respective impacts on indices ranging from the affordability of housing to water and air quality. Increasingly, health impacts analysis is being integrated into the software programs that are utilized to model and evaluate future development scenarios. Common scenario planning software systems include the following:

Smart Growth Index

MetroQuest

RapidFire

EnvisionTomorrow

UPLAN

WhatIf?

Under the federal transportation law, transportation construction projects must compete for federal funds, and health impact considerations can be incorporated into the criteria by which these projects are identified, scored, and selected. Normally, transportation alternatives analyses for regional transportation projects utilize only one land-use forecast, whereas scenario planning allows exploration of multiple land-use and transportation options in an integrated fashion, permitting comparisons among quantifiable impacts of various options. Environmental health-impact assessments are most effective in informing planning decisions when they are used to compare scenarios rather than make up-or-down judgments on a single project. Most health impacts are subtle and do not present black-and-white findings. Health-impact scenario planning is also most useful at larger scales, such as counties or regions, where decisions can be made to concentrate development in certain areas like transit stations and infill locations and limit development in other areas like exurban green fields. At these scales, factors related to location play as much of a role as those related to type of development.

Envision Utah (figs. 3.4, 3.5) was a pioneering use of scenario planning at a regional level. From 1996 to 1999 analysis and public discussion was carried out, and a set of actions to achieve an overall "Quality Growth Strategy" was supported by an extensive technical analysis of alternative transportation and land development scenarios. The Envision Utah analysis showed that in 2020, compared to the baseline, the Quality Growth Strategy will conserve 171 square miles of land, include a more market-driven mix of housing (by modifying some restrictive zoning regulations), result in a 7.3 percent reduction in mobile source emissions, include less traffic congestion, and require $4.5 billion less investment in transportation, water, sewer, and utility infrastructure.[19]

---

[19]American College of Preventive Medicine, *Four Truths.*

Figure 3.4
Envision Utah
scenario A
map showing
concentrations of
new development
in black.

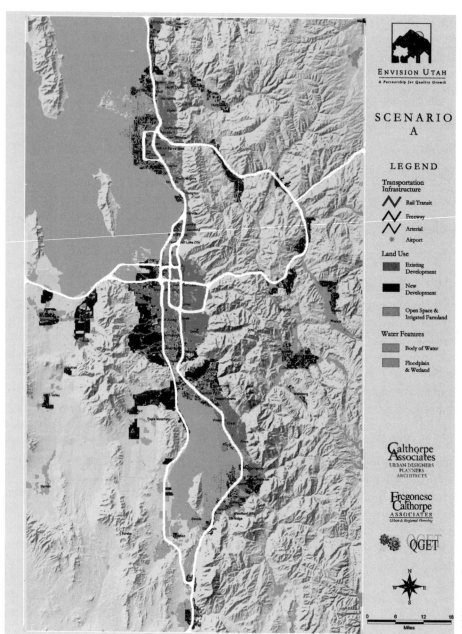

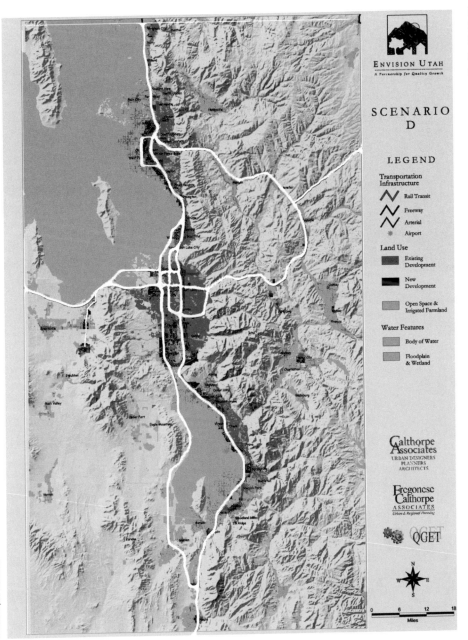

Figure 3.5
Envision Utah scenario
D map showing
concentrations of new
development in black.

Figure 3.6
Scenario
planning map
showing existing
conditions.

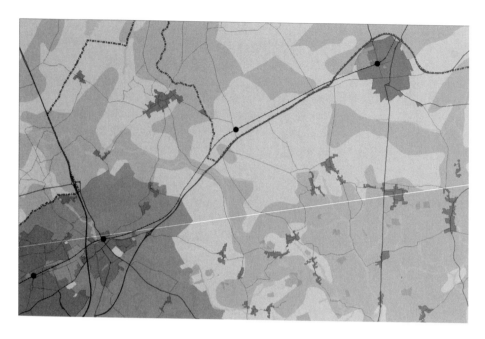

Figure 3.7
Growth scenario
map 1 showing
concentrations of
new development
in black.

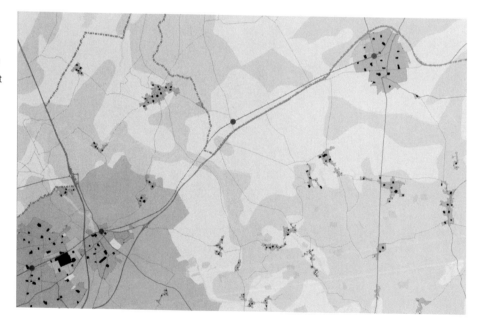

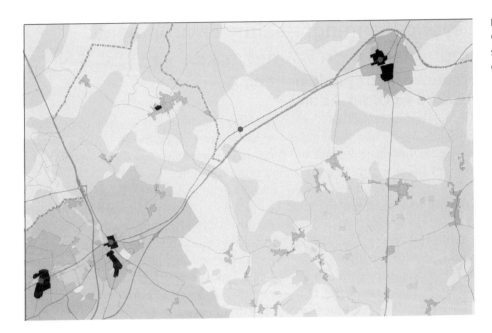

Figure 3.8
Growth scenario map 2
showing concentrations of new
development in black.

Figure 3.9
Growth scenario map 3
showing concentrations of new
development in black.

Beyond Planning: Healthy Environment Implementation Frameworks

Framework for Implementing Agencies Related to Older Adults

The primary implementers of urban development and social service delivery are real estate developers and community service agencies, respectively. Unlike planning and public health, real estate and social service implementers do not have shared histories and their institutional structures are very different.

A national network of Area Agencies on Aging (AAA) was established within DHHS under the Older Americans Act in 1963 to respond to the needs of Americans aged 60 and over in every local community. The fundamental mission of the AAA is to provide services that make it possible for older individuals to remain in their homes, thereby preserving their independence and dignity. These agencies coordinate and support a wide range of home and community-based services including information and referral, home-delivered and congregate meals, transportation, employment services, senior centers, adult daycare, and long-term care ombudsman programs. In most cases, the AAA play coordinating roles and pass federal and philanthropic funds through to local governments and community agencies that implement the programs. These implementing agencies, referred to as community-based aging programs, serve as focal points in the delivery of services to older adults in their respective counties. Services delivered through the Aging Services Network are available to any adult over the age of sixty, regardless of income.

Service providers and real estate developers define success differently: the former primarily measure in terms of positive outcomes in the populations served, and the latter in terms of positive returns on capital invested. The distinction in success measurements is not absolute, but in the final analysis service providers must show positive client outcomes to attract public and philanthropic funding, and developers must show positive cash returns to attract private investors. The cultural and institutional differences that stem from the different definitions of success can be significant.

In the past four decades, an entire sector of specialized nonprofit and public-private venture developers has formed to take advantage of a range of public subsidies dedicated specifically to housing and urban development. These specialized developers have found ways to balance investment return measures with public benefit measures, and they have successfully partnered with community service agencies to achieve these results. During this same time period, the private developers have tended to steer clear of community service providers and have chosen instead to operate solely as private business concerns.

The recent national economic recession has begun to shift the relationships between development sectors and community service providers. Cutbacks in public funding of all types have decreased nonprofit and public-private venture development as well as community services provision. Decrease in consumer spending has forced for-profit developers to look much harder for every possible resource that can be garnered in support of development projects. There are mounting reasons for community service agencies to develop means of partnering directly with for-profit developers without the benefit of public development financing to moderate the investment return needs of the developer. While the nonprofit or joint venture developer is able to leverage public funding through collaborative efforts with community service providers by increasing public benefit outcomes, the purely private developer must find ways of directly capitalizing community service provider contributions through either reduced capital and operating expenses or increased revenues. In exchange for these contributions, the providers can leverage their services to gain more of a proactive role in shaping and integrating into the wider built environment, and they could benefit from the fine tuning of product that for-profit developers undertake in order to successfully attract market demand.

Allowing private developers to gain direct private benefit from publicly and philanthropically funded services can produce reciprocal benefits for the communities served. A wide range of exchanges and trades can be negotiated with the private provider as illustrated by the following examples.

- In lieu of providing congregate meals for older adults in community facilities, service providers instead agree to fund full or partial meal vouchers redeemable in senior housing cafés and restaurants that are open to the public and orient outward toward the main street. Instead of funding a single purpose community cafeteria, or internal-resident-only dining facility, the steady stream of revenue helps seniors housing developers invest in the area's main street with businesses that benefit the entire community and serve older adults in a more intergenerational setting.

- A seniors housing development that agrees to integrate into an existing town center rather than an isolated green field location is awarded contracts to provide home services funded by the Older Americans Act to the surrounding community. These contracts make better use of the housing development's administrative and physical plant resources and open up the development to benefit a wider community.

- A community service provider that agrees to provide meal services and/or domestic assistance to an assisted living facility's residents is given access to a clinic or rehab facility within the development for use with their clients. This exchange makes better use of the service providers' administrative and physical plant resources, extends their abilities to provide services, and opens up the development to benefit a wider community.

All of these hypothetical examples illustrate not only a more efficient use of resources, but also a more effective, place-based approach to service delivery. In each case, both the seniors housing developments and the service providers are drawn into a more engaged and multifaceted relationship with the surrounding community. In this engaged posture, the community itself can bring additional resources to the process. More than one in four people age 65 or older in the United States volunteers regularly, and this represents a sizeable and talented implementation force.[20]

---

[20]National Governors Association Center for Best Practices, "Increasing Volunteerism Among Older Adults: Benefits and Strategies for States" Issue Brief (Washington, DC: NGA, May 2008).

To meet the changing needs of older adults and to expand the traditional aging network, communities across the country have been experimenting with the NORC model (Naturally Occurring Retirement Community). A NORC is defined as a community with a high concentration of older adults that was not specifically designated as a retirement communit. Many NORCs have a high enough density of older adults to achieve the economies of scale found in retirement communities. The NORC model recognizes where these densities occur and then marshals the purchasing power of a concentration of older adults to create services that were otherwise unaffordable or unavailable. Additional possibilities can be created by expanding the NORC model of collaboration to include intentional, privately developed retirement community facilities within a larger NORC community. A blended NORC and typical retirement community effort could result in a wider and deeper array of services for the community, as well as better returns on smaller investments for the developer. The Cluster Care model of home-based care developed in New York has already demonstrated that place-based service delivery can cut home-based care costs in half, when compared to services supplied to each individual in isolation.[21] Paring a NORC with a typical retirement community is a means of taking the Cluster Care model one step further. Such a partnership could serve to integrate institutional care into the physical and social fabric of neighborhood communities and mitigate the increasingly significant impacts that jarring transitions from one healthcare setting to another have on older adults.

While the traditional aging network and the services offered through the network are critical to supporting older adults in the community, as older adults live longer and healthier lives, place-based partnerships between private developers, communities, and service providers could play an important role in meeting a broader range of needs for a greater number of people.

Public Health and Public Space: A Framework for Specific Projects

In her 2001 Trust for Public Land report *The Health Benefits of Parks*, Erica Giles reviews the growing body of research that demonstrates the physical and psychological health benefits of parks and greens. She finds that exposure to plants, even potted indoor plants, can have beneficial effects, but that these benefits are greater when the contact is in the form of recreation or gardening in a public space. When public parks, greens, gardens, or trails are provided, Giles finds evidence that residents are more likely to exercise, that social capital is developed as a result, and that the social interaction itself promotes further exercise. Health benefits correlated to the presence of parks, greens, and trails include: better relaxation and coping skills; decreased levels of fear and anger; positive effects on blood pressure, heart rate, mood, day-to-day effectiveness, social behavior, cognitive functioning, and work performance; reduced crime; higher educational achievement; lower rates of asthma and teen pregnancy; and better responses to the community's needs by government agencies.[22]

---

[21]E. B. Fein, "The Packaging of Personal Care; In the New Cluster Concept, One Attendant Serves Many," *New York Times*, February 27, 1995.

Exercise is critical to remaining healthy and can preserve an individual's ability to manage activities of daily living longer. The design of the neighborhood can greatly increase the chance that an older adult will remain physically, mentally, and socially active and can greatly decrease the likelihood that he or she will suffer from depression. According to the *American Journal of Preventive Medicine,* the creation of or enhanced access to places for physical activity, combined with informational outreach, produced a 48.4 percent increase in frequency of physical activity, in addition to a 5.1 percent median increase in aerobic capacity, reduced body fat, weight loss, improved flexibility, and an increase in perceived energy.[23]

Environmental health professionals have been particularly engaged in public parks as healthy community assets. In 2002, the US Department of Health and Human Services (DHHS) and the National Recreation and Park Association (NRPA) entered into a Memorandum of Understanding to structure collaborative research programs to better understand how the two agencies could work together on obesity reduction initiatives. This collaboration has produced both research and policy initiatives advocating for expansion and better use of the public parks system.[24]

Park Design Factors

Parks can play a particularly important role in combating isolation-related depression and fostering social interaction. In order to foster social interaction most effectively, public and semi-public spaces within the community should be supervised, programmed, and differentiated.

Supervised space is provided informally by lining a gathering spot with windowed facades and activity areas. Maximizing "eyes on the street" or on the green space is a classic example of how a sense of safety can be developed with designed-in opportunities for informal supervision (fig. 3.10).

Programmed space is provided by structuring intentional uses within public spaces rather than leaving them entirely open to unstructured passive use. Programmed public space gives residents reasons to spend more time out in public. For older adults who may be self-conscious about the appearance of idling, a focused activity, whether pursued rigorously or not, can lend a sense of purpose to public space activity and thus can prolong the time spent in a public setting. The ability to remain an independent and contributing member of society as one ages is often tied to the quality and frequency of social interaction. Isolation-related depression can be a catalyst for other forms of physical and emotional decline and detract from the ability to live independently. Park programming can play an important role in ensuring that older adults stay engaged and have opportunities to socialize regularly.

---

[22]E. Gies, *The Health Benefits of Parks* (San Francisco: The Trust for Public Land, 2006).

[23]E. B. Kahn et al. "The Effectiveness of Interventions to Increase Physical Activity," *American Journal of Preventive Medicine* 22, no. 4S (2002): 87–88.

[24]J. Kruger, "Parks, Recreation, and Public Health Collaborative," *Environmental Health Insights* 2 (2008): 123–125.

Figure 3.10
Dover Kohl & Partner's Glenn Wood Park neighborhood center is a textbook example of a well-supervised common space.

Research has shown that gardening programs in public parks can produce many direct health benefits including better strength, endurance, and flexibility as well as lower blood pressure and muscle tension.[25] Raised planters and small community gardening facilities are becoming increasingly popular, providing both stress-reducing exercise and healthy and inexpensive or free produce (fig. 3.11). In one year, fifteen community gardens in New York City grew 11,000 pounds of fresh produce, of which they donated 50 percent to local soup kitchens and food pantries. In the same year, a single garden in the South Bronx grew 200 pounds of tomatoes and 75 pounds of peppers.[26]

Differentiated Space acknowledges and provides for stress points in group dynamics. A common point of stress is generational tensions between teenagers and older adults. Older adults may avoid areas that are teenager hangouts and thus perceived as unsafe, unfriendly, or too rambunctious. Teenagers may avoid areas perceived as uncool where too many older adults gather. These types of tensions may vary between places and cultures—and not always focus on teenagers and older adults—but their existence is common to the culture of place.

Mall and Lifestyle Center managers developed spatial differentiation to a science. As a retail space becomes a favorite gathering spot for older adults, the shop owners will quickly pick up on that fact in their sales logs and will either decide to further cater their products and services to that market segment, or develop programs and

---

[25]Gies, *Health Benefits of Parks*.

[26]"Just Food, 1999 Summary Report" cited in D. Englander, *New York's Community Gardens: A Resource at Risk* (New York: The Trust for Public Land, 2001).

Photo by Chrysoula Artemi (flickr.com/photos/chrysart/)

Figure 3.11
Penn South's Jeff Dullea Intergenerational Garden nestled in among high-rise residential buildings.

Photo by Steve Mouzon

Figure 3.12
Jackson Square in New Orleans utilizes hedges, fences, and streets that are closed to traffic to delineate and layer enough space to allow very diverse uses in close proximity. Everything from boisterous street performances to tranquil gatherings are successfully comingled in a confined urban space.

marketing to help counter it and bring a wider mix of customers into the store. It is not uncommon to see retail trends self-reinforce: teenagers begin to collect in an area, the surrounding retail recognizes this market and increasingly caters to it, teenager-oriented retail fuels the trend and encourages teenagers to further dominate the space, and older adults increasingly avoid the space.

The lesson in this common occurrence is that spaces do not always remain neutral and open to all. Designing spaces for social interaction must include anticipating and providing opportunities for differentiation, either by providing a wide array of smaller congregating areas distributed across the community, or by finding creative ways to subdivide larger public spaces so that they can be occupied differently by distinctly separate groups within close proximity. Social space is best thought of in terms of clutches that provide opportunities for the community to gather together, but gather differently: to collect but individuate (fig. 3.12). The clutches approach deters a single group's ability to monopolize a space and encourages a collective sense of neighborhood identity.

NEIGHBORHOOD WELLNESS AND RECREATION CHAPTER 4

Contributed by Jessica Wolfe, PhD, MPH, LEED GA

Urban Design and Wellness Industry Market Research

If seniors housing can be understood as institutional care models reaching out to more community-based settings, the fitness and wellness industry provides a very different view of the community reaching out to health services. Market demand for health and wellness offerings indicates that we want healthy routines integrated into our lives and that we are actively reaching out for institutions to support these routines. An industry that started out as a collection of health-food stores, spa resorts, and gyms is today rapidly closing the gap between wellness services and medical services—either by co-locating with medical facilities or offering minor, usually elective, medical services on site. The comparison of wellness industries and medical industries is telling: The former has developed purely as an expression of what we want and demand as consumers, while the latter has evolved primarily as an expression of things that we submit to out of urgent need. It is also telling as a comparison of our individual behavior as wellness customers with our collective behavior as payers of insurance premiums and taxes. Understanding healthcare as a combination of wellness routines and medical treatment could lead to more balanced individual and collective investments, as well as a more community-integrated manner of supply.

As a complement to public health research and programs discussed in the previous chapter, private wellness industry research and programs offer an alternative but complementary view into the association of well-being with the built environment. Focusing more on drivers of individual consumer behavior, this research also provides insight into detailed analysis of topics like curb appeal, the effective combination of product and service lines, and opportunities for cross marketing with other businesses.

The wellness consumer movement is helping to bridge the gap between institution-based medical delivery and the neighborhood settings of our daily routines by demanding more community-oriented approaches to fitness and health. This movement is affecting a shift away from a solitary focus on individual peak conditioning in gym settings to a wider framework for fitness that incorporates physical, emotional, social, and spiritual elements in more spa-like settings. Over the last few decades, fitness-related markets have noticeably diversified to include personal training workout facilities and family-oriented community centers, as well as physical therapy, weight loss, and holistic wellness specialty operations. This movement reflects the accelerating desire of residents across diverse settings to incorporate healthy routines into their daily lives. In the process, fitness facilities have begun to look less like traditional, stripped-down gyms and more like civic spaces that simultaneously foster social interaction and celebrate the larger built and natural environments. Indeed, across much of the country, "boot camp" fitness programs have abandoned customary structures altogether and have instead provided guided group workouts in public parks and squares. Wellness industry market research illustrates ways in which consumer preferences are thus driving the integration of wellness programming into the architecture, landscape, and urban design of any number of communities and settings.

The general field of wellness can be divided into several categories and associated business sectors. Wellness, for example, can encompass quality of life, longevity, and life satisfaction as well as actual health status and disease states. Wellness can also be viewed in terms of distinct components, including physical, emotional, social, and spiritual parts.[1] The business world has been quick to note the growing, multigenerational consumer interest in wellness, fitness, and antiaging across industry sectors as seemingly diverse as freestanding fitness clubs and hotel-based, therapeutic spas. Each of these sectors has the potential to contribute to both individual and community-based health, and market research on health and fitness, spas and hospitality, and health and medical technologies reflect the burgeoning financial opportunities underlying this diverse and expanding consumer base.[2] In 2010, revenues from the fitness industry alone exceeded $22 billion.[3] This figure does not include revenues from the related sectors of spa services, integrative medicine (alternative and complementary services not often covered by insurance), and other wellness amenities purchased widely at those sites or independently by consumers of all ages such as massages, private trainers, nutritional products, and the huge spectrum of health and wellness supplements bought over the counter. Combined, these products and services are estimated at well over $350 billion, with nearly continuous annual growth.[4] The large increase in dollars invested by businesses in wellness indicate that the private sector retail market already realizes that there is a personal demand for wellness and quality of life resources and that health and well-being are easily and enthusiastically accessed as part of a consumer's routine life, not solely through occasional visits to acute facilities for examinations and interventions based on the more traditional, disease treatment model.[5]

[1]A. King, D. Stokols, E. Talen, G. Brassington, and R. Killingsworth, "Theoretical Approaches to the Promotion of Physical Activity: Forging a Transdisciplinary Paradigm," *American Journal of Preventive Medicine* 23, no. 2 (2002): 15–25.

[2]Centers for Disease Control and Prevention, AARP, and the American Medical Association. *Promoting Preventive Services for Adults 50–64: Community and Clinical Partnerships* (Atlanta, GA: National Association of Chronic Disease Directors, 2009).

[3]Centers for Disease Control and Prevention, http://www.cdc.gov/nccdphp/sgr/ataglan.htm.

[4]Kalorama Information. "Key Technology Markets in Healthcare" (New York: MarketResearch.com, 2007), http://www.kaloramainformation.com/

[5]M. Furlong, *Turning Silver into Gold: How to Profit in the New Boomer Marketplace* (Upper Saddle River, NJ: Financial Times Press, 2007).

Aging and Wellness

As the science of exercise physiology advances and the baby-boomer generation approaches midlife, the health and wellness field has experienced an expansion of new training techniques, program innovations, equipment developments, and niche clubs targeting nearly every conceivable demand (fig. 4.1). By 2010, revenues for health and fitness clubs nationally topped $21 billion, an increase of about $4 billion from five years prior. Community-based nonprofits like the YMCA, already in the fitness business, began to actively cultivate older members through national outsourced programs like SilverSneakers, which, like the offering of daycare and infant swim programs, soon gained huge popularity.

Many of the programs successfully attracted older individuals because of the clubs' growing sophistication around programming for highly specialized needs such as mobility enhancement, arthritis prevention/remediation, rehabilitation, and flexibility maintenance. Interestingly, however, a considerable portion of membership appeal appears to stem from the built-in opportunity for routine social interaction. In fact, only 58 percent of fitness centers' revenues in 2006 came from membership fees; a striking 22 percent plus was generated through provision of other services, including private instruction, coaching, event and social participation, and merchandising of wellness products from clothing to nutraceuticals—foods and products felt by some to offer health and medical benefits.

The large number of retiring baby boomers, which will reach 77 million, has directly driven many of the observed changes in the marketplace and are estimated

Figure 4.1
Fitness centers today are highly programmed with specialized classes targeting everything from Pilates to spin cycling.

to account for over 50 percent of all retail spending in this arena.[6] The impact of this generation in the design, development, and accessibility of health, fitness, and recreational resources has been just as dramatic. Numerous studies confirm that individuals aged 55 or older are more fit than their predecessors, have a distinct insistence on higher quality of life, and believe that they will live longer and better if they participate in wellness activities.[7] The entry of the first of the baby boomers into what has traditionally been considered older age has given the largest impetus to the growth of the wellness and health industry. The most basic evidence for this has been the growing popularity of fitness clubs for this age group. At the end of 2007, fitness clubs boasted over 44 million members, with the fastest growing segment being those fifty-five and older. Membership targets for the larger fitness chains, aimed only ten years ago at members of the middle class, aged 18 to 34, have rapidly morphed in most cases to engage a much broader age range (often extending to those in their 80s), particularly with the advance of private instruction and customized, age-based and condition-sensitive programming.[8]

Wellness Trends in Continuing Care Retirement Communities

A spillover effect appears to be evident, that is, as the population ages and the baby boomers pursue higher standards of fitness, the senior housing sector has been forced to reexamine what amenities it will need if it is to continue to attract new residents to its communities. Continuing Care Retirement Communities (CCRCs), for example, once content to provide some limited on-site medical and nursing services along with limited fitness services (typically static equipment) now find that one of their strongest marketing elements lies in the broad menu of dynamic wellness, fitness, and recreational programs they offer to mature adults (figs. 4.2, 4.3, 4.4).[9] All segments of senior housing, as well as the rise of active adult communities, report that the demand for quality trainers and class teachers along with the latest in sports and fitness programming are extraordinarily high. In addition, members and residents expect these activities and programs to be provided in spa-like and club-like atmospheres and, in some cases, with actual medical and cosmetic services available at the same time. This pattern is further testimony to the growth of wellness programming as a core element of any type of lifelong neighborhood, whether urban or suburban, particularly when the goal is to retain residents across the lifespan and enable them to reach their maximal life quality.

The issue of whether baby boomers who seek lifelong fitness will prefer age-segregated living facilities is not the topic of this chapter, but it should be noted that a growing grassroots movement known as the Village to Village Network is rapidly expanding (see Chapter 11 for a more in-depth discussion of Beacon Hill

---

[6]Institute for the Future, *Boomers: The Next 20 Years, Ecologies of Risk* (Palo Alto, CA: Institute for the Future, 2007).

[7]IBISWorld.Industry Report, "Mature Markets: IBIS Market Research ReportWorld" (IBIS World, 2007), http://www.ibisworld.com/industry/home.aspx

[8]W. Thompson, "Worldwide Survey Demonstrates Fitness Trends for 2007," *CSM's Health & Fitness Journal* 10, no. 6 (2006): 8–14.

[9]American Institute of Architects, and the American Association of Homes and Services for the Aging, "Trends in Design: Showcasing Senior Living Designs, Products and Services" (Washington, DC: AIA/AAHSA, 2010).

Figure 4.2
The Williamsburg Landing
CCRC fitness center in
Tidewater, Virginia, resembles a
full resort clubhouse.

Figure 4.3
The Williamsburg Landing
cardio facility features ample
daylight and does not have the
hard floor surfaces or mirrored
walls typical of a peak fitness
facility.

Figure 4.4

The Williamsburg Landing pool is suitable for aerobics or lap swimming.

Glen Tipton

and the Villages network). To date, the availability and scope of fitness services varies widely by village/community and is sometimes represented only in the form of membership discounts to local fitness centers. Service menus are, of course, highly dependent on the members' interests and are strongly affected by the density and geographic locale where a village is formed. In more urban settings, access to a wider variety of fitness and wellness options is more easily obtained while retaining home ownership. In suburban and more rural settings, access to these resources may be more variable, and subject to the composition and market demographics of the larger community. In these settings, opportunities for daily fitness and specialized wellness regimens may be more challenging as individuals enter the later decades of their lives and discontinue driving. At that point, the use of shuttle services, in-home training, and newer, remote, or streaming video technologies are options for some and appear to be growing in popularity. However, given the relative newness of the Villages network it is not possible to know how aging in place will intersect with continued fitness activities on a large-scale basis. Still, the popularity of remaining in one's home or neighborhood appears to be worth the effort of making certain adjustments.[10] This area, in general, is one where considerable change and growth can be expected, from service and technology delivery models to residential offerings such as small houses, the Green House, cohousing, and so on. Further changes can also be expected from both evolving consumer preferences as well as the restructuring of reimbursement models at the federal and state levels.

---

[10]S. Brecht, S. Fein, and L. Hollinger-Smith, "Preparing for the Future: Trends in Continuing Care Retirement Communities," *Seniors Housing and Care Journal* 17, no. 1 (2009): 75–90.

Redefining the Lifelong Environment: Wellness in Community

The government and certain philanthropic health foundations have embraced the use of community and neighborhoods as ways to attract people to fitness activities in certain highly innovative ways. These include the use of social gatherings around group walks that are often publicized in print and on social networking sites, and the involvement of local businesses such as restaurants, grocers who provide healthy menus, and attractive educational materials on eating and exercise.

Advances in the fields such as behavioral economics and longevity have taught proprietors and residents alike that the promotion of healthy living through activities like group walking can be used to engage large sections of a community, going well beyond the walls of the facility to a kind of virtual wellness campus that can influence health outcomes. The challenge will be to help these communities in their efforts to preserve or improve existing infrastructure such as sidewalks, bicycle lanes, safe parks, and vehicular calming so that they can accommodate their diverse constituency and people as they age, rather than causing people to leave for more adaptive settings.

In addition to the aging demographic, this will be critically important as the cost of lifelong wellness rises. Despite the growing interest in healthful living and fitness economic and structural barriers remain. The cost of health club memberships continues to be a deterrent for some. In 2005, the International Health, Racquet, and Sports Association (IHRSA) reported that the average health club member had a household income of $82,900, which indicated an increase over the preceding year. Further, about one third of all health club memberships are held by households with incomes in excess of $100,000.[11] Thus, given current economic conditions, use of more specialized or extensive fitness resources may remain discretionary for many people, suggesting that the natural, built environment indeed is ripe with opportunities (fig. 4.5).

Main Street and the Arterial

The growing consumer demand for readily available wellness and fitness resources has impacted the way in which these services are organized and provided. The 1960s and 1970s saw the rise of the nonprofit community center in the form of multifaceted facilities like the YMCA and the Jewish Community Center (JCC). The majority of these centers were family oriented; a number had branches outside of major cities in the suburbs. Programmatically, the most common themes from this period were services for the young family, in particular, swimming lessons and summer camps for children. Typically, the centers occupied stand-alone structures along an arterial, reached largely by car (figs. 4.6, 4.7). The 1980s saw a notable increase in sophistication about fitness and wellness, particularly when TV and film celebrities like Jane Fonda and Richard Simmons popularized more niche, adult programming

---

[11]Thompson, "Fitness Trends."

Figure 4.5
A walking route laid out in Mableton's master plan including informative plaques and street furniture at strategic points (see Chapter 12 for a review of Mableton's planning process).

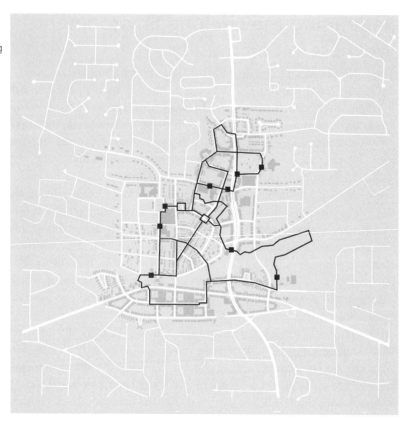

Figure 4.6
An aerial view of a typical suburban, "big box" community recreation center isolated at the edge of town. The facility is dependent on automobile access.

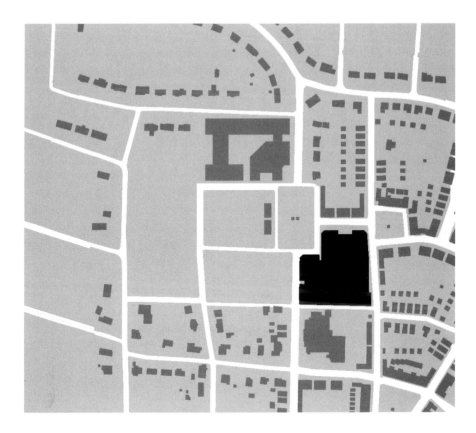

Figure 4.7
A plan of the Mableton's urbanized community center colocated in the center of town with the new elementary school.

like aerobics and step classes. Although historically popular among certain groups, weight training also began to gain popularity but was not widely recognized by the general public for its role in overall health until the 1980s and 1990s when resistance and flexibility training became popular. These fitness modes were increasingly embraced as scientific findings documented their direct and indirect benefits for longevity and general well-being. As these programs expanded, so did the typical footprint of a wellness center, growing from less than 10,000 square feet in the late 1960s to as much as 150,000 square feet today.

Niche Market Storefronts

Over time, the market for big-box, arterial community fitness centers has become increasingly competitive, following early dominance by several national and regional chains. Like the general move to big box retail in other retail sectors, large-scale chains found that the extensive market access provided by arterial locations could also be affected by transitory customer loyalty, high fixed overhead, and narrow operating margins. These issues contributed in part to the rise of smaller, local facilities that occupied smaller storefront spaces in strip malls and in town storefronts (fig. 4.8).

Figure 4.8

A corner fitness center in the middle of a neighborhood.

Often, these smaller, local facilities offer far fewer fitness options, and sometimes offer only one or two specialty programs such as yoga, Pilates, and spinning. This greater focus on particular forms of training appears to be contiguous with the growth in personalized medicine, genomics, and interactive health/wellness technologies, all of which emphasize individual characteristics and needs. Given the scientific advances, these trends are likely to expand in some fashion going forward.

By occupying storefronts, these businesses have the additional benefit of drawing walk-in customers who may be shopping at adjacent stores. Further, some consumers feel they add a highly personalized approach to well-being, with the perceived focus on the single customer. In some cases, these niche settings increase their draw by offering sought-after specialty services such as therapeutic massage or some mild aesthetic dermatologic procedures within scheduled physician hours. While sometimes succeeding in building greater customer loyalty, these smaller storefront boutiques are vulnerable to low foot-traffic volume, especially in nonurban settings or areas of low population density (fig 4.9), not to mention the rapidity of cyclical changes in fitness fads. Possible solutions may include the choice of dense, semi-urban settings and/or small settings that require little or no specialized build-out, thereby reducing initial outlay (fig. 4.10).

One example of a very successful storefront and niche operation is the chain Curves, Inc. In 2006, Curves, which had a smaller footprint and based itself in urban or suburban settings, had an estimated market share of 2 percent.[12] Targeting

---

[12]IBISWorld Industry Report. "Fitness and Recreational Sports Centers in the U.S.: Industry Market Research Report" (IBISWorld. 2007).

Figure 4.9
An auto-dependent fitness
center in a shopping center
development.

Figure 4.10
A community center embedded
in an urban neighborhood.

Photo by Mike Lydon

Figure 4.11
A neighborhood storefront fitness venue targeted to a niche market.

women unfamiliar or uncomfortable with the traditionally large, open-floor gym floors, Curves aimed to represent smaller, more personalized and confidence-building environments where women would try exercise and then feel enthusiastic about staying (fig. 4.11). These smaller settings appear to have had success in attracting first-time exercisers, including those who are concerned about their weight and/or are substantially overweight and thus reluctant to exercise in highly visible settings.

Employment Centers

In addition to neighborhood locations, there is also a trend to locate fitness, health, and rehabilitation resources within large employment settings. Where services are not provided on-site, the majority of large employers offer fitness center membership and may actively encourage their use as healthcare insurance premiums continue to balloon and the cost of missed workdays due to illness, injury, or disease becomes unsustainable. This benefit may appear in the form of work-provided health insurance, although it is subsidized by the employer and employee. In some cases, the employer is a healthcare system, seeking to improve the well-being of its workforce. The Mayo Clinic was among the first to construct a large, green wellness facility: the Dan Abraham Health Living Center, which focuses exclusively on employees' well-being and fitness. Located on the Mayo campus, it is an excellent example of an employer intent on carrying its lifelong health message to all of its customers.

Hospital/Wellness Facility Colocation

In the past decade, a number of fitness chains have explored the feasibility of colocating near or within community hospital and healthcare system campuses, a dramatic structural change from prior decades. By co-locating, some healthcare systems have found that they are able to establish more direct, personal contact and enhanced loyalty through co-branding. The ready availability and quick access to relevant medical specialty practices (e.g., orthopedics, cardiology) in a more consumer-friendly environment is also thought to be important. This model offers an example of how reworking the built environment around truly multifaceted programming provides "one-stop" wellness shopping for the savvy fitness shopper. It may also prove especially beneficial for the reluctant consumer whose primary care physician is concerned about the lack of fitness engagement through the reduction of some barriers to use.

This model appears to be popular in suburban settings when land costs and availability permit this configuration. It appears to appeal both to young families who are increasingly informed about health and wellness findings as well as the emerging baby boomer generation that closely tracks new scientific and popular trends related to aging. Industry benefits include broader branding opportunities for the healthcare facility, new revenue streams, and the chance to reduce acuity of problems by introducing or increasing amounts of preventive and rehabilitative health services early on. Similarly, some independent fitness chains have opted to lease space to specialty practitioners for clinics, ranging from peak performance training and private coaching to sports and medical injury rehabilitation.

A particularly good example of the rebranding and repositioning of a national, community-based fitness organization is the Y. Formerly known as the YMCA, this organization has redefined itself with updated materials, advertising, and signage and significantly broadened programming, in some cases reaching into medical, rehab, and health domains through clinics or subcontracting. These strategic initiatives reflect both the need and opportunity to attract customers of all ages and needs. In a number of cases, nonprofit organizations like these have made extensive efforts to colocate in a variety of novel community settings, from sharing space with newly built elementary schools in traditional neighborhood developments to universities (fig. 4.12).

Figure 4.12
An elementary school in Lake Nona, Florida, shares space with a fitness center.

Healthplex Associates

Green Facilities

A more recent trend in the evolution of fitness is a focus on living and exercising in healthy environments. Newly built structures or large renovations are, by law, required to meet ADA regulations for accessibility. Going beyond this, however, there is evidence that the growing number of green or sustainable buildings with extensive natural light and universal design reflect a strong demand by consumers to move away from a solitary emphasis on personal peak conditioning to spending more time in environments that themselves are healthful.

Environment and Obesity

Despite the dramatic increase in personal spending on wellness and fitness services, the country remains mired in an obesity epidemic. Behaviorally complex at the outset, body status and fitness levels are influenced by many factors, and what is recreational, fun, or compelling for one individual is anathema to someone else. Still, fitness and wellness programs have strong parts to play in the design and planning of the built environment across numerous dimensions: the choice to locate in a walkable environment, the attractiveness of the facility, the nature and extent of organizational outreach, and the amenities and programs targeting hard-to-reach groups. Some of the strongest current demand determinants are clearly disposable income and cost. After that, however, factors like weather conditions/geographical locale, consumer confidence and attitude, health/fitness awareness, local culture, and free time begin to play important roles.[13] Additional behavioral incentives come

---

[13]Thompson, "Fitness Trends."

from the growing number of employers or insurers who offer some form of prepaid health club membership as an inducement or potential offset for illness-related costs and skyrocketing health insurance premiums.[14] These variables comprise a striking change in attitude and behavior, compared to even a decade or two prior when exercise was generally viewed as an activity of interest to more limited groups, generally either professional or peak athletes, or those with extensive leisure time.

Community Fitness without Facilities

A number of creative communities have mobilized to instill a culture of fitness by using their existing, natural resources, regardless of structural density (fig. 4.13). Here a community adopts any number of specified healthy living objectives and seeks to engage as many people as possible, either by competing for a common goal such as total steps walked, or as a vehicle for meeting, socializing with, and supporting others. One good example is the newly launched "Blue Zone Communities."[15] The result of a public/private venture, Blue Zone Communities are defined as those that investigate and embrace specific best practice activity and lifestyle characteristics to enhance longevity. The first community, in Albert Lea, Minnesota, intended to meet a very specific set of outcomes. A few examples included a minimum 25 percent of the population participating in the program; the implementation by schools of specific food policies to reduce snack foods and encourage fitness; readily connected biking paths and social walking groups; and volunteers planting seventy community gardens. As is evident, this concept strongly endorses the use of existing, community open spaces for both planned and spontaneous fitness activities

Figure 4.13
Boot-camp fitness providers are increasingly providing fitness programming for public spaces.

[14]Association Resource Centre, *ISPA 2007 Spa Industry Study* (Lexington, KY: International SPA Association, 2007), 1–10.

[15]http://www.bluezones.com/programs/vitality-cities/.

for all ages, thus focusing on social integration and inclusivity for all. Programs like these, which engage the whole community and require relatively few concrete assets, are likely to be an integral part of the future of wellness in the United States.

Conclusion

Research and general observation show that a small proportion of people will exercise independently, but that the majority remains drawn to it for other reasons, typically social or entertainment/recreational value. This provides both challenges and opportunities for designers, architects, planners, and exercise specialists to figure out how to configure the built environment so that it can accommodate the largest and most diverse group of people across the various stages of life. A number of community-oriented fitness organizations have chosen to incorporate water parks to ensure the involvement of children and young families seeking recreational opportunities. These structures, while very popular and attractive, are costly and require considerable space that cannot typically be repurposed for use by other individuals. Pools, on the other hand, while also costly in terms of installation and maintenance, remain a strong draw across ages and are easily used by a wide variety of age and fitness types, simply by ensuring a walk-in end and movable lanes. Facilities that colocate on a hospital campus find they can easily accommodate the rehabilitation needs of patients during the typical workweek while still attracting employees and outside customers in usual peak times (prework, post-work, and weekends). Where weather permits, many of these aquatic settings employ sliding glass walls so that the activity atmosphere extends to the out-of-doors as well.

The issues of the types and styles of residential structures, neighborhood density, and the need for extensive volunteerism in many of these initiatives are issues that require further and considerable thought. Yet, it is clear that change is afoot. Market data confirm that today's wellness customer spans all age groups, from very young to very old, with the strongest participation by those seeking to age well or avoid the effects of aging for as long as possible. Across groups, ready accessibility and more seamless integration into daily, neighborhood life are requisite attributes for the busy individual or family, particularly where both parents are working or for mature adults who remain employed. Social interaction to foster behavior change, whether through actual or virtual, internet-based interaction remains a high priority for engaging in nearly all forms of wellness and fitness activities. Given these trends, it is now apparent that public health data showing the extreme importance of becoming or remaining fit across the lifespan seems increasingly consistent with consumer preferences as well as opportunities for innovative thinking in the design and planning of the built environment for years to come. This surprising alignment should provide for a firm platform on which to examine in far greater detail how wellness services are organized and dispensed in ways that are aesthetically, economically, and socially desirable as well as scalable and sustainable for the truly lifelong neighborhood.

PART II

NETWORKS AND DIVERSITY

The Neighborhood

The neighborhood, the district, and the corridor are the essential elements of development and redevelopment in the metropolis. They form identifiable areas that encourage citizens to take responsibility for their maintenance and evolution.[1]

THIS PART EXAMINES LONGEVITY AND URBANISM at the scale of the neighborhood. At this scale, older adult issues are different than those of the general population only by degree and not by category. Good urbanism at the community level raises the quality of life for all residents, but for older adults it is more critical and may determine whether or not healthy and engaged lives can be sustained in a community at all. Connection and diversity are foundational urban considerations for older adults, and they should be considered prerequisites to undertaking further lifelong neighborhood implementation.

In Chapter 5, connectivity and access are reviewed as subjects of both mobility and form. The structure of our transportation systems do more than just move us around; they provide the skeletal framework that determines the scale and weave of neighborhoods. Thoroughfares and transit systems must be designed and managed as shaping elements of the public realm and not simply as transportation features. The urban spaces that they shape are as important as the movement they facilitate.

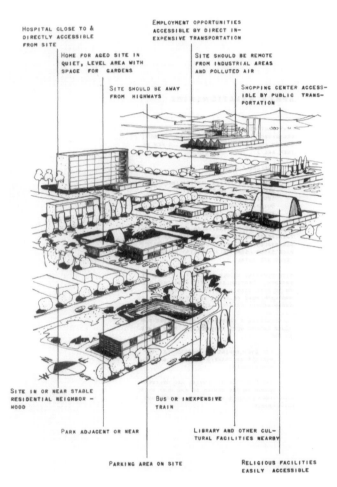

A 1953 advisory on locating seniors housing encouraged integration into existing urban settings.[2]

---

[1] Congress of the New Urbanism, *Charter of the New* Urbanism (Chicago: CNU, 1996), 1.

[2] US Housing and Home Finance Agency, *Housing the Elderly: A Review of Significant Developments* (Washingtgon, DC: Office of the Administrator, 1954)

In Chapter 6, building diversity is discussed. A neighborhood must have a range of dwelling types and a mix of uses to foster lifelong living. Before the widespread use of automobiles this type of building diversity occurred organically out of the basic necessities of pedestrian mobility. As an auto-dependent society, diversity of building types in close proximity is no longer a necessity for meeting daily needs. Many economic and regulatory forces make it difficult to provide a diversity of buildings in a neighborhood. Building diversity thus does not occur organically anymore and must be established as a highly valued goal of urban development if the cross sector, intergovernmental coordination now required to produce diversity is going to be achieved.

Experienced planners will recognize that there are no new, unique, or specialized responses to longevity in these subjects; they are well-understood and well-established goals of most mixed-use development approaches that are variously known as Planned Unit Development, Traditional Neighborhood Development, New Urban Communities, Mixed-Use Communities, Transit-Oriented Development, or Sustainable Urbanism. The neighborhood unit was first proposed as a foundational element of regional planning by Clarence Perry in his 1920 regional plan for New York. The concept has evolved over time: It was recast by Clarence Stein and Henry Wright around a central greenway in Radburn, New Jersey, by James Rouse around a retail mall in Columbia New Town development, and revisited once again by the New Urbanists around mixed-use, civically-oriented main streets. In all instances, the neighborhood serves as the central organizing element for aspects of the built environment that are regulated across many jurisdictions.

Part II adopts the same neighborhood unit concept, but utilizes lifelong health as an orchestrating theme. Longevity reorganizes our planning priorities—it does not reinvent planning. Considerations reviewed in Part II constitute an older adult agenda culled from general, well-established pools of good planning practices and elevated here, not as unique to longevity response, but necessary to longevity response. Because the issues considered are contained within a range of regulatory jurisdictions and are managed by a range of professionals, a lifelong agenda provides an opportunity to evaluate the end mix: to understand the composite relationships as an integrated whole rather than a collection of independent functions.

CONNECTIONS

One out of every four licensed drivers will be aged 65 and older by 2030.[1] Current transportation statistics clearly indicate the consequences of this percentage of older drivers on the road:

- Streets will be generally safer—older adults generate lower crash rates per licensed driver.

- Traffic will be more cautious—older adults are less inclined to engage in risky behavior while driving, are less likely to be under the influence of alcohol, and are more likely to wear seat belts.

Public perception that increasing percentages of older adult drivers will present traffic hazards is unfounded. We are at the most hazardous point in our life as drivers the day we are issued a license, and the risk we pose to ourselves and to others steadily declines across our lifespan. While the natural process of aging does lead to decline in the physical, cognitive, and sensory capabilities that affect a person's ability to drive, older adults have been shown to be more willing than the general population to self-regulate their driving habits based on their physical limitations.[2] Statistics show that it is the capacity for self-regulation (not multitasking while driving, and not driving while impaired by sleepiness, drug/alcohol influence, or emotions) that is the most critical element in driver safety. Older adults have an excessively high statistical rate of motor vehicle fatalities,[3] and given their propensity to act responsibly when operating vehicles, an older adult agenda for transportation and access should primarily focus on calming the driving behaviors of younger age groups rather than changing road and highway standards to better accommodate physiological conditions brought on by aging.

An even more affective agenda would focus on the many roles thoroughfares play in the built environment other than supporting motor vehicles. A vibrant neighborhood supportive of the entire lifecycle is a complex set of symbiotic relationships between social, economic, and spatial structures. The street network forms the basic armature for these relationships—it is the skeletal structure of community. The street network also shapes block structure, favors certain central areas, and has a determining influence on the perceived reach and weave of a community.[4] Connectivity is the primary indicator of street network integrity. A well-connected network (see figure 5.1) forms a grid with regular intersections spaced at comfortable

---

[1] A. Houser, *Older Drivers and Automobile Safety* (Washington, DC: AARP Public Policy Institute, August 2005).

[2] K. Ball, "Driving Avoidance and Functional Impairment in Older Drivers," *Accident Analysis & Prevention* 30, no. 3 (1998): 313–22.

[3] AARP Public Policy Institute, 2005.

[4] M. Mehaffy, P. Sergio, R. Yodan, and S. Nikos, "Urban nuclei and the geometry of streets: The 'emergent neighborhoods' model," *Urban Design International* 15 (Spring 2010): 22–46.

Figure 5.1
Poor connectivity of the neighborhood below the collector road makes it hard to walk from homes to destinations, while good connectivity of the above neighborhood creates a walkable environment.

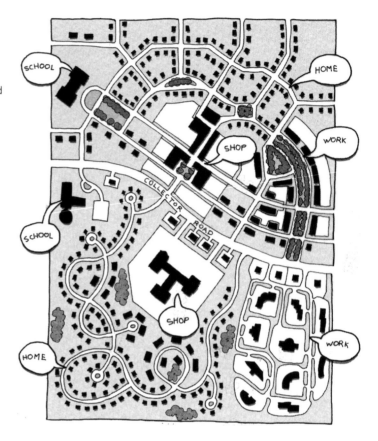

distances (200–500 feet is typical). The grid can be composed of winding roads or straight roads. Connectivity measures a street system's ability to

- disperse traffic, prevent congestion, and slow vehicle speeds;

- support a vibrant pedestrian realm;

- support easy movement between neighborhoods;

- support neighborhood retail opportunities;

- support the formation of social networks; and

- create a safe driving environment for people of all ages.

Unfortunately, street networks are rarely addressed as critical elements of a complex ecosystem and almost never as critical elements of a lifelong neighborhood. Most often streets are laid out, maintained, and occasionally redeveloped solely by transportation engineers and primarily for the purposes of motor vehicle access and congestion mitigation. An aging agenda for urban planning should start with ensuring that social, economic, and access issues are also considered when designing the street network. Connectivity is the most important of the urban design considerations covered in this section, but unfortunately, it is the consideration that is least often addressed as an aging issue.

Connectivity

While poor connectivity is not solely an older adult issue, older adults are more vulnerable to its negative effects and have more at stake in finding a solution than the general population. Too often, advocacy groups concerned with improving environmental quality for the disabled or elderly focus on small construction details and neglect the urban context. While signal timing, ramps, lever hardware, and other accessibility provisions all provide necessary accommodations for people of all abilities, connectivity is the single most important determinant in whether any pedestrian could or would want to be in the street at all. A poorly connected street network limits the customer catchment area for local retail and makes it difficult to establish a mixed-use neighborhood center. Poor connectivity makes it generally difficult to establish a pedestrian-oriented neighborhood at all. A poorly connected network is difficult to serve with transit and can isolate those who do not drive. Of particular concern for older adults who drive, a poorly connected network concentrates more traffic on high-speed arterials that are dangerous to enter from the lower speed local roads (fig. 5.2). Intersections between neighborhood streets and arterials can be quite frightening and hazardous for older drivers.

Connectivity is also a critical component in reversing the association of older adult communities with gated subdivisions. Gates originally went up around seniors housing developments in response to a misconceived notion of security. The perceived relationship between security gates and neighborhood safety has not been substantiated by crime statistics.[5] Lifelong neighborhoods' principles maintain that the segregation imparted by gated communities does more to damage to the

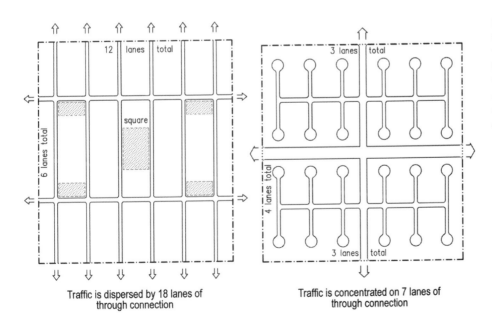

Traffic is dispersed by 18 lanes of
through connection

Traffic is concentrated on 7 lanes of
through connection

Figure 5.2
On the left, traffic is dispersed through a grid along eighteen lanes of through connection while on the right, traffic is concentrated from cul-de-sacs on the seven lanes of two connectors.

[5]E. Blakely, and M. G. Snyder, *Fortress America: Gated Communities in the United States* (Washington, DC: Brookings Institution Press, 1997).

neighborhood, isolate its residents, and impede the surrounding community than is warranted by any potential safety benefits of such security measures. There is a perception issue that must be overcome as well. Dispelling the association of older adult communities with gated subdivisions and marketing older adult communities as part of well-connected street networks is critical to the reintegration of older adult supports back into the community.

Reversing Dendrite Planning

Disconnected streets did not occur by random happenstance: they are an intentional product of the current dominant traffic planning philosophy (figs. 5.3, 5.4). This philosophy is entrenched in transportation departments at all levels—local, state, and federal—and it is necessary to understand its values and goals in order to introduce an effective counter approach. Traffic engineering has for more than half a century focused on what is known as a "dendrite" traffic system. The word's origins

Figure 5.3
A connectivity analysis of the existing fabric.

Figure 5.4
A connectivity analysis after the existing fabric is repaired.

are from the Greek word for tree, *dendrites*, and a tree's structure is a good image of the end goal of the planning system: a large trunk off of which progressively smaller branches stem outward. This tree-like approach to traffic planning has been favored over the last few decades, primarily for its ability to separate high-speed through traffic from lower-speed local traffic. Interstates serve as the trunk in the "road tree," which then branches off into progressively smaller thoroughfares: highway, arterial, collector road, and local street. These branches do not cross or interconnect with each other, but rather feedback toward the trunk for connections along the next higher order of road. These separated roads allow motorists going long distances to move at high speeds without interruption along the trunk, while also creating quiet and slow residential streets (the "twigs" at the outer canopy) for homeowners. The cul-de-sac is the ultimate example of dendrite planning at the neighborhood scale: a purely local street that is low speed, closed to through connection, and feeds all of its outward-bound traffic onto collectors.

The grid street system of regular blocks that is typical of most cities and towns developed before the 1940s is the counter point to a dendrite system. Rather than isolate local traffic from through traffic, the grid weaves them together. While the grid can support a hierarchy of streets ranging from boulevards to alleyways with different speeds and carrying capacities, it does so without completely isolating through traffic from local traffic: The separation is not absolute. As traffic backs up along a boulevard, motorists can disperse into the more local streets to find alternative routes around the traffic jam. It is exactly this kind of cut-through traffic that the cul-de-sac is designed to prevent.

Cul-de-sac development, loop roads, and other forms of dendrite traffic planning favor long blocks that do not connect to form a grid. Destinations within the neighborhood often have no direct paths connecting them, making in-between access routes long and walking difficult (fig. 5.5). Because separated local streets prevent nonlocal through traffic, they cannot support neighborhood retail that depends on drawing customers from a wide area in order to survive. Because dendrite systems also favor very long blocks and are less woven, they do not foster a sense of connection and relationship beyond the immediate neighbors that line the street.

Until relatively recently, the absolute value of this separated system went unquestioned. At the neighborhood scale, planners and homeowners alike generally held that local streets were more desirable, supported higher home values, and provided safer environments for children to play when the streets were completely separated from any through traffic. In recent years, however, an increasing number of studies have focused on this belief and found significant reason to question it. Joe Cortright's 2009 study for CEO's for Cities entitled "How Walkability Raises Home Values in U.S. Cities" found a positive correlation between home values and better-networked street systems. The corner may, in fact, be more valuable than the cul-de-sac.[6] A 2002 study by William H. Lucy and Raphael Rabalais entitled "Traffic Fatalities and Homicides by Strangers: Danger of Leaving Home in Cities,

---

[6]D. Darlin, "Street Corners vs. Cul de Sacs," *New York Times*, January 9, 2010.

Figure 5.5
Lack of connection between this neighborhood and its park results in a two-mile access route even for residents whose homes are directly abutting.

Inner Suburbs, and Outer Suburbs" finds that dendrite-structured suburban areas are less safe than grid-structured urban areas in terms of both homicide and traffic fatality rates. Though ads for cul-de-sacs advertise their safety, often picturing children playing in the street, research demonstrates that the opposite is true: The main cause of injuries and deaths to small children is being backed over by family members and friends rather than driven over by passers by.[7] Bill Hillier's 2004 article "Can Streets be Made Safe?" finds that allowing through traffic to permeate the street system decreases all types of crime by increasing the amount of supervision that can be provided by passing motorists.

These recent studies have questioned the validity of the association of dendrite planning with the safety, desirability, and profitability of neighborhoods—critical factors for the general population. For older adults, in particular, the dendrite system prevents establishing many aspects of the lifelong neighborhood that depend on the convenience, sociability, and walkability of lower speed local routes to activate a community. Dendrite planning biases the transportation system toward freight traffic and the needs of working adults who commute from residential areas to work centers regularly. Dendrite systems collect and concentrate high-speed traffic along

[7] W. H. Lucy, and D. L. Phillips, *Tomorrow's Cities, Tomorrow's Suburbs* (Chicago, IL: The American Planning Association, 2006).

arterials, while grids disperse traffic more evenly. Dispersed traffic is calmer, has lower peak speeds and shorter, more frequent intersection delays than collected traffic. Local trips within a community that are typical of the daily routines of retired adults and families with young children are more direct, more calm, and better able to support pedestrians and bicyclists along a well-connected grid.[8] Concentrated traffic is much faster and has higher peak-speeds and longer, less frequent intersection delays. Dendrite planning also relies more heavily on high-speed roads with complex entry and exit sequences that many older adults dislike. As people age, many find that navigating complex road environments and making rapid, complex decisions such as utilizing exit and entry ramps, merging and diverging traffic lanes, and multilane interstates becomes increasingly difficult.[9] Disconnected dendrite systems are more difficult to navigate, and way-finding impairments often experienced by frail older adults can make sustained living within the curvilinear geometries of typical loop and cul-de-sac neighborhood particularly difficult.[10]

Assessing Connectivity

There are a number of rule-of-thumb measures that balance pedestrian comfort and automobile mobility for optimum connectivity:

- Frequent intersection spacing, typically 200 to 500 feet apart and totaling 120 to 240 intersections per square mile.

- Small block sizes, averaging perimeter measurements of no more than a quarter mile or 1,320 feet.

- Number of street intersections per square mile is generous, ranging from 120 to 240.

- The ratio of four-way intersections to three-way intersections is an additional factor, as four-way intersections provide more connection than three-way intersections (figs. 5.6, 5.7).

While a good general indication, these measures do not tell the whole story. In some cases a development's transit orientation can provide significant regional connections that compensate for less local connectivity by joining an outpost community to a town center. Some early streetcar suburbs functioned by relying on light rail for a primary connection and less on streets to access destinations outside the neighborhood (fig. 5.8). Today, dense Transit-Oriented Developments are often developed along major regional commuter rail stops and the regional reach and draw provided by these stops can help offset deficiencies in the surrounding street network.

In other cases, a fused grid system is used to combine aspects of both dendrite and grid planning by establishing pedestrian grid connections between separate motor vehicle roads (fig. 5.9). Radburn, New Jersey, is one of the earliest and most famous

[8]W. Kulash, "Traditional Neighborhood Development: Will the Traffic Work?" Paper presented at 11th Annual Pedestrian Conference, Bellevue WA, October 1990.

[9]California Task Force on Older Adults and Traffic Safety, *Traffic Safety Among Older Adults: Recommendations for California* (San Diego, CA: Center for Injury Prevention Policy and Practice, September 2002).

[10]A. E. J. Morris, *a History of Urban Form: Before the Industrial Revolution* (Harlow, UK: Pearson Education Limited, 1994).

Figure 5.6
An intersection analysis diagram reveals the small number of intersections per acre and the high ratio of three-way to four-way intersections.

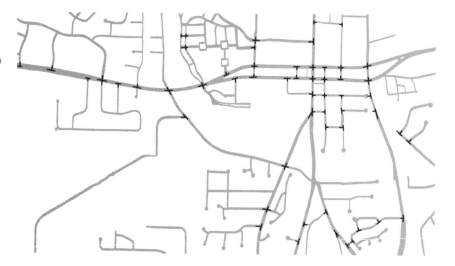

Figure 5.7
An intersection analysis diagram reveals the intersection per acre increase and better ratio of three-way to four-way.

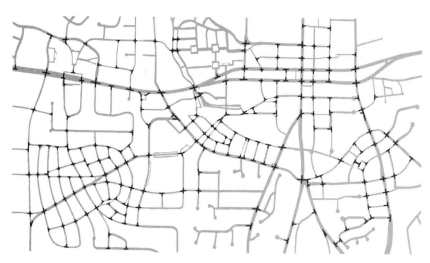

Figure 5.8
In 1984, the streetcar suburb of Fort Collins, Colorado, reopened one section of its streetcar route originally built in 1919 but closed in 1951.

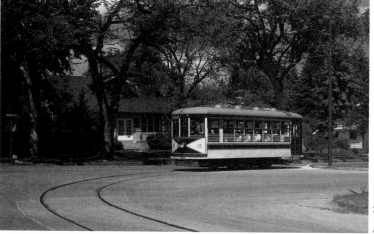

Steve Morgan

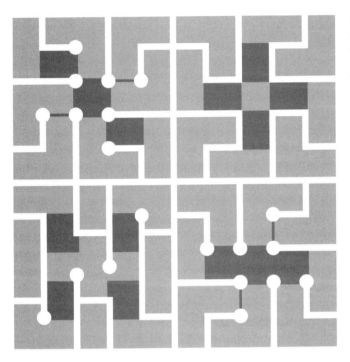

Figure 5.9
A concept diagram of various approaches to fused grid plans that prevent through connection by vehicles but allow pedestrians and bike traffic to flow through.

American examples of a fused system with pedestrian and bicycle paths provided along a continuous central greenway that is surrounded by cul-de-sacs. These pedestrian and bike connections can supplement deficiencies in the street network as well.

However, there is benefit to looking primarily at the street grid connections as the primary measure of connectivity. While there are multiple ways of providing pedestrian and biking opportunities as well as regional transit access, streets can multipurpose to a degree that paths and separated transit cannot. The intensity of use that goes on in this multipurpose environment adds vibrancy to the pedestrian realm. This vibrancy allows streets to support retail by providing service access, customer access, and a volume of through traffic that that trails and transit are not usually able to support in locations other than dense center cities. It also increases the intensity of social connection, mixing drivers and pedestrians in a close space and providing more opportunity for interaction between them.

The manner in which streets multitask provides the rich and layered experience necessary in creating an exciting retail environment. Mall and lifestyle-center development over the past fifty years has vastly improved the science of retail environment management, and it has been firmly established that an overall concentration of retail venues in a lively environment multiplies the likelihood of each of their success. A street can provide the volume of destination and service traffic necessary to support a lively retail environment, and the integration of this environment into a wider mixed-use community with a sense of place is proving to increasingly enhance retail prospects.[11]

---

[11] C. C. Bohl, *Place Making: Developing Town Centers, Main Streets, and Urban Villages* (Washington, DC: Urban Land Institute, 2002).

The Cost of Connectivity

In new construction, a highly connected street grid is usually the most efficient subdivision pattern. A grid usually provides more buildable lots and a more efficient ratio of street and associated infrastructure to buildable lot: Profit is thus maximized for a developer. Improving connection within an already developed area is a more challenging proposition. Eminent domain (seizure of private land for public purposes) is an expensive and extremely unpopular mechanism and is used only in rare conditions. Establishing connections across disconnected street systems often requires very skillful and strategic planning to minimize the need for property acquisition, and a long time frame that allows current residents to participate voluntarily and on their own schedule when acquisition of property is necessary.

Common Misconceptions about Connectivity

A common mistake made by both planning professionals and the general public is that density of either housing or retail is the major contributor to traffic congestion. In fact, the opposite is true. For the most part, density of housing shrinks the geographic area required to support retail and office destinations, bringing it closer to a larger majority of households, enabling more pedestrian access, and decreasing automobile dependence.

Rather than density, it is lack of connectivity that is the primary cause of traffic congestion (fig. 5.10). A well-connected grid disperses traffic along multiple routes rather than concentrating it on arterials that can clog up at peak demand times (fig. 5.11). Each additional connection and alternative route that is provided has the ability to siphon off traffic volume along the major roads as congestion begins to form.

A common objection to making additional street connections is the fear that they will allow cut-through traffic to come through neighborhoods, thereby creating hazardous conditions. In most cases, the street can be supplemented with traffic calming strategies that will mitigate this concern. However, this concern is legitimate when spot efforts are made to add an additional connection here and there without a broader public policy that

---

VIRGINIA'S CUL-DE-SAC REGULATIONS

In 2009, the Virginia Department of Transportation (VDOT) adopted new Secondary Street Acceptance Requirements (SSAR) that required developers to build well-connected street networks before the commonwealth could accept them into the public right of way.

The following describes the policies within the SSAR that were new to Virginia:

1. Area types: the division of the state into three categories based on long-term local, regional, and federal planning boundaries. The area types recognize the diversity of development and infrastructure needs throughout the commonwealth by establishing graduated connectivity standards for developments based on the area type in which they are located. These area types include compact, suburban, and rural.

2. Connectivity: standards to ensure connectivity of streets between adjacent developments and undeveloped parcels. Improved connection of newly constructed secondary streets to the existing street network and future developments will improve the network's overall efficiency.

3. Add streets to the system as network additions: the acceptance of new streets for a phase or an entire development as a single addition instead of acceptance of each street individually.

4. Pedestrian accommodations: standards to ensure that pedestrian accommodations are provided where appropriate.

5. Context-sensitive street design: revised requirements to provide initial designs that will serve as built-in traffic calming and ensure appropriate vehicular speeds. The SSAR also offers increased flexibility to use low-impact development techniques to help reduce storm water runoff.

6. Third-party inspections: the creation of an alternative to traditional VDOT inspection of additions to the secondary system.

New development proposals initially submitted to counties and VDOT after June 30, 2009, must comply with the requirements of the SSAR. As this legislation has time to gain influence across the state, connectivity will be significantly increased.

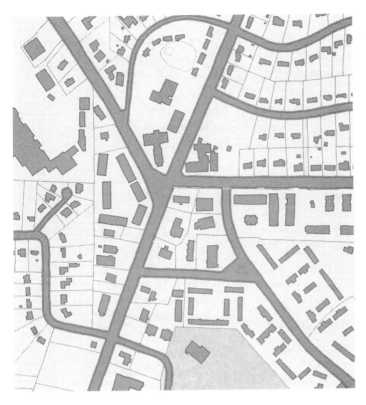

Figure 5.10
An intersection plan reveals the
lack of alternate routes around a
congested intersection.

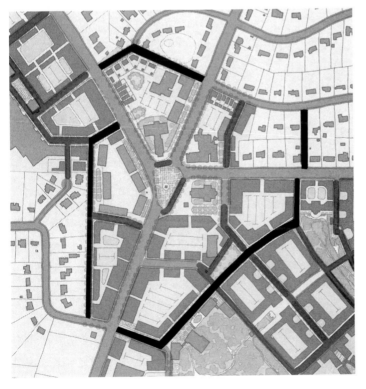

Figure 5.11
The proposed redevelopment of the
area provides new routes to bypass
the intersection when it backs up.

helps convert the entire regional system from total reliance on a few arterials to a robust network capable of dispersing traffic along a wide array of alternative routes.

Traffic volume does not necessarily conflict with neighborhood quality. A notable example is Dupont Circle in Washington, DC, which is structured around a very sophisticated, multitiered street grid (figs. 5.12, 5.13, 5.14). The circle separates the local street network on the surface from the high-volume/high-speed arterial that runs beneath. The result is a very desirable neighborhood with a vibrant pedestrian realm that manages to accommodate a volume of traffic each day that is equivalent to that of an interstate.

The traditional use of boulevards provides another example of accommodating high volumes of traffic while preserving connectivity. Traditionally, boulevards separated two or more center lanes of through traffic from parallel access or "slip" roads on either side. These separations were made by planted medians that helped preserve good street proportions and create an environment more accommodating to pedestrians. The slip roads restricted traffic to a lower speed than the central through traffic and served to collect frequent local roads to connections and gather them to join the though traffic at major intersections spaced much further apart (figs. 5.15, 5.16).

Figure 5.12
Dupont Circle provides a pedestrian friendly local-traffic network above grade and a high-volume through-traffic corridor below grade.

Figure 5.13
Detail.

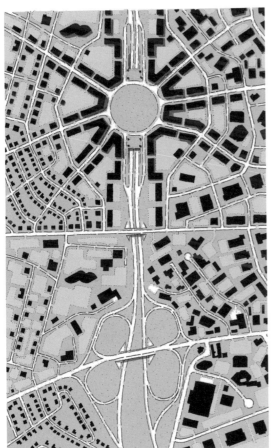

Figure 5.14
This diagram shows two ways of laying out a regional to local interchange: the clover leaf that is a ubiquitous feature of the nation's highway system, and a grade-separated version like that of Dupont Circle. The two interchanges have similar flow capacities.

Figure 5.15
This plan shows a section of an arterial converted into a boulevard with slip lanes. The slip lanes separate slower, local traffic from through traffic and facilitate on-street parking as well as better integration of local and regional thoroughfares.

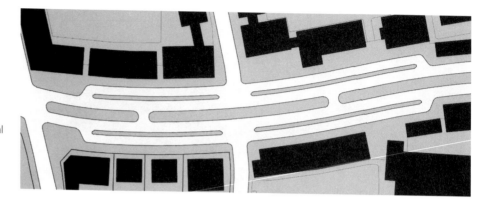

Figure 5.16
A typical plan and section of a boulevard with slip lanes.

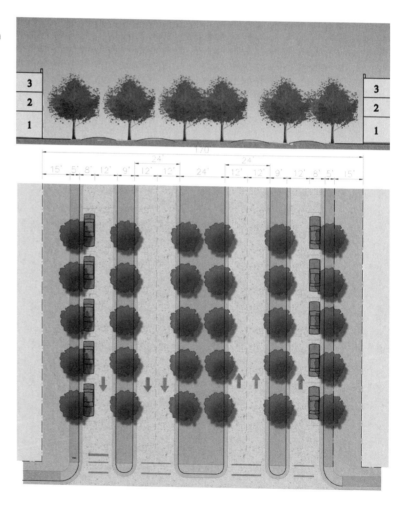

Lifelong neighborhoods are dependent on clearing up these misconceptions about connectivity: It is the primary tool for decreasing congestion, and street and neighborhood quality is not best maintained by limiting automobile access. Greater density and greater access both reduce, rather than increase, traffic congestion.

With conventional development practices, street systems are disconnected and restrict adjacent uses and neighborhoods from each other. People are required to use cars to get to places that are close-by, which results in traffic congestion isolating those who do not drive. Lifelong neighborhoods provide connected networks of streets and sidewalks. People have many routes to choose from to get to their destinations and may do so using a variety of means. The priority is to integrate all mobility options into a vibrant and cohesive built environment. The result is easy access to the necessities of daily life, whatever an individual's level of mobility.

Pedestrian Access and Transit

In planning for lifelong neighborhoods, pedestrian access and transit should be thought of as interrelated subjects—both parts of a continuous mobility network. Bus stops should be positioned in intervals that relate to walking distances so that as many residents as possible can leave their homes, get on a bus, and get off in a walkable distance from a wide array of destinations without needing to drive. When combined with pedestrian-oriented development, transit orientation can sustain individuals in their neighborhoods through life phases when automobiles are not the primary source of transportation for reasons of ability, finances, or choice (fig. 5.17).

While it may seem an obvious proposition that transit systems should mesh with walking routes and help people with their daily transportation routines, this

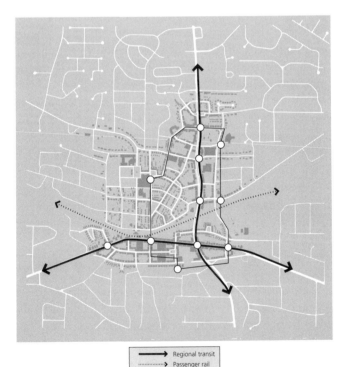

Figure 5.17
This circulator bus route connects a collection of pedestrian-oriented neighborhoods and allows their retail districts to function as a single unit: A pharmacy may be in one neighborhood, a grocery in another, and a hardware store in another, but all are easily accessed along the bus loop. This plan represents an optimum scale for circulator buses, allowing a single bus to run continuously with approximately twenty-minute head times.

Regional transit
Passenger rail
Circulator bus
Transit stop

Figure 5.18
Typical, regional-sized city bus can carry more than forty riders. It is made for relatively long hauls to regional hubs and is too large for neighborhood circulation in all but the densest of cities.

is not the goal of many transit systems (fig. 5.18). The primary focus of transit in most metropolitan regions is regional congestion mitigation rather than enhanced individual mobility.

As a strategic framework, congestion mitigation looks at peak hours of congestions—rush hours—and provides alternatives to individual car use for the most congested regional corridors. The resulting transit system tends to work well for the regional movement of workers—collecting riders in residential areas in the morning, bringing them to a central distribution hub, sending them out to big employment centers, and finally reversing the same journey to take them home in the evening. These systems are much less effective for those who are retired, are not employed, or work out of a home office and need transit for daily errands rather than commute to and from work. Even those who have intentionally moved to a mixed-use neighborhood for independence from the automobile may see their strategy fail when a health concern requires weekly visits to a specialized doctor whose office is across town. Congestion mitigation strategies do not effectively serve the transportation needs of anyone other than workers who live in a suburb and work in an employment center in another distant part of the region. Reorienting the focus of transit planning from congestion mitigation to individual mobility is particularly important for older adults who increasingly rely on public transportation as they age.

ADA and Paratransit

Even when public transportation is readily available in some areas, many seniors have difficulty using the system for a variety of reasons. In some neighborhoods, seniors may fear walking to bus stops and waiting for the bus in the midst of loitering youth. Based on an AARP senior housing study done in 2002, 20 percent of seniors avoided using public transportation because of the threat of crime. In a study conducted in Houston, Texas, close to 50 percent of elderly and disabled residents lived within two blocks of a bus stop, but they found use of the public transportation system nearly impossible due to lack of sidewalks, curb cuts, and bus shelters.[12]

ADA paratransit addresses some of these use issues. Paratransit is a flexible route, demand responsive transportation service typically provided by shuttle buses with accessibility provisions. Most paratransit services operate weekdays during normal business hours and require riders to make reservations at least twenty-four hours in advance. More than one hundred federal programs fund transportation services, with the majority of support coming from the Department of Transportation (especially the Urban Mass Transportation Administration) and the Department of Health and Human Services.[13] Title 49 Part 37 of the Americans with Disabilities Act of 1990 first required public transportation agencies to provide equal participation accommodations for passengers who were (1) unable to navigate the public bus system, (2) unable to get to a point from which they could access the public bus system, or (3) had a temporary need for these services because of injury or some type of limited duration cause of disability. These accommodations are required to specifically include "complementary" paratransit services to destinations within three quarters of a mile of all fixed-route transit services. Maximum waiting times for these door-to-door services are also mandated.

ADA paratransit requirements have been an unfunded mandate since they were first enacted. The service is a very expensive means of overcoming the barriers to access imposed by automobile dependent environments—often costing more than twenty dollars per average ride to provide. Longevity and the aging of the baby boomers will put an even greater demand on these services and will require more efficient and less costly means for their delivery.

Circulation Buses and Regional Buses

The image that comes to mind with the term public bus is that of a regional bus capable of carrying approximately thirty passengers (fig. 5.18). These buses serve regional transit demand, typically collecting passengers across a ten- to twenty-square-mile area on a five- to ten-mile-long linear spoke, delivering them to regional distribution hubs (fig. 5.19). Once at the regional hub, passengers can change to another regional spoke and head back out again to their destination. Regional buses are primarily intended to move the work force from residential areas to employment centers. They tend to be less useful for retired or home office workers who have a greater need for accessing daily needs that require short stops at scattered locations within numerous close neighborhoods.

A circulator bus, on the other hand, serves a local area and connects a group of neighborhood destinations. A circulator bus links neighborhoods into a single symbiotic cluster that shares various retail components and creates in aggregate a full range of local retail opportunities. Circulator buses are smaller than regional buses and typically shuttle no more than twenty people around an orbit of two to ten miles (fig. 5.20). In some cases, a small van provides sufficient shuttle service

---

[12]D. A. Howe, "Innovations In Aging-Sensitive Community Planning and Land Use Regulation," (Washington, DC: Brookings Institute, 2007).

[13]Ibid.

Figure 5.19
This schematic diagram illustrates
how a regional hub-and-spoke transit
system relates linear local bus routes to
regional heavy rail lines. This is a
hub-and-spoke system that
emphasizes regional commuter
congestion mitigation rather than
individual mobility.

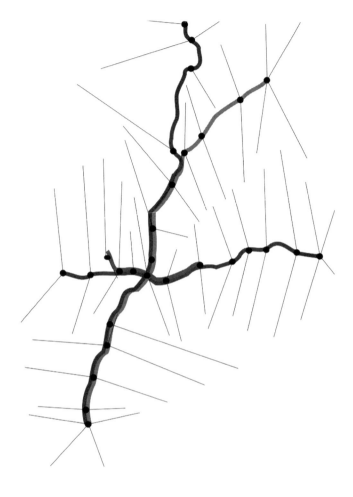

Figure 5.20
Mableton's proposed circulator
bus is scaled to allow a single
vehicle to run a continuous
loop in less than twenty
minutes. This allows the local
bus to make local stops and the
regional bus to make express
stops only.

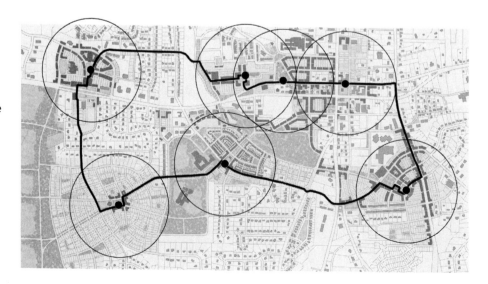

for an area. Shuttle buses are most often operated by Community Improvement Districts, self-taxing units of government usually formed, managed, and governed by the businesses within the district. However, as an increasing percentage of the population ages, circulator buses may need to play a greater role in public transit. An older adult agenda for transit should place greater emphasis on circulator buses and less emphasis on linear regional routes supplemented, to a degree, with ADA-mandated paratransit. Certainly the savings realized by less need for ADA paratransit would help offset the costs of supplying circulator buses.

In dense urban cores like Manhattan, there is less differentiation between regional and circulating bus systems. There is enough ridership to warrant a full-sized bus, even within a few neighborhoods, and multiple routes intersect regularly across a grid so that a great deal of potential routes can be accomplished without first traveling to big regional hubs. In urban cores, linear bus lines that cross regularly along the grid function both as regional spokes and, through a few easy transfers, circulating systems (fig. 5.21).

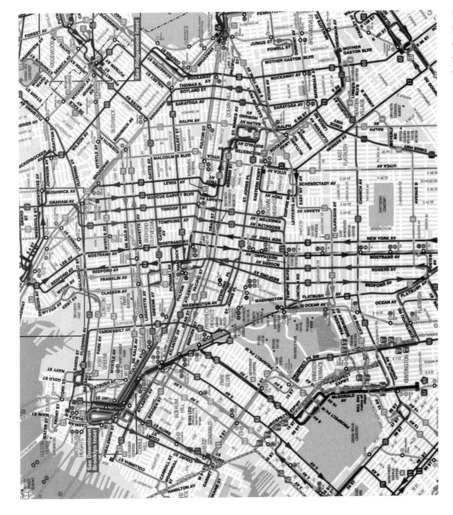

Figure 5.21
New York City's bus system is densely interwoven and thus supports local circulation trips as well as regional commuting.

Figure 5.22
Each type of transit has an ideal distance between stops. A well-planned transit system meshes transit types so that regional lines transfer to local circulators.

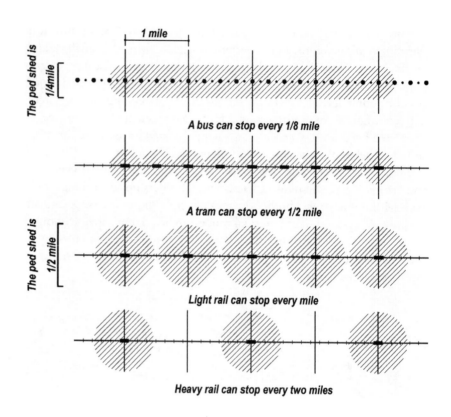

In less dense environments, circulating buses would be networked with regional buses to support better circulation locally while allowing the regional buses to operate as express routes that stop once at each occasional transfer point rather than the closer intervals required to accommodate pedestrians not included in a circulation system.

Gauging Pedestrian and Transit Mobility

Pedestrian and transit mobility is primarily gauged by overlaying circles on transit route plans. These circles are scaled to a half-mile radius and are a general indication of the area around a transit stop that can be comfortably reached by foot or wheelchair. Planners refer to this circular area as a pedestrian shed (fig. 5.22). Ideally, local transit stops will be positioned at intervals close enough to serve the majority of buildings in any area within the pedestrian shed of a stop.

In an ideal pedestrian and transit plan, each half-mile pedestrian shed would be centered on a small retail area that meets daily necessities, complete with a transit stop. Because this kind of retail requires a larger catchment area than can be supplied within a pedestrian shed, several of them could be linked together with small circulator buses that, once combined, would provide sufficient customers to make retail feasible. In this way, the network enhances the local retail and service network by drawing in larger customer catchment areas.

CHAPTER 6

DIVERSITY

Planning for Diversity

Both the housing stock and the neighborhood design of the post–World War II construction booms were conceived of and built for families. In the three decades following the war, families influenced the dominant household type. In 1960, 48 percent of all households had children and only 13 percent were single-person households.[1] Basic market forces, the strong desire of communities to attract families and their disposable incomes, and banking and land-use regulations allowed the construction industry to respond to the demands of this new and growing group at a scale not before seen in the United States. Housing these families would not have had to result in the challenges we face today except for the fact that the housing and neighborhoods built in response to this demographic were extremely uniform and inflexible. When the families turned into empty nesters and then aged into retirement, these homes no longer functioned in the same way. Large homes on large lots require maintenance that older residents did not have the desire, the ability, or the funds to maintain. Homes were pushed back from the street and away from each other leaving the common space of the street ill defined. Stairs and rigid floor plans created insurmountable barriers to changing bodies with a permanent or temporary disability. Single-use zoning has created homogeneous communities in which only one housing type—most often single family detached homes—are constructed. Large-scale developers could construct entire subdivisions at once, creating a community where all the homes are not only the same type but also are likely to share the same or a similar floor plan. When an older adult realizes that he is ready for a change, or when an older adult

BUILDING TYPES

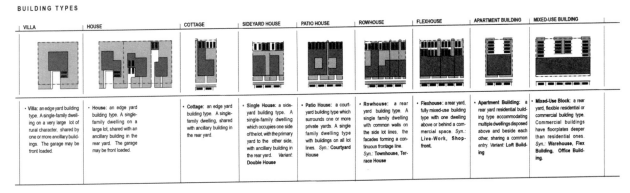

VILLA	HOUSE	COTTAGE	SIDEYARD HOUSE	PATIO HOUSE	ROWHOUSE	FLEXHOUSE	APARTMENT BUILDING	MIXED-USE BUILDING
• Villa: an edge yard building type. A single-family dwelling on a very large lot of rural character, shared by one or more ancillary buildings. The garage may be front loaded.	• House: an edge yard building type. A single-family dwelling on a large lot, shared with an ancillary building in the rear yard. The garage may be front loaded.	• Cottage: an edge yard building type. A single-family dwelling, shared with ancillary building in the rear yard.	• Single House: a side-yard building type. A single-family dwelling which occupies one side of the lot, with the primary yard to the other side, with ancillary building in the rear yard. *Variant:* Double House.	• Patio House: a courtyard building type which surrounds one or more private yards. A single family dwelling type with buildings on all lot lines. *Syn.:* Courtyard House	• Rowhouse: a rear yard building type. A single family dwelling with common walls on the side lot lines, the facades forming a continuous frontage line. *Syn.:* Townhouse, Terrace House.	• Flexhouse: a rear yard, fully mixed-use building type with one dwelling above or behind a commercial space. *Syn.:* Live-Work, Shopfront.	• Apartment Building: a rear yard residential building type accommodating multiple dwellings disposed above and beside each other, sharing a common entry. *Variant:* Loft Building	• Mixed-Use Block: a rear yard, flexible residential or commercial building type. Commercial buildings have floorplates deeper than residential ones. *Syn.:* Warehouse, Flex Building, Office Building.

Figure 6.1
This building type diagram represents the range of units that should be available in each neighborhood.

[1]M. Farnsworth Riche, "How Changes in the Nation's Age and Household Structure Will Reshape Housing Demand in the 21st Century," in *Issue Papers on Demographic Trends Important to Housing* (HUD, February 2003), 125–147.

[2]Ibid.

tries to take proactive steps to find a home more suited to his needs in advance of an accident or illness, he has to leave the community he has known and loved for years. Zoning has regulated that all the homes in his neighborhood are exactly like—the one he knows he needs to leave. Suburban development patterns have left him in a series of cul-de-sacs connected only to a major arterial road. Moving just two or ten miles away to downsize into a condominium or townhome and reduce his maintenance work and expenses requires that he leave the neighborhood association, park, walking group, or tennis partnership he has been involved with for several decades.

The demographics are shifting. In 2040, less than a third of households will be families with children and 30 percent of households will be made up of a single person. Examining the growth in the population over that same time period, 87 percent of new households will be households without children and only 13 percent of new households will have children.[2] This is a tremendous change from just forty years ago, and it requires a response on the same scale as the post–World War II construction boom. This response, however, will occur in a dramatically different context.

Again, we need to house a large population with specific needs, but this time it cannot simply be new construction on the edge of existing communities. Most communities cannot afford the infrastructure, and most older adults need to be close to other commercial uses. This time it cannot be a uniform stock. Individuals age differently and require different levels of support. Like housing for children and families, however, housing to meet the needs of the aging population has to provide more than shelter. It must be organized in a way that provides direct and convenient access to services. It needs to provide opportunities for social interaction and community building. It should facilitate healthy and active lifestyles. It must be located within walking distance of basic services so that residents have multiple ways to get around.

A strategy then, to meet the housing needs of the new demographic has to both reinvent traditional models of senior housing and retrofit existing communities to integrate housing options within. This will require a greater degree of attention to urban context, more emphasis on infill of existing communities rather than further expansion along green fields, and it will provide a greater opportunity for the integration of neighborhood retail (fig. 6.2). Governments could soon face the option of encouraging the retrofitting and redesigning of their suburbs or risk losing them to emigration and disinvestment. In 2000, 70 percent of the baby boomers were living in the suburbs comprising 31 percent of the entire suburban population.[3] The boomers will introduce the nation to the impacts of longevity on urban form, and in order to meet this new challenge, localities will need to reconsider how dwellings relate to each other, common spaces, stores, civic buildings, and multiple modes of transportation.

---

[3]W. Frey, *Boomers and Seniors in the Suburbs: Aging Patterns in US Census 2000* (Washington, DC: Brookings Institute, 2003).

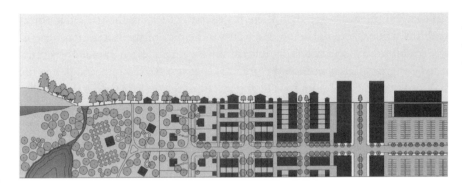

Figure 6.2
The SmartCode organizes along transect zones rather than use zones. Transects adjust zoning requirements based on the urban-to-rural context.

Zoning for Diversity

Zoning regulations often mandate homogenous subdivision developments by requiring singular and uniform development standards. Conventional suburban development zoning codes that segregate development by use and intensity often limit new subdivisions to one or maybe two building types. Municipal massing, setback, and architectural standards are often applied uniformly to all developments regardless of scale: whether they are on one acre or one thousand acres. The scale of development or urban-to-rural context does not inform or vary the standards. The relationship between various development intensities and building uses is not coordinated to create pedestrian-oriented communities. These deficiencies and blind spots in zoning codes exist not because the ability to regulate is inherently flawed, but simply because local governments are not accustomed to asking for or even allowing for anything more.

Intention Statements

As covered in greater depth in Chapter 3, intention statements can establish that the community values diversity of all types: economic, age, ethnic, racial, religious, or family structure. While it is not legal for government agencies to exclude people based on some of these diversity factors, there is a benefit to conspicuously repeating a preference for inclusion in an ordinance. Proactive statements have a way of surfacing resistance so that it may be addressed, whereas silence on these subjects facilitates quieter, institutionally cloaked practices that effectively result in exclusion.

Local governments seeking to generally increase building stock diversity or specifically increase the supply of certain forms of seniors housing in neighborhood settings can act on intention statements before a developer even appears, with "as-of-right" entitlements granted in specific, pre-identified districts in zoning maps and comprehensive development plans. This kind of proactive action to locate and allow certain uses in advance of an actual proposed project is an effective means of overcoming unpredictable "not in my backyard" (NIMBY) resistance. NIMBY is a problem that is well known by any local official who has tried to initiate changes in the built environment. Even when there is general consensus about overall objectives and intentions, oftentimes no one wants to be part of the initial steps toward change. Community objections to diverse development often include concerns about lowering property values to the potential negative traffic impacts. While the NIMBY problem can and does arise in any location, the desire to avoid drawn-out, expensive conflicts leads many developers to opt for peripheral locations where residents are less likely to put up a fight. NIMBY problems can thus not only stymie progressive action but also catalyze regressive action. Sometimes all that state and regional governments need to do is provide political cover from NIMBYs for local officials who want to do the right thing.

Allowing for Use Diversity

In many places across the nation it is illegal to walk to the corner and purchase a cup of coffee, prescription refill, or milk for breakfast. It is illegal because antiquated single-use zoning practices have made it impossible to provide daily-needs retail services within neighborhoods. Instead, single-use zoning codes prevent mixed-use development and push retail districts away from residential districts—usually to areas that can only be accessed by car.

Having basic services within walking distance is a great convenience for all residents but is particularly important for an aging population (fig. 6.3). A walk to the neighborhood store or coffeehouse provides exercise, opportunity for social interaction, helps decrease any sense of isolation, and perhaps most importantly allows for the possibility of staying in a community longer after losing the ability to drive. When a pharmacy can be located in the neighborhood or near enough to the home for local delivery, a nondriver can obtain a prescription refill without requiring their caregiver to take a day off from work.

A first step to reclaiming neighborhood retail is to address the basic limitations of the local land use and building codes to allow mixing of uses in a wide variety of community settings. Existing neighborhoods where most older adults live will have to retrofit and rezone areas for local commercial centers.

Zoning for Neighborhood Retail

From a zoning perspective, integrating retail back into neighborhoods can be accomplished through spot zoning, overlay zoning, and conversion to form-based code instead of use-based code (fig. 6.4). As a general rule of thumb, the more predictable and specific a community can make the zoning entitlement process, the better the result for everyone. Business investors will know what they can expect before purchasing a parcel and homeowners will know that the character of their community will be protected even as the uses diversify within it.

It is also important to consider what the various forms of zoning can do when choosing the right approach for a lifelong neighborhood initiative. Aging is a multifaceted issue best approached as a lens or litmus test for viewing a wide range of

TABLE 5E. SPECIFIC FUNCTION AND USE

	B3.4	B3.3	B3.2	B3.1	C
a. RESIDENTIAL					
MIXED USE BUILDING	□	■	■	■	□
MULTI FAMILY RESIDENTIAL	□	■	■	■	□
SINGLE FAMILY RESIDENTIAL	■	■	■	■	
SENIOR HOUSING	■	■	■	■	
ACCESSORY UNIT	■	■	■	■	
b. LODGING					
HOTEL (NO ROOM LIMIT)				■	□
INN (UP TO 12 ROOMS)		■	■	■	
BED & BREAKFAST (UP TO 5 ROOMS)	■	■	■	■	
SCHOOL DORMITORY		□	□	□	□
c. OFFICE					
OFFICE BUILDING		■	■	■	□
LIVE/WORK UNIT	■	■	■	■	□
d. RETAIL					
OPEN MARKET BUILDING	□	□	■	■	■
RETAIL BUILDING		□	■	■	□
DISPLAY GALLERY		■	■	■	□
RESTAURANT		□	■	■	□
KIOSK		■	■	■	□
PUSH CART				■	□
e. AGRICULTURE					
GRAIN STORAGE					□
LIVESTOCK PEN					□
GREENHOUSE	□				□
STABLE	□				□
KENNEL	□		□	□	□
GARDEN (PRIVATE FRONTAGE)	■	■	■		□
BEE KEEPING	■	■	■		□

	B3.4	B3.3	B3.2	B3.1	C
f. OTHER: AUTOMOTIVE					
GAS STATION				□	■
AUTOMOBILE SERVICE				□	■
TRUCK MAINTENANCE				□	■
DRIVE THROUGH FACILITY				□	■
f. OTHER: CIVIL SUPPORT					
CEMETERY	□	□			■
FUNERAL HOME		□	■	■	■
HOSPITAL				□	■
MEDICAL CLINIC		□	□	■	■
f. OTHER: EDUCATION					
COLLEGE				□	■
HIGH SCHOOL		□	□	□	■
TRADE SCHOOL		□	□	■	■
ELEMENTARY SCHOOL	□	■	■	■	■
CHILDCARE CENTER	□	■	■	■	■
f. OTHER: INDUSTRIAL					
HEAVY INDUSTRIAL FACILITY					■
LIGHT INDUSTRIAL FACILITY				□	■
TRUCK DEPOT					■
LABORATORY FACILITY				□	■
CREMATION FACILITY					■
WAREHOUSE					■
PRODUCE STORAGE					■
MINI-STORAGE					■
HEAVY MANUFACTURING					■
LIGHT MANUFACTURING		□	□	■	■

■ BY RIGHT
□ BY WARRANT

Figure 6.3
This function and use table is typical of a SmartCode ordinance that organizes around transect zones rather than building-use zones. As shown in the table, transects 4 to 6 allow mixed uses.

urban planning and design decisions. Spot zoning is not similarly multifaceted. It provides only a one-time exemption from typical zoning requirements for a single development proposal. Overlay zoning is better but is most effective when it provides for a single special use or small collection of special uses. Overlay zoning is commonly used to provide opportunities for specialized age segregated senior housing to be developed to a greater density than would normally be allowed of general population housing. The overlay approach lends itself to providing opportunity to integrate this kind of specialized form into existing communities. Form-based code is often the most effective tool for addressing the multifaceted concerns of a lifelong neighborhood. Rather than allow a onetime exception or provide wider opportunity for a specialized urban form, form-based code orchestrates a wide range of built environment considerations in order to produce a diverse but cohesive whole environment. The focus of form-based code on the consistency and holistic integrity of the whole environment mirrors the multifaceted focus of a lifelong neighborhood approach.

Spot zoning is enacted on a lot-by-lot basis as landowners apply. It is the least predictable and least defensible means of accomplishing the purpose, and therefore it is the least likely method for adapting communities to better serve older adults. Analysis of existing communities developed over the past fifty years under single-use

Figure 6.4

A neighborhood retail and civic square can be accomplished very economically and efficiently. This neighborhood center in New Town at St. Charles, Missouri, provides a post office, a small grocery, and a town hall in three buildings clustered around a corner square.

zoning ordinances often reveals that spot zoning was practiced widely when the zoning ordinances were too restrictive or when political influence shaped entitlement decisions rather than master plans or zoning ordinances. The lack of predictability that goes with spot zoning is especially difficult on retail. Potential retail investors need to know before they purchase a parcel whether or not it will support their business rather than after they have purchased it and presented development plans to the regulating entity. Nearby homeowners cannot be assured that the retail facility will build in a manner that is compatible with their homes when it is allowed an exemption or variance from the governing code. Perhaps the most significant drawback to spot zoning neighborhood retail is the inability to develop the intensity of compatible retail uses in the right configuration when the opportunity to operate in a neighborhood is given out erratically on a case-by-case basis. A successful retail environment is difficult to develop at any scale, but especially at the neighborhood scale where the geographic market catchment area may be very small. Success depends on uses that are most compatible and best configured so that they create sufficient intensity across all business hours and create cross-market drawing power. It is very difficult in most neighborhood environments to gather compatible, symbiotic businesses on a spot, case-by-case manner. Rather, doing so requires a multisector effort to understand and envision the neighborhood's retail potential and bringing together the various and necessary stakeholders to carry out the that cohesive vision.

Overlay zoning can be adopted by the local land-use regulating authority to allow certain types of retail uses in certain conditions for communities that adopt the ordinance for a specific geographic area. Overlay zoning may generally stipulate conditions under which retail uses may be developed by right without further conditions, or they may be "plan contingent"—requiring review and approval of the specific plan and adherence to this once entitlements are provided. In providing opportunity for retail as an overlay, there is more predictability and better defensibility when compared with spot zoning. The zoning can be enacted in an area before a specific project is being proposed and can be an enormous asset in attracting the targeted kinds of business desired by the community. An overlay-zoning category is available to the entire area under the jurisdiction of the zoning authority, but is only enacted in areas when a community or project developer requests its adoption. In general, overlay zoning is better when it is adopted by a community with an overall vision for the end results rather than by a developer who has a single business interest in the area. Community-driven overlay zoning can take additional steps of preapproving the desired types of retail and services as a means of recruiting those businesses. Another proactive measure that can assist in recruiting appropriate retail and services is to provide a plan book of community-compatible building forms that are preapproved for certain uses and possibly even receive expedited permitting service from the building department. A locally appropriate community-based skilled nursing facility building type could be provided, for example, that would not require a special-use permit application. Pattern books and stipulating specific desired uses are good examples of provisions that can be made in the zoning code to help proactively recruit the kinds of neighborhood retail and service developments that would be most beneficial to older adults.

Form-based code is the most robust and holistic zoning approach for retail integration. Because form-based code primarily emphasizes the shape, form, and character of the whole place rather than the individual use of each property, the approach is often better suited than conventional zoning for retail and service integration in the community. Form-based codes were developed by practitioners who advanced the cause of pedestrian-friendly, traditional neighborhood development planning principles; hence, they are typically more focused on the pedestrian scale than automobile scale when regulating street and building details. A form-based code usually addresses public spaces like the street, sidewalks, and parks, and then organizes the individual private developments so that they contribute to and shape the public areas in a consistent way that is inspired by the local character of a place. A good example of the difference between a form-based code and a conventional code is that a conventional code might rely entirely on setbacks that require minimum separation distances between a building and a property line with no maximum limit, whereas a form-based code would be more likely to put an emphasis on build-to lines that limit the maximum setback and require a minimum amount of building mass at the build-to line. The setback requirements primarily ensure that one building doesn't intrude onto the space of another, while the build-to requirements are primarily focused on orchestrating individual buildings so that together they produce a whole street with a vibrant pedestrian realm.

Form-based codes are particularly helpful in reintegrating the retail and services needed by older adults into residential neighborhoods because they can help assure diversity of use without fragmentation of community character. This is an important consideration when residents are most familiar with strip-mall retail, which they typically don't want in their communities. The objection is founded—retail of this type is destructive to neighborhood character if it is not brought into a more pedestrian-friendly, neighborhood-oriented form. When retail and service building types are compatible with the surrounding homes and contribute to the neighborhood character instead of destroying it, more communities opt to integrate them into traditional neighborhood settings.

Single-use zoning has prevented the integration of retail into neighborhood settings for so many decades now that the majority of the retail and service industry will need to reinvent itself to fit into a current neighborhood setting. Retail and service business models have come to depend on the regional markets that can only be accessed along arterial roads and attracted with large, big-box stores like Home Depot or Walmart to anchor a development. Where the smallest big-box operation may not be able to function below a minimum of 30,000 square feet, many neighborhoods will not be able to accommodate more than 2,000 square feet or provide enough customer base for more than a few convenience items.

On the other hand, older adults can provide an important market segment for retail, particularly when they are retired and not working on the same peak retail demand periods typical of working adults (e.g., 9:00 A.M., 12:00 P.M., and 5:00 P.M.). In an ideal circumstance, a neighborhood café might provide a morning coffee and breakfast to-go venue for parents dropping off children at school before heading to work. From 10:00 A.M. until 3:00 P.M. the café might cater to older adults, even sponsoring senior-specific meet-up events. From 3:00 P.M. to 5:00 P.M. the café might function primarily as an after-school hangout spot for teenagers and also serve parents returning from work in the evening who are looking for a place to have dinner. Neighborhood retail requires these types of multiple market shifts throughout the day in order to survive. Niche markets are harder to serve at that scale. Older adults can play an important role in the daily cycle of retail shifts, particularly if they provide a good customer base in residential areas for those otherwise dead midday hours when working adults are at their jobs and children are at their schools.

Integrating retail and service provision back into the neighborhood will require both zoning reform and entrepreneurial innovation. Older adults can be both advocates for this change as well as an important part of the market that will fuel the change. There are already good examples of mixed-use neighborhood development sprouting up in most regions across the country, and as the business models are understood better and perfected, those communities that have proactively adopted zoning ordinances that support neighborhood-based retail will be the first to receive the investment.

Allowing for Housing Diversity by Building Type

Zoning ordinances should seek to increase the availability of townhouses, apartments, and condos within single-family zoned areas to preclude the de facto generational segregation by housing type. Growing communities should have a goal of mixing smaller and larger units within close proximity in order to fit the needs and desires of the full spectrum of citizens. Particular attention should also be given to establishing the base requirements for entitling as-of-right residential supportive and care housing. It is often very difficult for designated senior housing types such as assisted living and congregate housing to gain zoning approval. These types of senior housing developments mix residential uses with service uses and thus

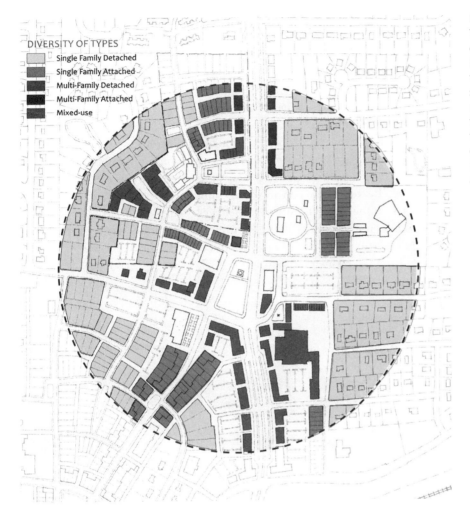

DIVERSITY OF TYPES
- Single Family Detached
- Single Family Attached
- Multi-Family Detached
- Multi-Family Attached
- Mixed-use

Figure 6.5
This housing diversity diagram exhibits a good mix of housing types with buildings that accommodate both shops and apartments in the neighborhood center to single family homes at the edges of the pedestrian shed. This mix ensures that every period of a life cycle is accommodated with an appropriate housing type.

trip ordinances that focus on use as a distinguishing and differentiating element. Compromise is frequently necessary regarding building use classification, height, and site coverage, as well as parking for staff, residents, and visitors.

Proactive zoning changes can be made to better accommodate older adults who are no longer active and who need more support to remain in a community. These may include allowing home-care outpost offices in the neighborhood, possibly as a use category in zoning ordinances that is less restrictive and more flexible than typical commercial or office designations. Another possibility is to allow some types of community-appropriate skilled nursing residences—the Green House or small home-care facilities covered in Chapter 6. Understanding that many of the dominant forms of institutionalized care facilities are not yet suited for community integration, local governments might consider a special designation for small houses and Green House care facilities that are appropriate for integration into a neighborhood setting, thereby allowing those facilities to build without additional special permits provided that they meet the design and programming criteria required by that designation.

Accessory Dwelling Units   The most immediate way to insert a more diverse range of homes into an existing suburban neighborhood is to allow the construction of accessory apartments or "granny flats." The City of Santa Cruz Accessory Dwelling Unit (ADU) Development Program is a good example of how local governments can encourage and facilitate this type of housing diversification program. The Santa Cruz ADU initiative seeks to promote infill development to provide more rental housing opportunities, concentrate growth in the city center and discourage further expansion in its surrounding green belt, and concentrate growth to make public transit more cost effective to supply. The City of Santa Cruz defines an ADU as a secondary living unit on a single-family home property that has separate kitchen, bedroom, and bathroom facilities. The ADU can be attached or detached from the primary residence (fig. 6.6).[4]

Figure 6.6
The grouping of accessory dwelling units at the rear of properties along a mid-block alley associates them with an alley community rather than with the main house. These are known as alley houses.

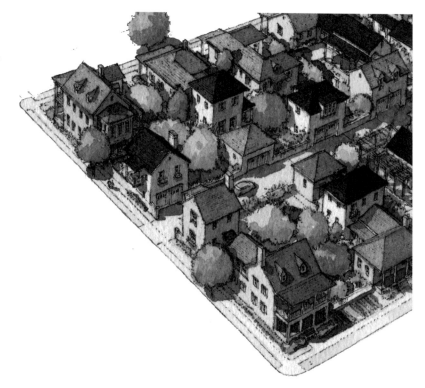

---

[4]http://www.cityofsantacruz.com/index.aspx?page=1150.

Santa Cruz managed the implementation of the ADU Development Program with great care, accompanying it with a public education campaign focused on the role the units could play in increasing the stock of affordable rental property while providing rental income to home owners to help single family housing remain affordable. The City was also provided quality control assurance by both cracking down on the proliferation of poorly constructed, illegal ADUs, while encouraging well constructed ADUs with the provision of technical assistance, sample prototype design concepts, a manual, a video, and a loan program offering up to $100,000 for the construction of ADUs.[5]

A variation on ADU initiatives is the Elderly Cottage Housing Opportunity movement (ECHO). Originally developed in Australia, ECHO units are temporary accessory apartments, raised on either wheeled trailers or demountable modular homes. These units are owned and managed by a company rented to households with an older or friend. The "mother-in-law" moved into this totally separate apartment. Upon her death the modular apartment would be removed. The company that owned the unit would then rent it to another family somewhere else. Though AARP began advocating for the use of ECHO units in the 1980s, regulatory barriers and costs associated with installation and removal of temporary units dampened widespread adoption of this strategy. ECHO units did not prove cost effective or expedient in comparison to simply adding an extension to a home. Recently however, MEDCottage, a group out of Salem, Virginia, has lobbied for statewide legislation to support ECHO housing and has launched a nationwide effort to market portable, modular units that come equipped with a number of care technologies including monitors that track vital signs, interior temperature, and any falls or accidents (fig. 6.7). Caregivers are able to unobtrusively monitor the occupant from the primary residence. Additionally, a lift track comes preinstalled in the ceiling to help impaired and frail residents get in and out of bed and to the bathroom without requiring heavy lifting by the caregiver. Additional attention is paid to even and continuous floor illumination to reduce trip hazards and to the heating and air systems to keep air quality as high as possible. MEDCottage is betting that the combination of statewide legislative efforts and units with tailored assistive technologies and design will overcome the previously experienced barriers to widespread market adoption of the ECHO concept.

Lifelong neighborhoods require strategies that yield a rich diversity of townhouses, apartments, and condos, as well as detached homes, accessory apartments, and some supportive and skilled care near enough to ensure a continuous care environment within the community (figs. 6.8, 6.9). Pairing these diverse dwelling types with retail, office, civic, and service uses creates complete neighborhoods that are at the heart of lifelong neighborhoods.

---

[5]Ibid.

Figure 6.7
The MEDCottage is an updated version of the Elderly Cottage Housing Opportunity (ECHO) concept originally developed in Australia.

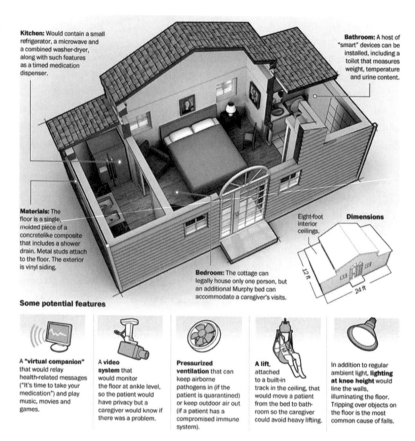

Kitchen: Would contain a small refrigerator, a microwave and a combined washer-dryer, along with such features as a timed medication dispenser.

Bathroom: A host of "smart" devices can be installed, including a toilet that measures weight, temperature and urine content.

Materials: The floor is a single, molded piece of a concretelike composite that includes a shower drain. Metal studs attach to the floor. The exterior is vinyl siding.

Eight-foot interior ceilings.

Dimensions

12 ft
24 ft

Bedroom: The cottage can legally house only one person, but an additional Murphy bed can accommodate a caregiver's visits.

Some potential features

A **"virtual companion"** that would relay health-related messages ("It's time to take your medication") and play music, movies and games.

A **video system** that would monitor the floor at ankle level, so the patient would have privacy but a caregiver would know if there was a problem.

Pressurized ventilation that can keep airborne pathogens in (if the patient is quarantined) or keep outdoor air out (if a patient has a compromised immune system).

A lift, attached to a built-in track in the ceiling, that would move a patient from the bed to bathroom so the caregiver could avoid heavy lifting.

In addition to regular ambient light, **lighting at knee height** would line the walls, illuminating the floor. Tripping over objects on the floor is the most common cause of falls.

Figure 6.9
This diversification strategy diagram demonstrates schemes for infill and subdivision of large single-family lots.

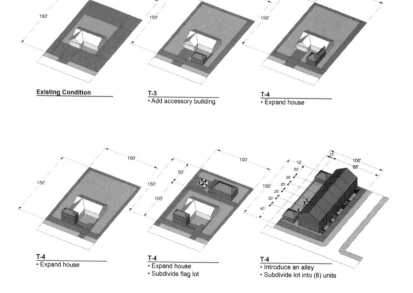

Existing Condition

T-3
• Add accessory building

T-4
• Expand house

T-4
• Expand house

T-4
• Expand house
• Subdivide flag lot

T-4
• Introduce an alley
• Subdivide lot into (6) units

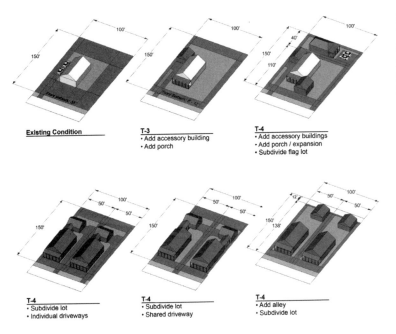

Figure 6.8
This diversification strategy diagram demonstrates schemes for infill and subdivision of large single-family lots.

Building Codes and Housing Diversity

Although the intention of this book is to examine longevity at the urban rather than architectural scale, the omission of single-family homes and multistory attached homes from federal accessibility laws has created an urban problem that must be addressed at the building code level. Local governments are seeking to ensure accessibility coverage by enacting additional building code requirements to supplement the federal standards and zoning, which provides a good means of phasing these requirements based on priority areas. Cobb County, Georgia, for example, required that "Easy Living" standards be met by all residential units constructed within a senior-housing overlay zone district. These included the following:

- One-Level Living: Locate all necessary living features (kitchen, bath, fireplace, laundry, etc.) on one level. Or, ensure that lower floor of home could be adapted for possible one-level living—this may mean converting a dining room to a bedroom or converting a closet to a main floor laundry room with at least one entrance accessible without stairs.

- Bathrooms: Require blocking in bathroom walls to ensure ability to retrofit for elderly safety (e.g., grab bars). Require 5-foot turning diameters in bathroom, kitchen, and closet layouts to allow future modifications for wheelchair accessibility, higher bathroom counters, lever faucets and mixers with anti-scald valves, temperature-controlled shower and tub fixtures, stall showers with a low threshold and a shower seat, and nonslip bathroom tiles.

- Kitchens: Kitchen cabinets with pullout shelves and lazy Susans, lower cabinets with large drawers instead of fixed shelving, easy-to-grasp cabinet hardware

(C-pulls instead of knobs), task lighting under counters, stovetop with front controls, easily accessible refrigerator and freezer, adjustable upper and pull-out lower shelves (fixed shelving cannot adapt to changing needs), and color or pattern borders at counter edges to indicate boundaries.

- Safety Features: Encourage safety features in homes such as handrails on both sides of the stairs; a peep hole at a low height; gas sensors by the stove, water heater, and gas furnace to detect leaks; strobe light or vibrator-assisted smoke and burglar alarms for hearing loss; and lower windowsills, especially for streetside windows and for use as an emergency exit.

- Doors: Doorways 36 inches wide with offset hinges on doors, levered door handles instead of knobs, and patio doors and screens that are easy to open and lock.

- Lighting: Increased incandescent general and specific task lighting, light switches at 42 inches instead of 48, luminous switches in bedrooms, baths, and hallways.

These building code requirements are relatively minor and inexpensive adjustments in housing production, yet the difference when enacted across an entire neighborhood and community can substantially forward lifelong goals.

Conclusion

In order to support lifelong well-being, a neighborhood must have a diverse range of buildings in terms of both use and type. AARP reports that an increasing percentage of older adults are "stranded at home"—unable to afford or operate a car, left without sufficient access to transit and therefore the ability to shop for daily needs nearby, and are isolated from their social networks. This stranding is, in large part, a function of planning policies that have segregated buildings by use and type. Segregating stores from homes and work thus pushes places to dwell, work, participate in civic activities, shop, and re-create all to different parts of town.

Isolation-related depression is an increasingly common problem among older adults and it can have debilitating collateral effects that when combined contribute to rapid declines in both physical and emotional states. Aging in distant, inaccessible environments is an expensive proposition, and one that is rapidly becoming infeasible for a wide percentage of the population. Older adults isolated in sprawling suburban communities not only become less able to engage and contribute to the community as their physical or financial state limits their mobility, but the community is also equally challenged in efforts to reach out to and support older adults. For those stranded with limited mobility options, paratransit, home care, Meals on Wheels, and the whole collection of Administration on Aging funded services strain to keep up with the dispersed demand. Isolation shifts many supports provided routinely by neighbors in close environments entirely onto the public health and social systems in distant environments. Travel distances can quickly require more resources than the provision of care itself.

Zoning policies, established first in intent and thereafter in enforced regulations must allow and encourage an adequate diversity of commercial, residential, and civic uses to ensure that daily needs can be met in walking range. There must be an adequate diversity of residential types to ensure that residents can change homes as their needs change across lifetimes without being forced to leave the community altogether in search of an appropriate home. Both forms of diversity are essential to creating compact communities that draw civic, social, and shopping opportunities into accessible proximities for those who cannot operate automobiles.

PART III

SENIORS HOUSING

EVOLUTION IS INEVITABLE IN THE SENIORS housing field. It is often said that getting old and eventually dying is not for the weak—it is a Herculean endeavor. It is no surprise that we ritualistically try to reinvent the last phases of life at each generation; joie de vivre compels us to resist the inevitable. Grown children's desires to provide the best for their parents also drive change. Each successive generation of Americans has tried to do its best in caring for the preceding generation, even as the understanding of what is best changes: initially, healing spa retreats; then sterile environments; then increasingly laboratory-like medical facilities; and now the more familiar neighborhood environments wherein chronic disease can be better managed by improved daily routines. Seniors housing has evolved as our ideas of healthcare have evolved, often at the cutting edge of change and fueled by a willingness to try the new with the hope that it will be better than what we know of the old. The ritual of aging is that of reinvention, not of tradition, and the senior housing industry has deep-seated motivations to be continuously and radically innovative.

Our attitudes about older adults also change. At the beginning of the twentieth century older adults were the venerable stewards of institutional wisdom and continuity: the chairs of boards, and the chiefs of community organizations. By the second half of the twentieth century, older adults were retirees, relieved of those sorts of institutional burdens and deserving golden years of quiet leisure. As we wade into the twenty-first century, the baby boom generation seems intent on forming a new creative

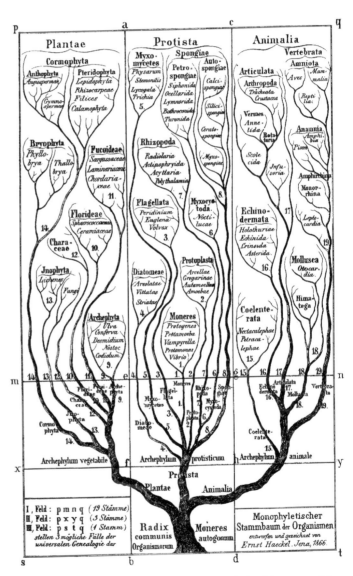

Ernst Haeckel's tree of life describes evolutionary relationships among living organisms as diversifying. Haeckel postulated that all life evolved from a common origin that divided into three kingdoms—plant, animal, and microbes—that then continually subdivided over time.

class: less focused on leisure than on expression, engagement, and personal growth. Older adults appear to be imagining roles that are neither dominating and venerable, nor retiring and leisurely, but rather are looking to mix it up, to defy specific social categories, and in their individual pursuits possibly even meld lifestyles with their millennial generation children.

The overarching premise of Part III of this book is that as the seniors-housing industry has evolved, it has created buildings, services, and community-wide features that are uniquely tailored to support an aging population. In many ways, the very existence of these specialized communities is a direct response to deficiencies in the general urban environment. They provide a level of access and support needed by older adults that is unavailable and unsustainable in the wider community. The industry has established simple models (independent living, assisted living, skilled nursing, and so on) for what are, in reality, very complex relationships between the real estate, finance, and healthcare industries. They represent the best we can muster: complex integrated approaches to fulfill the needs of older adults. The lifelong neighborhood approach is not a rejection of existing senior housing development models, but rather an application of their core value propositions to a more dispersed and community-integrated context. Without the involvement and integration of the senior housing and care industries a "good neighborhood" cannot undergo metamorphosis into a lifelong neighborhood. Seniors housing has raised the bar for caring environments, and every generation has always sought out the newest and the best that can be provided in exchange for the hard work of aging.

With these changing perceptions about healthcare and aging in mind, Chapter 7 first examines the evolution of the senior housing type as an evolving cultural form that has led up to the lifelong neighborhood concept. The senior housing type is reviewed as a progression from a building to a suburban senior housing campus to a self-contained, fully realized version of a traditional neighborhood development. Lifelong neighborhoods can thus be seen as a logical next step in evolution in which the components of a senior housing development are pulled apart enough so that they can be woven into the community fabric. Rather than conceiving of senior housing as a single, isolated development, lifelong neighborhoods borrow on and contribute to the whole neighborhood, not just the property on which a seniors facility is constructed.

Chapter 8 further builds on this theme by looking at the role market studies can play in opening the seniors housing industry. Market studies are commonly viewed as reactive gate-keeping functions. A developer proposes a project, the market study evaluates its comparative risks, and a go or no-go recommendation is made that influences the ability to raise financing. From the investor's point of view "the decision to lend without appropriate market analysis is no more than gambling."[1]

This conception of the market study as a limited risk analysis primarily for the investor's benefit may at one time have been largely true, but today the role of the market study is much more expansive and creative: an early analysis of the whole market potential rather than a final review of a finished proposal's feasibility.

---

[1] G.I. Thrall, *Business Geography and New Real Estate Market Analysis* (New York: Oxford Univ. Press, 2002), 4.

Market studies have taken more proactive roles in identifying opportune locations, evaluating consumer preference trends, and generally participating in the visioning of new development. Future innovation in the seniors housing market will be more focused on analysis of existing environments and understanding how market trends relate to the nuances and complexities of location and community. Given the state of the economy and the current extreme risk aversion of the financing industry, it is highly unlikely that a new basis for modeling health and housing relationships could be developed from scratch in the immediate future. Innovation is incumbent on the creative and convincing application of familiar means and methods to new contexts. The market study is essential in this endeavor.

Chapter 9 establishes a typology of senior housing components so that they can be understood as discrete modules that can be deployed in a community setting rather than contained within a single assembly. In addition to detailing the components of seniors housing, services and public policies that are drawn on to better support community-based aging are listed, and each seniors development component is accompanied by a list of service and policy items that might be drawn on to help facilitate integration into the community.

EVOLUTION OF SENIOR DEVELOPMENT TYPES

CHAPTER 7

Contributed by Glen A. Tipton, FAIA

As the experience of aging is reinterpreted by each successive generation, the physical spaces and methods of care provided for older adults have also changed. Perhaps the most notable change is the shift over the past few decades from charitable giving to the vulnerable to programs that emphasize empowerment and independence as guiding principles. Despite this process of generational reinterpretation, there are traditions embedded in both the physical spaces provided for aging as well as in the methods of care. These traditions are persistently manifested in each new interpretation of aging and in the spaces created for older adult care. This chapter reviews some of the critical archetypes of place-based aging supports in order to understand the morphology of aging in the built environment.

Early Senior Care Models
Almshouses

Between the seventeenth and twentieth centuries the destitute were often housed in almshouses: early outreach centers usually associated with a church or wealthy patron (fig. 7.1). Without any other form of explicitly designated social support, older adults who were unable to provide for themselves often came to these establishments for shelter, nourishment, and care. Good examples in Europe include the Christ's Hospital Almshouses in Abington, England, which included Long Alley, Brick Alley, Mr. Twitty's, Wharf, St. John's, and Tomkin's Almshouses, the earliest portions of which were established in 1446.

The very modest home of Jeanne Jugan in Saint-Pern, France, serves as a less institutional counterpoint to the early almshouses (fig. 7.2). In the mid-nineteenth

Figure 7.1
Foster's Almshouses in Bristol, England, opened in 1482 to provide housing and care for the "old and infirm." The building functioned as an almshouse until 2007, when its operations were moved to a modern facility in North Bristol.

Chris Downer

Figure 7.2

Jeanne Jugan's home in Saint-Malo, France, where Little Sisters of the Poor was organized to take in older adults needing care. Today, Little Sisters of the Poor provides skilled nursing homes all over the world.

Glen Tipton

century, Jeanne Jugan formed a Christian community based out of her small cottage home to care for and take in abandoned elderly women. By her death in 1879, the community had grown to 2,400 members and had franchises across Europe and North America. At this point, Pope Leo XIII approved the constitutions for this community as the Little Sisters of the Poor, and both the order and the focus on senior care provision was replicated worldwide. Jeanne Jugan was canonized in 2009 and given the name Sister Mary of the Cross in recognition of the mission she developed out of her small home in France.

Early Medical Model

In America, the earliest versions of the nursing home were similarly built by wealthy individuals and religious orders in the nineteenth century. These facilities were patterned after what was considered the standard of a healthcare facility, the hospital. Johns Hopkins Hospital, for example, was established in 1873 by Baltimore philanthropist Johns Hopkins (fig. 7.3). It was hailed as a model of a clean, efficient, and healthy hospital design where modern medicine could cure what in earlier years would have ended life.

When the Keswick nursing home was chartered in 1883 by the Maryland General Assembly, its founders took design cues from the prominent hospitals of the day. Along with the emphasis on cleanliness, an antiseptic and overtly institutional atmosphere was created. But Keswick's very name at its founding—The Keswick Home for the Incurables—drew a strong distinction from the hospitals it was patterned on. This was a place that patients came to die rather than be cured. By overlapping the image of a care institution with the image of old people waiting to die, this designation of patients as incurables had a significant negative effect on the

Figure 7.3
Built in 1873, Johns Hopkins
Hospital set the standard
for American hospitals. This
established the hospital as the
primary environment for medical
treatment.

image of senior care facilities. The image of warehouses for death permeates today's public image of nursing homes.

Surveillance and the Early Nursing Home

In early hospitals and nursing homes, the need for surveillance played a significant role in shaping the architectural type. Without electronic call systems or video cameras, attendants were only able to effectively monitor patients when they could maintain direct visual connection. This led to large, open multibed wards that were supervised from central nursing stations (figs. 7.4, 7.5). Activities like bathing and toileting, which required significant assistance, were provided for in centralized facilities.

Privacy Emerges as a Concern

Those who could afford more services eventually demanded greater privacy, so the smaller quad or double occupancy room design evolved. The architectural type shifted from open, clear span wards to axial wings of double-loaded corridors. Still lacking of any electronic signaling system, surveillance was maintained down the long hallways of wings that converged on centralized nursing stations. Though the patients gained some privacy by tucking into rooms on either side of the hallway, they could still catch the attention of the nurses by ringing a bell, or later by lighting a signal over the door. In the early days, it is said that patients would sometimes signal the need for help by throwing a shoe or washcloth into the hallway for the nurses to see from their station.

Figure 7.4
An example of an early medical
ward, before privacy became
an issue in hospital design. The
rooms are open and spare to
allow the staff to easily monitor
patients.

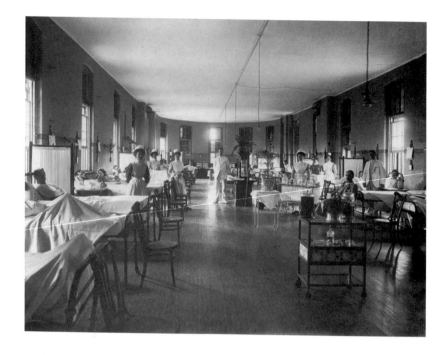

Figure 7.5
The late-nineteenth century Presbyterian
Hospital in Philadelphia is an example of the
emergence of a trend to organize wards
around a central nursing station command
point. This placed the hospital staff front
and center and relegated the patients to
the periphery. The Green House care model
and the Culture of Change initiative have
spearheaded efforts over the past decade to
finally shift this model and emphasize the
residents rather than staff in the care home.

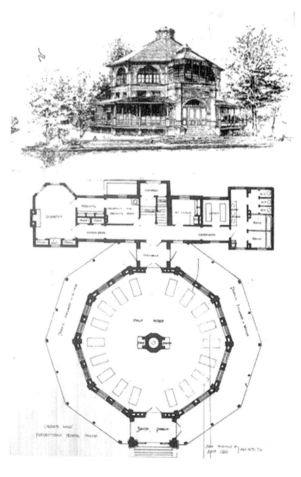

Institutional Neglect

After social security was enacted, followed by Medicare and Medicaid, access to nursing home care was publicly underwritten for those who needed it. It should be noted that with these public programs, 65 became institutionalized as the official retirement age: the first time a specific age rather than physical condition became the threshold for senior status.

With government funding comes regulation. Eventually, the nursing home industry became one of the most heavily regulated of all business types in the United States, in many ways more regulated than even jails and prisons. As a result of the emphasis on safety and liability mitigation, security concerns took priority over individual dignity. The comparison has been made often between the architectural form of a prison and that of a nursing home: Both prioritize security and close supervision from central hubs at the intersection of wings. This era of highly regulated, barebones economy, prison-like environments had the effect of shifting the perception of nursing homes from the type of nurturing community embodied by almshouses, to prisons for neglect. Building form and regulatory requirements managed to change the image of the nurse from Jeanne Jugan to Nurse Ratchet of the movie *One Flew Over the Cuckoo's Nest.*

Through the years, despite the fine care provided by many for-profit and non-profit entities alike, the nursing home became a symbol of institutionalized warehousing of old people. This institutionalism was enhanced by a well-meaning regulatory effort to enact minimum space requirements for nursing homes. While these minimum standards prevented some inhumane conditions, they also had the negative effect when combined with minimal funding for construction of becoming de facto maximum limits. Hence, very tight bedrooms, toilet rooms, bathrooms, and multiuse public rooms were produced, further enhancing the public image of a nursing home as a fearful place to avoid at all cost.

Early Urban Renewal

In postwar years, both nursing homes and general senior housing became programmatic components of the larger urban renewal campaigns funded under Title 1. Architects and planners led very brutal initiatives to affect urban renewal through slum clearance. Entire neighborhoods were demolished and replaced with dehumanizing super block towers (fig. 7.6). These massive cookie-cutter high-rise structures became vertical slums, devoid of any social characteristics of fundamental urban neighborhood development. Urban renewal projects funded by Title 1 were in high gear when government funding was first released in volume for senior housing and care facilities, and the architectural and urban forms of urban renewal were incorporated en masse into the senior building types. Ironically, urban renewal nearly ended urbanism in this country as the flight to the suburbs began. It also left a lasting negative impression on the public's view of senior housing and care facilities.

Later Urban Revitalization

This phase of ill-conceived urban intervention ended forcefully with the demolition of the Pruitt-Igoe Housing Project. For senior housing and care facilities, however, the high-rise tower form first developed for the urban renewal campaign continued

Figure 7.6
Paul Rudolph's Crawford Manor Seniors Housing development. The mechanical, hinge-like massing and corduroy masonry set a tone for much of the senior housing developed under Title 1 in the 1960s.

Benjamin Northrup

to be employed. Interestingly, even as Hope VI and other US Department of Housing and Urban Development (HUD) funding sources provided incentives to move away from super block high-rises to low-rise neighborhood models for public housing, senior housing often continued to follow the tower model. High-rises did offer security and more urban environments for older adults, but as all other forms of publicly funded housing went low-rise, the towers became increasingly isolated from the surrounding neighborhood fabric. Ultimately, this set the stage for seniors to be segregated in their own gated facilities.

Diversification of the Senior Housing Type

As the nursing home was solidly cast into large towers, alternatives to this institutional medical setting were also being explored. The industry recognized that aging was not a singular condition and that the economy-at-scale model did not always result in efficient use of funds. Providers found that care environments that were more tailored to various types and degrees of needs could be more cost effective than the one-size-fits-all approach of the hospital-like nursing home. In order to enable the development of alternative approaches, many states adopted rules for the funding and provision of shelter and modest services in smaller, congregate housing settings (fig. 7.7). These tailored, congregate care models became known variously as assisted living, independent living, and supportive housing, all of which strove to increase self-sufficiency through the provision of a limited range of nonmedical supportive services in a residential setting. Congregate housing is neither a nursing home nor a medical care facility. It does not offer twenty-four-hour care and supervision, nor does it take on an inclusive custodial care role for residents. The model is considered congregate because each resident has a private bedroom but shares one or more other facilities such as kitchen, dining, or bathing facilities with other residents. Endowments and nonprofits lead the way in developing congregate housing alternatives to operate in these newly adopted regulatory openings. As the congregate model grew more popular and its relative efficiency was demonstrated by endowment-funded nonprofits, state and federal programs stepped up to encourage all providers, for-profit and nonprofit alike, to develop congregate housing for seniors through direct grants, tax credits, and other attractive financing terms.

These congregate housing facilities were typically multistory elevator buildings, but a few single-story group home models were also developed. The multistory

Figure 7.7
A barebones congregate building that is an example of the early emphasis on construction economies and affordability.

building was most often arranged with a double-loaded corridor with studio and one-bedroom apartments on either side. Over time the studio units proved to be very unpopular and were phased out, as two-bedroom units were phased in. As with earlier nursing homes, regulations established minimum property standards and these minimum requirements soon became the normative condition in a competitive funding environment. Public funding cost control regulations also set caps on the amount of non-unit, amenity space to be permitted in the building. Congregate housing thus quickly found its way to marginal costs and barebones environments.

Active Adult Communities

As noted earlier, rather than setting senior status to a physical condition, the Social Security Act instead established the age of 65 as a threshold for retirement. This age threshold had the effect of ushering large amounts of healthy and able-bodied workers into retirement. In addition, many post-war industries, unions, and governmental organizations had established generous pension plans with early retirement options, and many of the "GI generation" happily opted to exercise their early retirement options. The sudden wave of relatively affluent, able-bodied retirees led to the emergence of a new development facility type for seniors, the active adult community. These communities were the first fully urban approaches to provide specifically for aging across an entire community, and their early examples pioneered unique urban structures.

Lured by a desire to retire at a younger age in warmer climes with a recreation-based lifestyle of golf and tennis, early retirees beat a path to these communities that sprung up all over the sunbelt of the United States, especially in Florida and Arizona. These communities emphasized the active lifestyle to distance themselves from the institutional image of nursing homes and the over-65 definition of senior congregate housing. To reinforce this differentiation, these communities soon became known as 55-plus communities, owing to the age-defined restrictive covenants of residency. As the Social Security Act had established 65 as a threshold for senior status, the Fair Housing Act (FHA) of 1968 similarly established 55 as another senior threshold. The Fair Housing Act, which generally barred housing discrimination, provided an exemption for those 55 and older. Under the law, housing and communities could be restricted to residents above the age of 55 and not be considered in violation of anti-age discrimination laws.

Real estate developers soon also learned that active adult development would be preferred by jurisdictions. By limiting residence to those 55 and older, there would be no added burden on the local school system by such a development. The active lifestyle suggested that little additional burden on emergency health services would be required. And to reinforce the image of security and age segregation, these communities were often gated, thereby reducing an added burden on the local police force. The perks of additional tax revenue without a great deal of service expense proved to be a lucrative proposition for local governments, which in turn began to pursue active adult community developers with incentives. Soon, every state in the union had growing numbers of these communities. Names like Del Webb and The Villages became synonymous with the 55-plus, active adult, gated-community.

Most active adult communities were dominated by single-family homes with many recreational outlets: golf courses, swimming pools, tennis, and other sports amenities. For several decades, the Fair Housing Act required that significant facilities and services had to be provided for the elderly in a community that was age restricted, and this requirement usually resulted in a community clubhouse that provided space for private and community gatherings, and increasingly some form of fitness facility. There was typically little emphasis on healthcare on-site.

Continuing Care Retirement Communities

By the late 1960s senior housing and facility types diversified to address specific niches within the senior market, and while this provided much more choice in tailoring a living environment appropriate to an individual's current condition, the limitations of this model were becoming apparent. Multiple moves to other facilities were required as a resident's condition deteriorated, or as more often was the case, as a resident would come into a congregate care facility at the onset of frailty and not be willing or able to move when their need for medical care increased. Active adult communities and congregate care housing were both increasingly occupied by very frail residents who needed higher levels of care than their community could provide. As frail older adults became a higher percentage of the residents, fewer active adults were interested in moving into the facility. This cycle led in the 1960s to the development of a second urban model that provided both active adult housing and a range of skilled nursing facilities on-site (fig. 7.8). This urban model became known as the Continuing Care Retirement Community, or CCRC. In its early years it was also known as the Life Care Community because CCRCs often operated effectively as an insurance policy to assure guaranteed access to increasing levels of care, including long-term nursing care, for the rest of one's life (fig. 7.9).

The earliest of these CCRCs were sponsored by nonprofit organizations and were most often sited on large campuses with a maze of interconnected one-story apartments. However, some early CCRCs were also high-rise single buildings. Often the common areas were quite large, with a range of specialized spaces for services and

Figure 7.8
An early example of a campus-type CCRC developed on a green-field site and operated as a self-contained village set apart from the surrounding community.

Glen Tipton

Figure 7.9

An early high-rise CCRC developed as a single hospital-like building.

Glen Tipton

amenities. Since these were private pay and typically financed without government subsidy, there were no minimum space requirements or other controls on the size of units or amount of space allocated for common functions. This was a purely market-driven product and the market responded well.

Some early CCRCs offered guaranteed care for life in exchange for the resident's entire net worth, regardless of the amount: hence the name "life care." This proposition proved ill-conceived for some of these developments, resulting in a few well-publicized scandals involving the financial failures of early CCRCs. These failures led to increasing regulation of the CCRC as a form of consumer protection. Many states are now heavily involved in both the regulation of and review of every aspect of CCRCs.

To assure that such failures are rare, these controls require high levels of presales and many other assurances. The typical CCRC is not purchased; rather, the resident pays an entry fee that is either fully or partially refundable, or declining refundable over a fixed period of time. For the wide array of services including meals, the resident pays a monthly service charge. Alternatively, a rental model is used. There are a few equity purchase models and even fewer cooperative models.

The typical CCRC of today has somewhat changed from its earlier ancestors. It still provides a combination of housing, services, and care. They come in a variety of settings from single-story individual homes with community buildings and a health centers to interconnected mid-rise elevator buildings and all-inclusive high-rise buildings and various combinations thereof (figs. 7.10, 7.11, 7.12). A typical CCRC has a total of around 350 dwelling units and skilled nursing beds.

Figure 7.10
Jefferson, a newer, high-end
CCRC in Arlington, Virginia, is
a self-contained city.

Figure 7.11
Detail.

Figure 7.12

Marsh's Edge, a resort-like Continuing Care Retirement Community on St. Simons Island, off the coast of Georgia.

Glen Tipton

Evolution of the CCRC Market   Over time, market demand has changed to reflect the traditional housing market. Independent living units have generally increased in average size. The typical CCRC resident comes from an existing and usually owned single-family home, town home, or condo, and prefers a unit as similar to their previous home as possible. The CCRC must respond with units that have curb appeal to these new residents, but do so while incorporating all FHA accessibility requirements, which are generally shown to detract from first impression of a new residence. The resulting independent living unit thus typically disguises its accessibility features to the fullest extent while promoting as many new home amenity features as possible.

The once popular studio unit has all but disappeared. Before the onset of the 2008 economic recession, unit sizes showed no sign of slowing growth. In the wake of the economic downturn, sizes have begun to moderate. For example, in urban settings where land cost is generally higher, unit sizes are sometimes below average to permit more units per acre to be built, thereby justifying the higher land cost.

Another significant change in the CCRC market has been the range of services and amenities provided. The GI generation of people old enough to have fought in World War II defined the early CCRC market, and as stated earlier, this generation highly valued recreation and leisure. The next generation was the smaller "silent" generation of people who were children during World War II.[1] With a much greater demand for more choices and an interest in fitness and wellness, this new silent market has caused both new and existing CCRCs to reinvent themselves.

---

[1] This moniker was coined in the November 1951 issue of *Time* in an article titled "The Younger Generation," which reads, "By comparison with the Flaming Youth of their fathers & mothers, today's younger generation is a still, small flame. It does not issue manifestos, make speeches or carry posters. It has been called the 'Silent Generation.'"

The demand for choices covers a wide range of subjects from unit plans, finishes, and appointments to choices of dining venues on-site (fig. 7.14)—from bistros to buffets, from cafés to demonstration cooking—all replacing the single-minded GI dining hall (fig. 7.13).

The emphasis on fitness and wellness has redefined how CCRCs are perceived. Today's CCRC typically offers the full complement of facilities to serve all aspects of wellness: physical, intellectual, social, emotional, spiritual, and vocational. Amenities typical in today's CCRC include indoor swimming/aerobics pools (fig. 7.15), fitness equipment (fig. 7.16), group exercise rooms, spas, lecture halls,

Figure 7.13
A typical high-end GI generation dining hall with an emphasis on formality and elegance.

Figure 7.14
A typical high-end silent generation dining area with an emphasis on variety and informality.

Figure 7.15
The pool has become a central focal point for many seniors housing developments. It functions as a luxurious amenity and supports aquatic aerobics programs that are extremely helpful in supporting older adult fitness.

Glen Tipton

Figure 7.16
A typical fitness center in a seniors housing development, emphasizing day lighting and exterior views rather than the TVs and mirrors found in a typical peak fitness facility.

Glen Tipton

libraries, cyber cafés, pubs, chapels, and arts and crafts studios. The typical CCRC also provides some form of higher acuity care. This varies from state to state, and the original long-term nursing care model has evolved over the years through such terms as domiciliary care, personal care, and residential care, among others.

Assisted Living

A Continuing Care Retirement Community manages contradictory psychological needs. On the one hand, virtually every resident would prefer to remain in their own independent living apartment as long as possible, and age in place. While the philosophy of the CCRC is to encourage the resident to age in place, there is also the obligation to ensure both the resident's safety and that of his or her neighbors. As a result, an intermediate assisted living component began to emerge in the early 1980s in CCRC campuses as a way to provide a safer, more service-enriched environment than independent living, but less intensive than that of the nursing center. This assisted-living model is based on a Scandinavian model of smaller, residential care.

Initially, this was entirely offered by for-profit developer/operators to private paying customers who typically were the adult children of a senior. The creative residential design helped ease the guilt on the part of the adult children when recommending their parent move to a facility (fig. 7.17).

The early assisted living facilities were stand-alone to resemble large Victorian or Georgian mansions. Their resident rooms, newly recategorized from patient rooms, were small studios, sometimes double occupancy. Each had an adjoining toilet room with a shower and included a kitchenette to provide a semblance of the home the resident left behind. These arrangements also provided greater levels of dignity and privacy than the typical nursing room. The assisted-living facility boasted a large amount of public space, in part because it was marketed to an affluent private pay clientele, and in part because it was not yet regulated to a minimum standard, marginal cost form. Where the nursing home had a dayroom and dining room that often doubled as the same activity room, the assisted-living facility had a library, ice cream parlors, arts and crafts classes, country kitchens, and family rooms (fig. 7.18).

Figure 7.17
Christian Healthcare Center in Wyckoff, New Jersey, is typical of early low-rise assisted living facilities with an emphasis on residential architectural vocabularies, which set it apart from the skilled nursing facilities of the day.

Figure 7.18
The interior common spaces of Marsh's Edge CCRC in St. Simons Island, Georgia, emphasize homelike scales and detailing.

Glen Tipton

The tremendous initial success of the assisted living facility attracted significant Wall Street investment in the 1990s and markets were quickly saturated by developers who believed this need-driven market would never be exhausted. In fact, many markets were exhausted and a glut of financially troubled assisted living developments soon fell into bankruptcy.

Although there were some well-run and financially stable assisted living facilities, the volume of troubled ones ultimately led to regulation. Because assisted living provides services at a level below that which nursing provides, at a lower cost per day, most jurisdictions encouraged the development of this type of facility to keep older adults from being prematurely admitted to a nursing facility. Despite the regulations, many CCRCs recognized the market perception of the benefits of a deinstitutionalized care environment and the need to add such a service and environment in their facilities. Many states now offer Medicaid waivers as an incentive for would-be residents to use assisted living in lieu of nursing, in recognition of the benefits of the lower operating cost of assisted living.

In recent years, as the assisted living industry has matured and the CCRCs have added it on campus, the typical CCRC assisted living apartment unit has evolved to be much like a small independent living unit, with larger kitchenettes, separate bedroom, and walk-in closets (fig. 7.19).

Memory Support

Assisted living originally evolved as a response to declining physical abilities as a limited form of daily assistance with activities of daily living (ADLs)—much less intensive than skilled nursing assistance. Within the range of assisted living services,

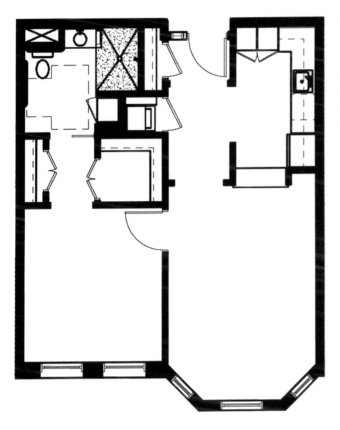

Figure 7.19
A typical barebones assisted living residential unit floor plan. Even at the economy level, it is important to provide at least a small kitchen to emphasize a degree of independence and continuity of daily routines.

a specialized form has emerged to serve the large percentage of people who suffer from mental function decline known variously over the years as senility, dementia, or, more recently, Alzheimer's Disease. This group of older adults includes more than 45 percent of the population over 80 years of age. This form of assisted housing is known as memory support.

Memory support facilities go beyond assistance with activities of daily living and have practice particularly in responding to the sometimes erratic and irrational behavior that can accompany memory loss. They usually segregate memory loss residents when these erratic behaviors are manifested to avoid disturbing other residents who may be physically frail but mentally strong (fig. 7.20).

During the past decade, an increasing number of stand-alone, dedicated memory support facilities have emerged with strong market response, owing to the increasing diagnosis and awareness of these degenerative diseases. In addition to stand-alone facilities, both assisted living facilities and CCRCs have added specialized wings or buildings dedicated to memory loss residents. As more has been learned about the physical and behavioral needs of older adults experiencing memory loss, homelike residential facilities serving between ten and sixteen residents have been developed and are known as household memory support care (figs. 7.21, 7.22).

Figure 7.20
A perspective drawing showing the elevation of a small house-care facility. Ten residential units are provided per floor and two or more of these houses must be grouped on a block in order to conform with skilled nursing regulations.

Figure 7.21
This is a plan of a floor in a small house-care facility showing the grouping of the units around a central living area.

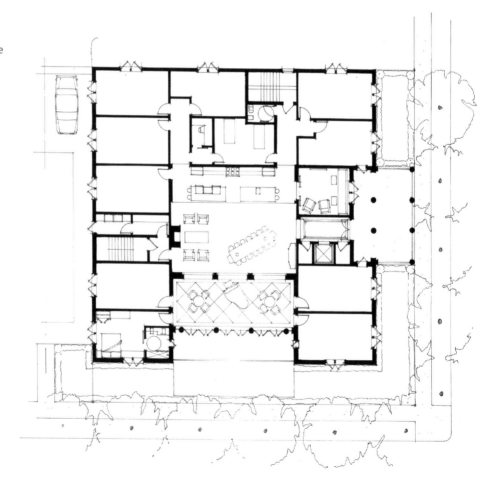

Figure 7.22
This is an elevation of a small house-care facility showing the potential for ground floor retail. Without ground floor retail, the style is appropriate for T-3 to T-4 settings, while the inclusion of ground floor retail makes it appropriate for T-5 to T-6.

Figure 7.23
The Garfield and Redford houses designed by Perkins Eastman are long-term care facilities based on the Green House model. Located in Redford, Michigan, each Green House has a homelike setting that is limited to ten residents per house.

Courtesy Perkins Eastman and Christopher Lark

Figure 7.24

This plan organizes around an open common area with kitchen, dining, and living room areas. The kitchen, which is typically sequestered in a separated support space, is a central element. The preparation of food is an important social and communal process in the Green House model, and residents are able to participate in the cooking.

Courtesy Perkins Eastman

The Green House

A parallel movement, with roots in the Eden Alternative championed by Dr. William Thomas, has begun to revolutionize the nursing home as well. Dr. Thomas's heavily stylized operational and physical model is called the Green House. The model espouses no greater than ten residents per house (figs. 7.23, 7.24), which is mandated to be freestanding, although it is often grouped in collections of several of these houses.

The Green House Replication Initiative, as it is now known, has garnered increasing support, even among regulators and traditional institutional operators. However, not all similarly scaled care homes are part of the Green House project. There are many CCRCs and other care providers who have selectively adapted the Green House concepts to their operations. When not part of the Green House Initiative, these small house-care facilities vary in numbers of residents housed, from ten to sixteen, and often combine houses with a shared service care.

All of these changes are intended to provide a more resident-centered form of care, wherein the residents' needs and contributions are the center of attention and great care is made to place the pragmatics of staff and service delivery in the background. Much like the movement in the developmentally disabled care environments of the 1980s, which liberated those persons from an institutionalized life to a more normalized residential life, all of these changes have attempted to allow the older adult to hold on to important aspects of home life.

THE LIFELONG
NEIGHBORHOOD MARKET

CHAPTER 8

Market Study Elements of Critical Importance to Lifelong Neighborhoods

The market study for various types of senior housing and care communities is based on a series of elements that are typical of most forms of real estate development analyses. A review of numerous books on real estate market analysis reflects the consistency in these elements, although there are certainly differences in the drivers for each development type. Common elements include the following:

- site evaluation

- market area/service area definition

- competitive environment

- demographics

- economic conditions

- demand and absorption analysis

Over the years, consensus has emerged about the drivers for evaluating each element of the market study for age-restricted housing, but those drivers are a reflection of the relative singularity of the type as well as the expectations of age-based, rather than experience-based behavior. The traditional drivers for each element are presented in table 8.1.

It is necessary to conduct an examination of each of the market study elements while focusing on creating environments where people can successfully age and move through a well-integrated continuum of need. Although lifelong neighborhoods are just emerging as a concept and therefore don't provide a substantiated body of experience for documenting behavior, we can still anticipate potential modifications to some value drivers based on the knowledge amassed thus far.

Site Evaluation
Visibility   Visibility may not be as significant a factor in a lifelong neighborhood as it is in a traditional seniors housing development. The components of a lifelong neighborhood that are intentionally designed to serve the older adult market may not need to stand out and distinguish themselves from the other elements of the community. In fact, one of the positive features of such neighborhoods is the way in which specialized housing forms, such as assisted living and nursing and even independent living, become relatively invisible, thereby eliminating the stigma associated with needing care and support. Integrated wellness models will

Table 8.1

AGE-RESTRICTED HOUSING	
STUDY ELEMENT	Value driver
	Factors particularly influenced by the lifelong neighborhood model are underlined
SITE EVALUATION	Visible to drive-by traffic
	Access to major roads
	Access to public transportation
	Proximity to services, including social, cultural, recreational, and healthcare
	Configuration/topography
	Zoning requirements
MARKET-AREA DEFINITION	Importance of local draw
	Perception of site/neighborhood
	Relationship to highway systems
	Natural geographic features
	Jurisdictional boundaries (county/state)
	Psychological boundaries
	Influence of sponsorship
	Urban/suburban/rural differentiators
	Preopening sales/leasing data
COMPETITIVE ENVIRONMENT	Defining competition by product type and economic target market
	Comparing features including age of property, overall size, unit size/mix, service program, pricing structures/amounts charged, ownership/sponsorship, levels of care, occupancy, wait list, absorption
	Location relative to subject of study
	Positioning
	Planned competition (expansions, new development) and timing and approval status
DEMOGRAPHIC TRENDS	Overall population trends
	Population by age segment (typically 55+, 65+, 75+)
	Households by age (typically 55+, 65+, 75+) and income
	Housing tenure
	Age and disability statistics
	Adult child (influencer) household trends (45–64-year-olds who may want an older family member to live closer)

Table 8.1 Continued

AGE-RESTRICTED HOUSING	
ECONOMIC CONDITIONS	Home values
	Employment/unemployment trends
	Economic development patterns
	Health of the economy
DEMAND AND ABSORPTION	Sizing the market based on age, income, frailty level, household size, housing tenure, and home value
	Factoring in competition
	Acceptable penetration rates
	Absorption influencers and pace

further support the ability to create a seamless environment that offers the benefits of preventive care.

Access   Access and connectivity will continue to be an important part of site evaluation, as was discussed in greater depth in Chapter 5. Lifelong neighborhoods stress the importance of access on multiple fronts: transit, well-connected street networks, as well as pedestrian and bike paths. Access is not only a valuable asset in drawing a market for seniors housing, it is also essential to supporting neighborhood retail, community connections, and other important elements of a lifelong neighborhood.

Proximity to Services   An increasing movement toward home-based care will also permit lifelong neighborhoods to meet the changing needs of their aging populations. Active adult communities typically do not provide any healthcare services directly. They are rarely even co-located with an assisted living or continuing care retirement community. As a result, this necessitates the use of home-care services, as residents age and their needs increase. Existing senior housing providers, particularly those offering independent living, have found an increasing insistence on aging-in-place by residents unwilling to move through the continuum within the facility or out of the facility to obtain higher levels of assistance and healthcare support. During the last decade, many owners/operators/sponsors have entered the home-care business in order to respond to their own resident preferences and, in many cases, to serve those who do not choose to move to their facilities.

Market Area Definition

Local Draw   Most older adults do not move, but for those who do, it is often because the adult children are concerned about the ability of the aging family member to obtain the services and care they require. This may be compounded by the aging person's isolation. The lifelong neighborhood model is highly responsive to one of the basics of defining the market area for senior housing: the desire of most people to stay as close to "home" as possible. As noted earlier, even with the existing models of age-restricted housing and care, the majority of residents make their choices based on relative proximity to where they live now. In many cases, this is already where their children are residing, as well. In a lifelong neighborhood, the concerns about isolation can be minimized, and elements of the neighborhood can be designed to meet increasing care needs. Thus, lifelong neighborhoods respond to the already documented pattern of staying in community and may, in fact, increase the proportion of residents who try the housing models available to them. The basic value drivers that have been used in the past for analyzing the market remain viable and support the ideas of retrofitting existing buildings when possible or even creating new, in-fill development that meets the needs of the community's aging population.

Despite the substantial growth in all types of communities for older adults during the last half of the twentieth century and early twenty-first century, most people prefer not to move at all. The Census Bureau reported that only about 5 percent of those age 55 and over move annually, compared to 17 percent of those under 55.[1] And the move rate actually declines as age increases. Among movers 55 and older, half remain in the same county, which supports the idea that people would prefer to age-in-place because of the strong ties and connections they have built in a community during their lifetime. AARP's study of livable communities reported that the vast majority of adults over 50 "would like to be living in the same local community five years from now." This varied only modestly based on age: Among those who were 65 and older, nearly 90 percent responded positively to this statement, and among those aged 50 to 64, nearly 80 percent responded positively.[2] This is also true of the desire of those age 50 and older to remain in their current residence. A 2008 survey of homeowners 75 and older reported that nearly 61 percent expect to stay in their current home for more than ten years.[3]

Most movers to senior housing communities also do not move very far from home. The Independent Living Report (ILR)[4] study indicated that new residents moved a median of 10 miles from their former residences. Other national studies confirm the fact that a large proportion of movers did not relocate a substantial distance. Table 8.2 reflects a number of interesting findings. Regardless of the type of community, it appears that only approximately 20 percent of residents have moved a distance greater than 25 miles. Not surprisingly, a greater proportion of those moving to the more need-driven products (including freestanding assisted living and assisted living colocated in a community with independent living) attract a greater number of residents from within 5 miles as compared to independent living units that are part of a CCRC. This reflects a greater level of mobility for those still functioning well enough to make the move to the CCRC. Another interesting finding is that the closest family member of those who have moved to assisted living

[1]US Census Bureau, "Current Population Survey, 2003: Annual Social and Economic Supplement," in *Geographic Mobility 2002 to 2003* (March 2004), 20–549.

[2]AARP, *Beyond 50.05 A Report to the Nation on Livable Communities: Creating Environments for Successful Aging* (Washington, DC: AARP, 2005).

[3]Brooks Adams Research, *Special Issue Brief: A Statistical Survey of Senior Homeowners* (Washington, DC: American Seniors Housing Association, Spring 2008), 9.

[4]American Seniors Housing Association, *The Independent Living Report* (Washington, DC: American Seniors Housing Association, 2009).

Table 8.2

DISTANCES FROM PRIOR RESIDENCES					
	IL in CCRC	Freestanding AL		IL/AL	
Number of Miles	**Distance from Previous Home (%)**	**Distance from Previous Home (%)**	**Distance from Closest Relative (%)**	**Distance from Previous Home (%)**	**Distance from Closest Relative (%)**
<5	27	40	36.7	43.5	37.8
5–10	20	20.4	24.4	20	18.9
11–24	26	20	17.8	15.3	13.3
25+	20	19.7	21.1	21.2	30

Sources: Continuing Care Retirement Communities 2005 Profile

2009 Overview of Assisted Living

is also living nearby. Just below 40 percent are within 5 miles of the facility, and 19 to 24 percent are within 5 to 10 miles.

Competitive Environment

Positioning   One of the most significant opportunities that exist for serving older adults in an age-integrated lifelong neighborhood or community is that it is an environment that embraces all ages, thereby diminishing, if not eliminating, the objection that seniors have to "just living with other old people." This offers the potential for a uniquely positive positioning strategy that emphasizes life experience and local connectivity. Although this can't be quantified in a traditional market feasibility analysis that is based on supply and demand calculations, it can be demonstrated through well-crafted consumer research.

The lifelong neighborhood concept is also more open to the creation of local affiliations and partnerships than is typical of a stand-alone seniors housing development. One of the major trends today in senior housing is the consolidation and formation of multifacility networks and providers (similar to the hospital consolidations that occurred in the last decade or so). Existing organizations, both for-profit and nonprofit are looking for ways to enhance their reach and revenue streams, frequently beyond existing sites and properties. Many of these organizations have established reputations and constituencies and have built trust within their markets, which can strengthen new options that become available for seniors in lifelong neighborhoods. Opportunities for smaller scale, in-fill developments are enhanced if potential affiliates or partners already have much of the operational infrastructure on a larger campus within or near the market area.

Demographic and Economic Trends

The presentation and analysis of demographic data will always form an underlying basis for the market analysis of virtually any housing and/or care related product. Household formation is a driver in analyzing housing that is not age restricted.

Understanding the size of the trends of age-defined segments of the local market will continue to be critical to making decisions (both developmental and financial) about products that serve an aging market. What is most important is that the demographic analysis reflects the actual defined market area rather than relying on national or even statewide data and projections. Each market is "local" and the demographic dynamics (growth, stability, trends) of that locality are critical to decision-making. While age alone may not be predictive of behavior, it is indicative of the potential depth and nature of the market. For example, a market area dominated by low-income aging residents is unlikely to form a sound basis for developing high-end market rate housing, although mixed income (low and moderate) economic segments may readily mix. A market area, such as some of the highly urbanized renter-dominated areas in the Northeast, may not support the development of for-sale or entrance fee products. Significant out-migration of the working-age population may be an indicator that senior family members will follow them rather than remain in place, unless sufficient local resources are available to support their continued residency.

Values of existing homes will be an indicator of the ability of older adults to afford a move. It is important that the pricing for both active adult communities and other forms of senior housing be affordable to a large segment of the local target market. Older adults will not want to spend the entire proceeds from the sale of their home to either purchase a property in an active adult community or pay an entrance fee in a CCRC. This obviously affects pricing. All these elements of the demographic and economic analysis are important in understanding the local market area today and in the future.

Demand and Absorption

Sizing the Market   One of the key questions in market analysis is what the proper assumptions are in sizing the market. Probably the most significant assumption relates to age. Traditional minimum age assumptions are reported in table 8.3.

Will age-integrated, lifelong neighborhoods break down some of the barriers to attracting younger segments of the population to the age-restricted components? Although the Fair Housing Act sets the minimum age for senior housing and care facilities at 62, one of the greatest difficulties has been in attracting the "younger"

Table 8.3

MINIMUM-AGE ASSUMPTIONS	
Product	**Minimum Age**
Active adult communities	55
Independent living (freestanding, or in combination with other levels of care)	75
Assisted living/dementia care	75
Skilled nursing (driven by Medicare eligibility and state bed-need methodologies)	65

elders to specific age-restricted senior housing and care communities. We may be able to look forward to reaching those in their early 70s who object to moving into properties that are designed just to serve the old. Is it even possible to attract those below the age of 70? It seems quite likely that the various residential products available in lifelong neighborhoods will cross all age lines. For example, the influx of people to cities that are successfully reviving their residential and retail cores tends to occur among millenials starting their careers and who do not yet have families and empty nesters of all ages (though typically over 50). The features that are attractive to both groups are similar and include walkability, immediate access to retail, entertainment, and cultural venues, and the simple blend of many age groups. Whether this will be replicated on smaller scale suburban and rural lifelong neighborhoods remains to be seen, but it seems a reasonable expectation.

Penetration Rates   A further question is whether higher project penetration rates will be achievable because of the increased desirability of living options within the lifelong neighborhood. Historically, very low penetration rates for new development (five percent or less of qualified households net of competition) were the norm and served as the benchmarks accepted by financial markets. Higher penetration levels have been considered acceptable for products such as assisted living, which are more need driven and thereby assumed to be required by a larger proportion of the population. A white paper entitled "Demand Terminology: Finding Common Ground" was published in 2008 based on the work of a task force of industry experts. The primary goal of this task force was to reach consensus on certain definitions for the basic terminology and methodology used in senior housing when conducting demand analyses for independent living units. This project reinforced both the methodology and the interpretation of quantitative outcomes for independent living. Terminology such as *project penetration rate* (the percent of net qualified households that must be captured to fill the proposed units) and *market penetration rate* (the percentage of age- and income-qualified households within the defined geographic market area assumed to reside in the existing competitive units at 95 percent occupancy) were established as guidelines for "measuring" potential market strength.

While there is relative consistency in calculating demand or market depth for independent living and assisted living in senior housing settings, little consistency exists in the approach to calculating demand for active adult communities. Virtually no benchmarks for acceptable levels of project or market penetration exist.

Absorption Pace   One of the most difficult elements to project accurately is absorption rate. In general, in real estate absorption refers to the number of units that will be sold or leased each month. Typically, absorption reflects recent experiences in the local market for similar types of developments, particularly those still being actively marketed. The pace of absorption will be affected by the quality of the project, its location, and its strengths and weaknesses, compared to similar developments as well as the health of the real estate market. The budget for marketing and the experience and capabilities of the market staff also have major impacts on absorption. Obviously, projecting absorption can be quite difficult in a market where there has been no recent comparable development and there are first time projects being undertaken by the developer. Interestingly, the white paper referred to previously does not even use the term *absorption*. Instead, it addresses the "velocity of presales" and "fill rate":

> The presales velocity is the rate at which properties are able to be pre-leased or presold in a given area within a specific time period. A presale is defined as a 10% deposit towards the upfront payment for the unit selected.[5]
>
> The fill rate measures the rate at which units in a project fill (i.e., residents move into the community) once the community opens.[6]

Factors That Contribute to Residency in Age-Restricted Communities

Several books have been written elaborating on the details of each of these elements in studying the market for senior housing, and they have, to a great extent, reflected the common industry practices and benchmarks. However, in *Analyzing Seniors' Housing Markets*, Brecht makes reference to the argument against simple age segregation put forth by David Wolfe in *Serving the Ageless Market*. He writes, "Age is a correlate, not a determinant, of consumer behavior in maturity markets and hence should not be used in defining and predicting specific consumer behavior of older people."[7] This has undoubtedly been true during the decades of the emergence and growth of seniors housing and care as an industry (starting in the late 1960s) as well as the active-adult-community market in the last two decades, although most market studies for various types of age-restricted housing and care have placed greater emphasis on the framework of age as the drive of demand. This has been reinforced by the requirements of the lending community that has sought standardized practices and benchmarks for conducting market feasibility studies to be used in supporting the financing transaction. The only "behavioral" determinant that has entered into the value proposition in financing seniors housing has been the required level of presales (typically 70 percent of the independent living units) in senior housing communities, which are primarily independent living and typically charge some type of substantial up-front fee). Rental independent living, assisted living, and nursing care are rarely able to, or even expected to, pre-lease at this level before the financing takes place.

The argument for the value of the experience versus the "care" or services offered can be summed up by contrasting the two most common statements heard throughout the senior housing industry. Marketing personnel across the industry will tell you that the statement "I'm not ready yet" is the objection they hear most frequently from prospective residents. Undoubtedly, the same thinking informs the

---

[5]David B. Wolfe, *Serving the Ageless Market: Strategies for Selling to the Fifty Plus Market* (New York: McGraw-Hill, 1990), 86.

[6]"Demand Terminology: Finding Common Ground," unpublished white paper 2008.

[7]Wolfe, *Serving the Ageless Market*, 86.

vast majority of seniors who never even consider a move to senior housing. By contrast, the most frequent comment made after moving in and adjusting to the new lifestyle is "Why did I wait so long?" The latter is a testament to the quality of the experience rather than the value of real estate proposition. Wolfe writes about the "gateway to experience principle," a positioning strategy that senior housing providers are only now starting to focus on as their marketing message.

The aging baby boomers will have a profound effect on the senior housing industry. Current models of senior housing are viewed as "not for them" by the adult children who are still influencing their older family members to make the move. This huge generational wave that is ready to come ashore in the housing and healthcare market will influence and create the new shapes to come. As with all generations, they represent many market segments looking for different types of experiences, rather than a single monolithic group called "the elderly." In fact, they will eschew being referred to as "seniors" or "the elderly" as they reinvent the ever-lengthening aging process. Two recent studies of family members of those seniors currently living in various forms of senior housing do indicate that among people familiar with such communities through personal family experience show a strong interest in considering such options when they need them in the future. Seventy-seven percent of respondents in the National Survey of Family Members (NSFM) of Residents of Continuing Care Retirement Communities indicated they would consider a CCRC for themselves in the future.[8] Senior Living for the Next Generation reported that 72 percent of respondents would consider a move to a senior living community in the future.[9]

How will this generation shape the housing and care options of the future— the not so distant, as well as ten to fifteen years out? And how do the benefits of new forms of aging environments impact the analysis of market opportunities? How do the principles of "urbanism" respond to and influence the quality of life and lifestyle sought by the coming generation? One of the underlying principals of lifelong neighborhoods is that they embrace the notion that most people want to remain a part of the community in which they have lived most of their lives. This enables people to make decisions based on position influencers rather than having to overcome the negative image of age-segregated housing communities. Lifelong neighborhoods reinforce the need for older adults to remain well integrated in communities, where they can enjoy life-affirming experiences and continue to make contributions commensurate with their interests and capabilities.

Beyond the framework of a typical market feasibility study, we must increase our understanding of what the factors are that either cause or prevent older adults from moving. Through an examination of these perceived benefits and drawbacks we can plan the development or enhancement of communities that welcome and enable many generations to participate in a lifelong living environment. In 2001, the American Housing Survey (AHS; designed by the US Census Bureau and the Department of Housing and Urban Development) began asking questions about

---

[8] *National Survey of Family Members of Residents of Continuing Care Retirement Communities* (Mather Lifeways Institute on Aging, Brecht Associates, Inc., Ziegler, 2011), 6.

[9] *Senior Living for the Next Generation* (American Seniors Housing Association, 2011), 31.

"fifty-five-plus" communities and was able to differentiate three types of housing for this market segment: age-qualified active adult communities, non-age-qualified owner-occupied communities (which are not explicitly age-restricted but nevertheless occupied by adults age 55 and over), and age-restricted rental communities.[10] While these broad categories may include senior housing designed for the older segment (legally, the Fair Housing Act has also created a category of housing for those age 62 and over) including CCRCs, independent living, and assisted living, we cannot be sure that information from the residents was specifically captured by the AHS. However, one privately funded national study, The Independent Living Report (ILR)[11] did focus on residents of independent living communities designed for the older segment of the market. This study presented results from 942 completed surveys of people who recently moved to properties randomly selected from the top 100 metropolitan statistical areas (MSAs) in the country. It included entrance fee CCRCs, rental CCRCs, combined independent living and assisted living communities, and freestanding independent living communities. Another recent national survey of homeowners 75 years of age and older shed additional light on how this segment of the market views their living situations. In 2008, the American Seniors Housing Association (ASHA), the same organization that published the ILR, published a special issue brief entitled *A Statistical Survey of Senior Homeowners* (SSSH), with the stated goal of understanding more about how senior homeowners perceived the home sale process. Although this survey was conducted just prior to the full impact of the recession, the housing market had already begun to decline and the responses of participants shed additional light on many issues covered in this chapter. *Right House, Right Place, Right Time*, written by Margaret A. Wylde, provided valuable insights into reasons why people move, based on a national survey of those 45 and older who have or are planning to move. Finally, two current national studies contribute data from family members of residents who are living in various types of seniors housing regarding their thoughts about their own future choices about housing and care. These include the *National Survey of Family Members of Residents Living in Continuing Care Retirement Communities* (NSFM) published by Mather Lifeways Institute on Aging, Brecht Associates, Inc. and Ziegler and *Senior Living for The Next Generation: A View Through The Lens of the Experienced Adult Child (SLNG)*, published by the American Seniors Housing Association.

For those who do move, there are a number of reasons they repeatedly give to marketing and development professionals, and these reasons have been supported and reinforced by national research. These factors can be characterized as falling into three broad categories:

■ real estate

■ lifestyle

■ health

---

[10]NAHB and MetLife Mature Market Institute, *Housing for the 55+ Market* (Westport, CT: MetLife Mature Market Institute, April 2009), 5–6.

[11]*The Independent Living Report*, 11.

Real Estate

Downsizing   Many older homeowners reside in homes where they have lived for many years as they have raised their families. The SSSH survey indicated that the average length of homeownership was twenty-four years among respondents, and 38 percent had lived in their home for thirty years of more.[12] With their family now grown and gone, these empty nesters are typically residing in homes with significantly more space than is needed or wanted. And, frequently, the larger grounds on which these homes were built are no longer desirable. The desire to downsize into more manageable space is a common theme among those who talk about and eventually move away from the family home.

Although the AHS and ILR approach the question of downsizing differently, both reflect the desire of many older adults to live in a smaller home. During the period from 2001 to 2007, the AHS revealed a declining percentage (from 5.9 to 0 percent) of those moving to age-qualified housing did so because they wanted a larger place. Further, the extremely small proportion indicating this as a reason for moving supports the notion that downsizing (or at least remaining in a home of similar size) is a factor in making a move to age-qualified housing. The 2007 data reveal a substantial contrast between different age segments. A much smaller proportion (1.6 percent) of the oldest group (75 and older) cites this as a reason for their move than the youngest segment (55 to 64), of which 8.4 percent indicated the desire for a larger place as the reason for their move. The ILR is much more direct with regard to the issue of downsizing and 6 percent of respondents listed the desire to downsize and simplify their lives as a reason for their move. When asked what might prompt a future move from their current home, 14 percent of senior homeowners responding to AHSA's survey indicated that they "have more space than they need" as a factor.[13] Finally, according to Wylde, as age increases the desire to move to a smaller home increases. Of those age 55 to 64, over one-third indicated a desire for a smaller home as a primary or secondary reason for moving, in contrast to over half of those age 75 and over.[14]

In the SLNG five percent of respondents indicated they would specifically consider a move to a senior living community because they wanted a smaller house with no maintenance.[15] A broader question of what would prompt a post-retirement move from a current residents resulted in 61 percent pointing to the desire to downsize.[16]

Less-Expensive Housing   Obviously, the largest cost associated with owning a home is the monthly mortgage payment. With increasing age comes the increasing likelihood of owning a home mortgage-free. Several studies confirm that nearly

---

[12]Brooks Adams Research, *A Statistical Survey*, 7.

[13]Brooks Adams Research, *A Statistical Survey*, 11.

[14]M. Wylde, *Right House, Right Place, Right Time* (Washington, DC: BuilderBooks, 2008), 54.

[15]*Senior Living for the Next Generation*, 32.

[16]*National Survey of Family Members of Residents of Continuing Care Retirement Communities*, 26.

three-quarters of homeowners age 75 and over own their home mortgage free, so this significant element of the cost of living is no longer a factor for most people in that age group. The results of having paid off the mortgage provide greater flexibility as well as substantial equity for older homeowners. While this can manifest itself in a strong desire to remain in their existing home, it also affords them the option of selling it and downsizing to something more manageable with the cash realized from the sale. Despite the substantial declines in home values during the period beginning in 2007, the length of time that older homeowners have lived in their homes translates into a large increase in its value and the owner's equity. However, one of the problems that have been hampering the move to senior housing has been the unwillingness to accept the fact that the home is worth less than it was at the market's height in the mid-2000s. Holding out for those mid-decade prices limits both the sellers and the buyers who are unwilling to pay what appear to be inflated prices.

Even with the mortgage paid off, the other carrying costs of maintaining a home can be very high, particularly for older, less energy-efficient homes and homes with grounds that must be maintained. The suburbanization of America provided large homes on large lots where many chose to raise their families. The costs associated with such properties remain high over time.

The SSSH reported that 8 percent of respondents felt they would move when they could no longer afford their home. Those moving to age-restricted rental housing are more likely (13.1 percent) to be looking for less expensive housing than those who moved to active adult (7.5 percent) or other 55-plus owner occupied housing communities (5.5 percent).[17] According to Wylde's research of those age 45 and over, "31 percent who were planning to move, compared with 17 percent of those who had moved, said the reason for moving was to reduce expenses."[18]

Minimizing Upkeep As noted earlier, maintaining the home and grounds represents a large burden for older homeowners. Not only can it be costly, but it is often difficult to find reliable people to provide these services when needed. Fundamentally, all forms of housing for older adults address this issue. One of the basic services common to everything from active adult communities to CCRCs and independent living communities is that the common grounds and amenities are maintained through either a contract between the homeowner's or renter's association and a professional maintenance organization, or the property's own maintenance staff. In all senior housing communities, this service extends to interior community spaces and the residential units themselves. One telephone call leads to the necessary maintenance being performed.

This factor was not addressed at all in the AHS but represented the top reason (14 percent) why those living in independent living made the decision to move. In fact, this was the only reason among the top ten identified by this study that could be attributable to real estate versus other lifestyle and health factors. The SSSH reported that 26 percent of respondents cited the burden of home maintenance

---

[17]Demand Terminology, 30.

[18]Brooks Adams Research, *A Statistical Survey*, 57.

as a factor that would contribute to a possible decision to move in the future.[19] A significantly larger proportion of those surveyed for *Right House, Right Place, Right Time* indicated the desire for low maintenance as a primary or secondary reason for moving. This was the most significant reason for moving for approximately 70 percent of all three age groups starting with those 55 to 64 years of age.[20]

Better Quality Housing The desire for a better quality house or apartment ranked high among reasons to move in 2007, particularly among those age 55 to 64 (15 percent), as compared to the oldest (75 and over) segment of whom 6.8 percent cited this as a reason. The proportion of those citing better quality housing was higher among those moving to a single-family home as compared to multifamily housing.[21]

Since many older adults have not moved for several decades, they tend to be in older homes that may be in need of repair. Respondents to the SSSH survey of homeowners aged 75 and older revealed nearly 40 percent had been in their current home for more than thirty years or more, yet 41 percent of respondents said that they were not prepared to spend any money on home improvements or repairs to attract a purchaser to their home. Another 25 percent indicated a willingness to spend less than $1,000.[22]

Lifestyle

Closer to Family Significant factors contributing to the decision to move among those age 55 and over are "family/personal reasons," including the desire to live closer to other family members, particularly their children. This is related to a number of factors. The most obvious is the desire to maintain close family ties and be able to visit with grandchildren. In addition, caregiving to aging family members is a growing responsibility in this country.

Among movers 55 and older in 2007, regardless of product type, approximately one-fifth cited family/personal reasons as the reason for the move. This was the second most frequently mentioned reason cited for their move to independent living. Even more compelling evidence of the importance of being near family was presented in *Right House, Right Place, Right Time*. Survey respondents (who included those who had moved within two years or who were planning to move) increasingly cited this as a primary or secondary reason for moving as age increased. Among those aged 55 to 64, 30 percent referred to this reason, compared to 42 percent of those 75 and older.[23] The NSFMRLCCRC reported that 52 percent would consider a post-retirement move to be closer to family and friends.[24] Being closer to

---

[19]Brooks Adams Research, *A Statistical Survey*, 11.

[20]Brooks Adams Research, *A Statistical Survey*, 54.

[21]*Demand Terminology*, 28.

[22]Brooks Adams Research, *A Statistical Survey*, 1.

[23]*Continuing Care Retirement Communities: 2005 Profile* (Washington, DC: American Association of Homes and Services for the Aging, 2005), 56.

[24]M. Wylde, *Right House, Right Place, Right Time*, 54.

one's family is often cited by marketing personnel as the reason why their residents have made a move. A number of those who are 75 or older may have already made one move to be closer to family by moving to an active adult or other community targeting the 55-plus market and therefore have already achieved that objective.

Increased Opportunities for Socialization

Of course, the desire to be closer to family and friends discussed earlier relates, among other things, to an expectation that this will produce increased opportunities for socialization. However, when considering the older segment of the 55-plus population, this factor becomes even more significant as the chance of losing one's spouse and friends increases. A total of 54 percent of respondents to the ILR study mentioned companionship, having a social life, and relieving boredom as reasons for their move, thus reinforcing the importance of socialization to the older population. When asked which housing choice offers the most opportunity for socialization comparing a CCRC to a single-family home, 82 percent of respondents in the NSFM selected a CCRC versus 16 percent for a single-family home. One of the elements that are consistent to nearly all forms of housing for seniors is the ability to gain access to social activities without having to drive a car or even walk a substantial distance. The mix of residential and community spaces along with the staffing and programmatic elements of senior housing result in many daily opportunities for social interaction, whether during meal time or in formal or informal gathering places and activities.

Increased Sense of Security

Another motivating factor that is not directly explored in the AHS is the desire for security. Certainly the fact that so many communities that are designed for the 55-plus population are gated with staffed security personnel at the gate indicates that the desire for security is important, even if it is not actually a motivator for the move. In fact, security is one of the "soft" amenities, or qualities of active adult communities referred to in "Developing Active Adult Retirement Communities" published by the Urban Land Institute. Referencing the *National Directory of Lifestyle Communities*, 43 percent of communities included had automatic gates, a security guard, or both of these; 34 percent had roving patrols within the community.[25] Security figured as a partial or primary reason among survey respondents reported in *Right House, Right Place, Right Time.* Among all survey respondents aged 45 and older, 30 percent of those who had moved and 29 percent of those planning to move indicated that better security was a factor.[26]

In the ILR report, "gaining a sense of security, physically, fiscally and/or mentally" was cited as one of the top-ten reasons for moving. CCRCs and other forms of senior housing that attract the 75 and older segment of the population are designed to respond to this need for security. Eighty-eight percent rated a CCRC more secure than a single family home in the NSRM report.

The substantial and varied staffing, including in many instances medical personnel, provide a basis for residents (and their family members) to feel confident that their

---

[25]D. R. Suchman, *Developing Active Adult Communities* (Washington, DC: Urban Land Institute, 2001), 93.

[26]*Continuing Care Retirement Communities*, 55.

needs will be met, even as those needs increase, particularly in the area of healthcare. The CCRC is designed to address this, with its options ranging from independent living to assisted living and ultimately, nursing care. Other communities that may combine independent and assisted living, or assisted living and nursing care also respond to the concern that needs for supportive and healthcare services are likely to increase in the future. Financially, the type of CCRC providing the greatest level of security is what is known as a "lifecare" or "extensive contract" community. In this model, residents pay an entrance fee and ongoing monthly fee "in exchange for the right to lifetime occupancy of an independent living unit and . . . residents who require assisted living or nursing care may transfer to the appropriate level and continue to pay essentially the same monthly fee they had been paying for independent living."[27] This type of contract allows them to plan for future needs in a structured way that features cost containment through a form of facility-based, actuarially sound self-insurance.

Health
Access to Healthcare Services
Closely aligned with a form of "security" is the desire to have access to healthcare services. The ILR reflects this in that three of the top ten motivators to move, related to healthcare, are either for themselves (9 percent cited "personal health problems and/or not being able to take care of themselves") or a resident's spouse (5 percent). Having levels of care available was also cited by 5 percent of respondents. When thinking about what might prompt a future move from their existing home, 50 percent of homeowners age 75 or older cited "deteriorating health."

Once again, the CCRC is the senior housing product designed to best provide for future healthcare needs because of its inclusion of both assisted living and, more particularly, skilled nursing care. In addition, many of these communities also offer specialized memory care units designed to serve those with Alzheimer's disease and other cognitive disorders that lead to memory loss and loss of functionality.

Despite the fact that those who move to active adult communities don't consider themselves old, knowing that access to healthcare is readily available, yet not on the campus itself, contributes to the sense of security. Locating an active adult community within "a reasonable distance of a hospital and in close proximity to medical office"[28] is important and may also offer outreach or wellness programs that are of benefit to the residents. In a study of Americans age 50 to 64, 92 percent indicated that, "quality healthcare facilities are an important factor in considering where they will live" in the future.[29]

In the SLNG report, 51 percent rates as important that they would want the security of having access to care and supportive living if and when they need it in their later years and 42 percent say they will consider senior living when they

[27]*Continuing Care Retirement Communities*, ix.

[28]*Demand Terminology*, 76.

[29]American Seniors Housing Association, *Housing and Financial Security for Leading Edge Boomers* (Washington, DC: American Seniors Housing Association, 2005), 12.

start needing assistance with day-to-day personal tasks. Among respondents in the NSFM study, 97 percent rated on-site healthcare services as an important/very important factor when considering a CCRC for themselves in the future.

Need for More Supportive Services   While many seniors do not require healthcare services per se, independent living and assisted living levels of care respond to the need for more supportive services. Independent living communities offer meals, housekeeping, and scheduled transportation, and assisted living also provides assistance with ADLs such as eating, bathing, dressing, toileting, transferring (walking), and continence.

Factors That Deter Older Adults from Moving to Age-Restricted Communities
Cost

A major distinction between active adult communities and senior housing is the cost factor. With active adult communities, particularly those that are offered on a for-sale basis, the cost is limited to the purchase price of the residence and the monthly maintenance fee. Typically, the monthly maintenance fees are primarily associated with the upkeep of buildings and grounds, and they may also include staffing of the community center. Fee increases are usually tied to the cost-of-living index and include necessary capital improvements of common facilities and grounds over time. However, the control of those costs is in the hands of the Resident's Association rather than third-party operators, which gives voice and control to the owners themselves. Even rental active adult communities are typically not subject to sizeable rent hikes.

On the other hand, senior housing communities are service intensive and rarely involve ownership by residents. As such, costs go well beyond those typically associated with the carrying, maintenance, and upkeep of real estate. For example, The State of Seniors Housing reported that for communities that participated (including independent living, assisted living, and CCRCs) in 2007, the median annual expense per unit, per year was $30,234. The cost per resident per month was $2,400. Of the annual operating expenses per resident, only 15 percent were directly related to the real estate (including taxes, property insurance, repairs, and maintenance).[30]

The concern about moving to an independent living community cited most frequently in the ILR by residents (16 percent) was related to the "associated costs and the fear that the costs may increase over time." This fear is not unfounded. According to the US Census Bureau, median income decreases with age, as is clearly reflected in table 8.4, which demonstrates that those age 75 or older, the age when

---

[30]American Seniors Housing Association, *The State of Seniors Housing 2008* (Washington, DC: American Seniors Housing Association, 2008), 65.

Table 8.4

US MEDIAN INCOME IN 2009 BY AGE

US Median Income 2009 by Age Cohort

Age Cohort	Median Income ($)
55–59	59,656
60–64	55,866
65–69	40,223
70–74	37,994
75–79	31,030
80–84	28,178
85+	24,522

Source: Claritas

most move to senior housing, have a median income of roughly half of the youngest group in the 55-plus cohort.

The Employee Benefits Research Institute estimates the breakdown in sources of income for this group (figure 8.1).[31] This breakdown clearly illustrates that for those 65 or older the majority of income is derived from sources such as Social Security and Pensions and Annuities. These sources are not subject to significant increases. And, as the economic recession of 2008 to 2009 demonstrated, income sources such as assets and earnings are subject to substantial decreases. The limitations of seniors' income and concerns about being able to afford housing and care

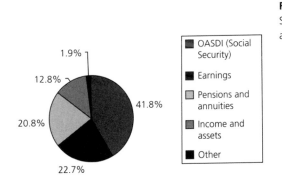

Figure 8.1
Sources of income for Americans age 65 and older

OASDI (Social Security)

Earnings

Pensions and annuities

Income and assets

Other

---

[31]Employee Benefits Research Institute Estimates from current population survey, January 2006 Supplement, published Oppenheimer Fund Investor Education Series, *Lessons for Boomers from Today's Retirees.*

in the future have an undeniable impact on decisions to move. Yet a study published in 2007 by the American Seniors Housing Association concluded that "the current cost of living for age and income qualified seniors with incomes between $30,000 and $75,000 living at home is remarkably similar to those costs for similar services offered by quality market rate rental independent living communities."[32]

Fears about financing their future healthcare needs are high among the concerns "leading edge boomers" pointed to when asked what they worried about as they got older, that is, past the age of 65. Nearly 60 percent indicated being worried (very much or somewhat) about having enough health insurance, while 55 percent feared not having enough money for long-term care. Nearly 40 percent feared becoming a financial burden.[33]

Respondents to the NSFM reflected these fears. When asked about their greatest concern regarding retirement, 24 percent cited outliving their savings and 13 percent indicated being able to afford healthcare.

Don't Want to Live in a Place for Older People

The expected market penetration rates are low for all forms of housing for older adults, whether they target the younger group such as active adult communities or the older segment such as CCRCs and assisted living communities. AARP's *Beyond 50.05* report indicated that 85 percent of those age 65 to 74 want to stay in their current residence for as long as possible and an even greater percent (86 percent) of those age 75 or older responded positively to this question.[34] This relates to many factors including the desire to live in an age-integrated community. The vast majority of those 55 and over do not want to live in a community that legally limits the age of residents, and many feel that by being surrounded only by older adults, they, too, will feel "old."

Feel They Are Not as Frail as Other Residents

Even among the older population there exist biases against those who are in ill health and are frail, and this is frequently based on fear of one's own future. Six percent of those who had recently moved to an independent living residence indicated that "age of residents" was a concern when making the decision to move.

This is particularly pronounced in active adult communities, which almost never include associated CCRCs, assisted living, or nursing facilities on the same campus. The younger segment, even those who choose to move to an active adult community, does not want to see or be reminded of their own potential frailty; hence, historically these different types of age-qualified communities have not shared a single campus. In some cases, the products for the older market have been located on out-parcels or adjacent to the campus of an active adult community.

---

[32]American Seniors Housing Association, *How To Successfully Challenge Common Misconceptions About the Cost of Independent Living* (Washington, DC: American Seniors Housing Association, Fall 2007), 2.

[33]N. Carn, J. Rabianski, R. Racster, and M. Seldin. *Real Estate Market Analysis: Techniques and Applications* (Englewood Cliffs, NJ: Prentice Hall, 1988), 9.

[34]AARP, *Beyond 50.05*, p. 48.

Don't Want to Give Up Their Independence

One of the greatest perceptions that prevents seniors from moving to seniors housing is that by doing so they will be giving up their independence. The organized programming such as required daily meals and even scheduled activities results in the fear that choices are being limited and daily activities are being "institutionalized," which contributes to this fear. "I'm not ready yet" is a commonly heard expression in response to senior housing, even among those who actually choose to move to such a community. The ILR reported that 11 percent of respondents were concerned about losing their freedom and independence. The NSFM report showed that 41 percent viewed a CCRC as affording a resident more independence versus 59 percent who viewed a single-family home in this way. Interestingly, once they have adjusted they often say, "I don't know why I waited so long to make this move," suggesting that their perceptions and fears of senior housing were unfounded.

Don't Want to Leave Family, Friends, Home, or Neighborhood

While the desire to be closer to family and friends is a major motivator for a move to age-restricted housing of every type, the fear of leaving family/friends and the neighborhood also weighs heavily for some. This was the second most frequently cited reason among those who had, in fact, moved (15 percent), indicating that the pull or motivator factors had outweighed this concern. For those who don't make the move, it is likely that this is a significant issue in preventing people from making the move.

As noted earlier in this chapter, among movers ages 55 and older, 50 percent moved within the same county. This supports the importance of maintaining local ties and connections that have frequently been built over much of an adult's lifetime.

Lifelong Neighborhoods and Influencing Factors

In *Beyond 50.05: A Report to the Nation on Livable Communities Creating Environments for Successful Aging*, AARP defines a livable community as "one that has affordable and appropriate housing, supportive community features and services, and adequate mobility options, which together facilitate personal independence and the engagement of residents in civic and social life."[35]

The lifelong neighborhood concept supports the following qualities:

- sound neighborhood structure

- diversity of accessible and appropriate housing

- convenient places to shop for daily needs

---

[35]AARP, *Beyond 50.05*, p. 25.

- vibrant, accessible pedestrian realm

- diverse social gathering spots

- healthy living

- dispersed wellness programming

- continuous employment and volunteerism

- support services and continuing care available as needed

Many of the words found in these concepts were discussed earlier in this section in relation to the reasons why older adults move to various forms of age-qualified housing, particularly senior housing. The concepts of Livable Communities or life-long neighborhoods are responsive to the overwhelming majority of people who want to be able to age successfully without leaving their community. Both under-score the values of being home to multiple generations, promote aging in place, ease of pedestrian access, and varied housing types that all favor right-sized homes.

These types of communities afford residents numerous and varied opportunities for socialization through gathering places that can range from the front porch to the neighborhood coffee shop, bookstore, or fitness center. Through the design of streetscapes, lot sizes, home design, and pedestrian transportation systems, a sense of community rather than isolation is emphasized, which not only enhances social-ization but also increases the security of the residents.

Historically, various types of age-restricted and seniors housing have typically been located in rural and suburban settings where land has been available for the developments on the scale that was considered necessary. As such, while services may have been conveniently located to these communities by suburban standards they were still located miles away and access necessitated the use of cars and vans. As such, walkability was not necessarily considered to be an important factor in selecting or valuing a development opportunity, since most suburbanites had spent a lifetime getting in the car to do anything.

By contrast, the concepts that inform livable communities or lifelong neighbor-hoods respond to the changing preferences of the baby boomer generation that is now coming to the age that has historically been the market for age-targeted or age-restricted active adult communities. By 2021, those boomers will form the tar-get market that has historically moved into senior housing communities that offer significant supportive and even healthcare services. From all anecdotal evidence, the boomers do not see themselves in the same way that previous generations might have. The word "senior" is anathema to them and the very notion of moving to a community of the type that is now available exclusively for "old people" is unap-pealing. The catch phrase "not your father's Oldsmobile" comes to mind when we think about the aging boomers and their response to their self-image and many of the existing housing types now available to them.

As boomers continue to reinvent themselves and their lives, they are likely to seek housing environments that support their needs. What will this entail? Research shows that although the age of retirement has decreased in the last several decades, for various reasons the boomer generation is likely to continue working. While employment patterns will change, emphasizing self-employment and part-time work, many boomers are expected to remain in the workforce. As such, they will want to reside in communities that facilitate access and connectivity. Downsizing may be redefined as "rightsizing" as boomers look for housing models that emphasize manageable size, quality, and utility of design and proximity to friends, neighbors, and services.

Evidence of this trend can be found in the growth of traditional neighborhood developments and transit-oriented developments that link together the fabric of life, work, and play. The trend of returning to urban environments also reflects these changing preferences, as two distinctly different generations make up a substantial portion of households moving to the cities. They include the millenials, who have now completed college and are entering the workforce as well as the empty-nesters, who no longer need the large home or the benefits of suburban school districts.

The desire for right-sized homes is a growing trend reflecting not only the current economic recession and housing crisis, but also the basic desire to create a smaller home that fits the changing needs of an aging population. One need only look at the "cottage" industry created by Sarah Susanka, author of the *Not So Big House* series. Her original book has led to a series of related books, which all emphasize Susanka's principles of "build better, not bigger."

SENIORS HOUSING COMPONENTS

CHAPTER 9

With Contributions from Susan Brecht and Duncan Walker

As reviewed in Chapter 7, seniors housing development has made great strides in moving from hospital-like configurations to more familiar neighborhood forms. As the look and style of seniors housing is normalizing, it is becoming easier to integrate into neighborhood settings. The distinction between care provided in seniors housing developments and care provided in the community is beginning to blur. Many providers who have traditionally provided market rate services in seniors housing settings are now also offering home-based and community-based services. In an article published in the *Seniors Housing & Care Journal*,[1] the authors presented the results of a survey of approximately 350 midwestern CCRCs. More than half indicated that they expect to be offering services by 2013 to those living outside their developments, and 17 to 30 percent of these properties are already doing so.

The next step in seniors housing evolution can be to open to the surrounding community and join with the public sector in upgrading and enhancing the

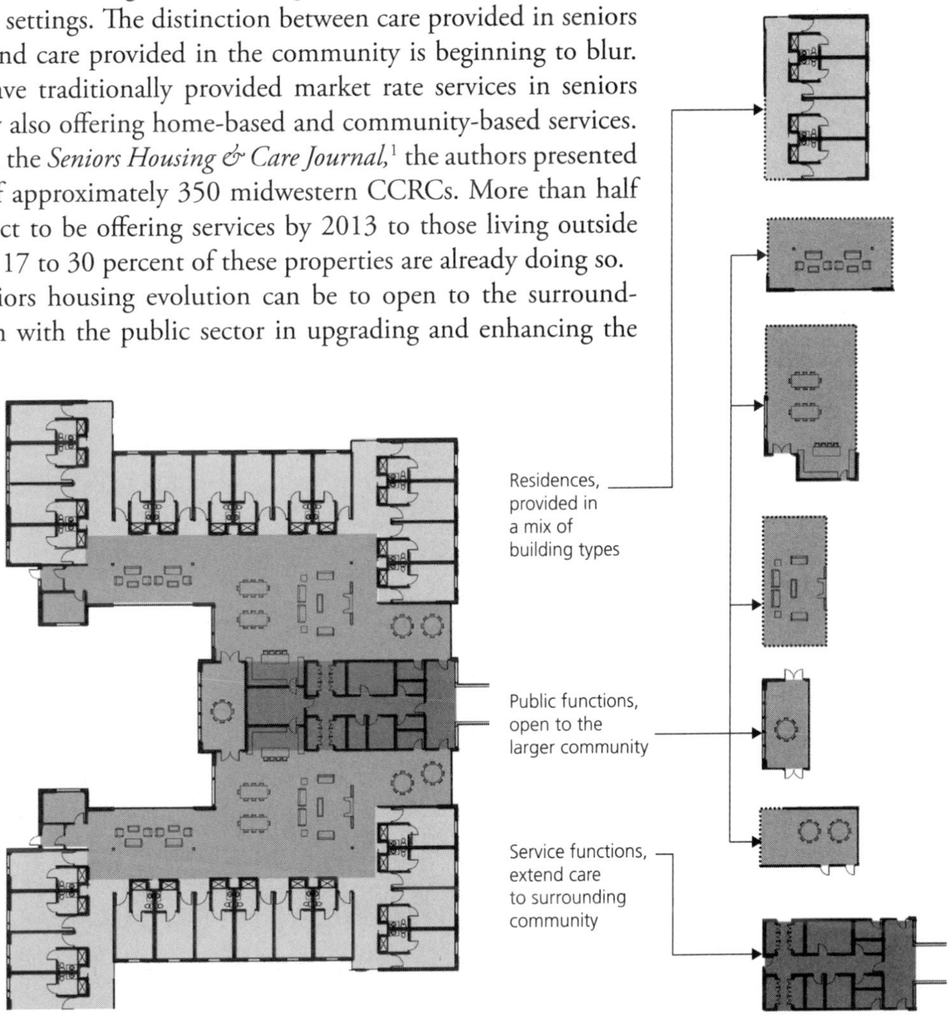

Residences, provided in a mix of building types

Public functions, open to the larger community

Service functions, extend care to surrounding community

Figure 9.1
A senior facility is an assemby of private, public, and service components that can be redistributed between the building, the block, and the entire community.

[1] S. B. Brecht, S. Fein, and L. vHollinger-Smith, "Preparing for the Future: Trends in Continuing Care Retirement Communities," *Seniors Housing & Care Journal* 17 (2009): 84.

general built environment. The wider community would benefit from access to the kinds of supports and environmental considerations provided in specialized senior environments and the industry would benefit from sharing the cost of community facilities, services, and amenities with a larger customer pool than the one or two hundred residents of the single development. Ideally, the larger community and the specialized providers will find ways to meet in the middle, coordinate resources, and provide an upgraded service-rich environment for all.

As reviewed in Chapter 8, seniors housing business models currently represent complex packages of services and buildings resulting from a careful stitching together of real estate and healthcare industries. The financing mechanisms that have been developed to bring these otherwise unrelated fields together are equally complex. The packaged approaches to health and housing coordination have a tremendous value to any effort at upgrading a whole community and there is an advantage to preserving the basic structure of the package when opening it up to the entire community.

In order to help further the goals of opening seniors housing and better relating it to the neighborhood, the following pages present taxonomy of the building and space components typical of a seniors development package. A more modular approach would look at how some of these components could support multiple programs—some internal to the development, some available to the larger community. In some cases these facilities could be provided by the private developer and opened to the larger community on a fee basis, and in other cases the facilities might be publicly provided and made available to the private development in exchange for fees or in-kind contribution of services. The modular approach would emphasize this type of give-and-take of both space and services within the surrounding community. The goals of these exchanges would be to extend the reach of seniors housing services, gain efficiencies of scale for operations, and form relationships that break down the distinction between the development and the larger community. Aging-in-place could come to mean a wider array of possibilities that include remaining in one's current home, moving to a home that is more suitable, or taking up residence in a care facility when more acute care is needed. The place referred to would be that of the neighborhood rather than the home itself. The fullest realization of a lifelong neighborhood would accommodate all of these options under the banner of aging-in-place.

Initiating Lifelong Neighborhood Design with a Market Study

Neighborhood-integrated seniors housing models are much more dependent on careful tailoring to existing community assets and needs. The market study can play an expanded role in understanding local conditions and addressing niche markets. In their more expansive role, market studies navigate between what is known about existing developments and what is known about evolving consumer and supply trends, and the studies help establish the highest and best way to move forward with a new or redeveloped community. When market studies are conducted early in the planning process, they explore what the market can financially support, along with the exploration of what the property can physically support. By evaluating the target market characteristics, the competition, and the overall demand, design decisions can be refined regarding the size and composition of the development elements and its specific attributes and pricing.

A thorough, site-specific market study provides results that offer guidance to the design team. For a single-use site such as a residential development, the study should result in recommendations on the total number of units that can be absorbed in the next five years, and the type of housing units, unit sizes, pricing, and amenities that are feasible. For age-restricted housing developments, recommendations can also address the type and use of common areas that will be necessary to attract the target market. Further refinements of certain types of age-restricted housing (such as assisted living and nursing homes) may be dictated by state regulation. For mixed-use developments that may combine housing for various age groups as well as recreational, retail, and office space, the results of the specialized market analyses must be integrated by the development and master planning team. Further, both the age and economic target market for the development, which is recommended or confirmed through the market study, will have an impact on design in order to reflect appropriate pricing and affordability.

Those with the responsibility of marketing a development find tremendous value in market studies. Studies can support the establishment of brand identity for the development by identifying and pursuing a niche that may not have already been served in the market. A study's demographic data should be presented not only for the entire market area (primary and secondary) but should be disaggregated by other measures such as census tract or zip code. By providing this level of information, marketing professionals can make informed decisions about allocating marketing dollars and efforts. A study should further identify the characteristics of the target market by age, income, and home values, and it might also disaggregate the population by housing tenure (owners vs. renters). Finally, marketing professionals look to market studies to inform them about who the competition will be and what they will offer. This critical data help to properly position, market, and sell the development.

Ultimately, the market study is used to support financing transactions. Single-use developments may be easier to finance than mixed use for a number of reasons. It is not uncommon for developers to have existing banking relationships for projects that may be similar to what they have built in the past. Furthermore, financing sources and even departments within an institution vary depending on the type of development. For example, a particular financial institution may provide a construction loan on a for-sale housing development through their real estate lending division, yet an assisted living or nursing home would be more likely to be financed through the healthcare lending or even commercial real estate department. A mixed-use development crosses those lines in terms of land use and might require separate financing transactions. With regard to FHA-insured lending, there are different programs for different uses and each has its own underwriting criteria, including the specifics of what the market study must address. For example, the FHA 221(d)(4) program is available for rental market-rate independent living for seniors but cannot be used to finance a project that is primarily assisted living. Under FHA's 232 program, a project must either be assisted living or nursing care, but it cannot allocate more than 20 percent of its units to independent living. Each program has separate market study guidelines and is reviewed by different divisions within HUD.

Yet in breaking down the transactions into the component parts, the viability of the overall mixed-use development may be overlooked or misunderstood. While it may be unlikely to expect that financing will incorporate all elements of a lifelong neighborhood, the lending community will need to be educated about the value added to their part of the transaction by combining the benefits of all of the complementary land uses.

Making the Case

More than a compilation of data and statistics, a well-done market study must tell a story. While the data and statistics are clearly important components of the story, their interpretation and the context that a well-defined inquiry, including qualitative information provided, must form the basis for supporting development (or altering or abandoning it, as necessary). The story that is crafted for the creation or enhancement of lifelong neighborhoods and new urban communities may be in its infancy. Professionals involved in conducting studies must produce a compelling, reasonable, and well-documented story in order to support those who are using it to plan and design communities, create meaningful affiliations, and attract good partners that will ensure success.

Seniors Housing Components

In the following pages, the typical components of a CCRC are reviewed. These issues are summarized for each type:

Form The general type of buildings that can accommodate the program. These may range from single-family homes to shops to high-rise buildings.

Typical increment What is the smallest building that can accommodate the minimum program necessary to getting started? If the program is spread among multiple buildings, what is the smallest increment required for operating efficiency?

Description Additional information on the building or program.

Purpose Mission of the building and program.

Community alternative In a neighborhood-integrated setting, what buildings and programs existing in the community that might be drawn on to supplement or replace the building type?

Optimal proximities Additional program spaces that need to be adjacent or close by.

Illustrations A neighborhood-compatible building example is shown for each building type to provide a picture of the scale and massing that would need to be utilized to work into a pedestrian-oriented neighborhood. There are five basic building types (figs. 9.2, 9.3, 9.4, 9.5, and 9.6).

All components reviewed can work within the building type shown, and examples are provided for how they can be organized to fit within a neighborhood. Additionally, a standard neighborhood disposition diagram is provided for each type. Areas where the building and program could be optimally placed are shaded in gray.

Figure 9.2
A small two-story town center building type.

Figure 9.3
A large two-story town center building type.

Figure 9.4
A three-story town center building type.

Figure 9.5
A community center building type.

Figure 9.6
Example of building type.

Figure 9.7
Disposition in
Barnes Square.

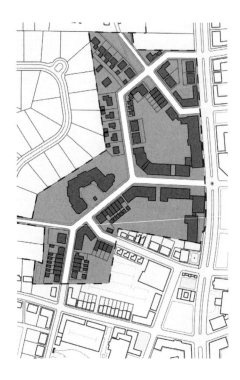

This Barnes Square diagram (fig. 9.7) is provided to show where the building or building space is planned in the proposed Barnes Square development. This neighborhood-integrated CCRC is further discussed in Chapter 12.

When the component is typically a space within a building rather than a stand-alone structure, the "town-center-in-a-box" building concept illustration is shown (figs. 9.8, 9.9). The town-center-in-a-box is an efficient, low-cost means of providing neighborhood-based retail and community programs including the following:

- A convenience store with groceries

- An ATM for convenience banking

- An inexpensive place to eat, including booths and a counter:
  - The commissary of the restaurant could stock the staples of a grocery store, so that the two businesses can be combined.
  - The counter might be designed for use as a demonstration kitchen for healthy-cooking classes.

- A general activity hall with a mailbox room:
  - The mailbox room can provide the functional daily destination that brings people out to walk and socialize.

- A bus shelter in the form of a covered porch or a seat within the store, providing a pleasant, dignified place to wait for the bus

Figure 9.8
Town-center-in-a-box
elevation.

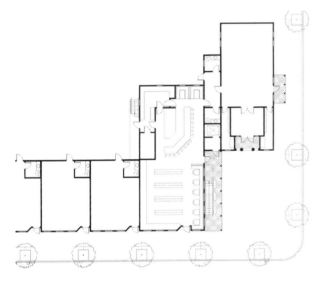

Figure 9.9
Town-center-in-a-box
plan.

■ Flexible office and retail spaces upstairs and to the side that could also be used for geriatric clinic programs:

● In larger neighborhoods, other shops could be added to this plan—a drugstore being among the most useful.

The town-center-in-a-box concept is useful for thinking about how typical program spaces of a senior housing development could be reorganized to fit into a neighborhood center better, and potentially remain open all day or during particular hours for access by the general public. The concept is operationally efficient, and it depends on only one employee to supervise and operate the entire facility at a basic level. Accessed by older adults during the day and younger adults in the evening, the businesses could become very cost efficient. This design is well suited to support a Mather Café—the new model of senior center that is being implemented across the country.

A.1 PERMANENT HOUSING TYPE: ACTIVE ADULT

Figure 9.10
Disposition in
Barnes Square.

Figure 9.11
Areas appropriate
for building type.

Form Any form of housing, same types and sizes as general market housing; should support single-level living.

Typical increment Fifty units.

Description Identical to regular housing types except a preference for single-level living that may impact certain unit-type density yields.

Purpose Provides living accommodations focused on the needs of people with grown children who want less household maintenance responsibilities and may have to deal with mobility issues in the foreseeable future.

Community alternative The active adult housing unit varies little from the units supplied in the general market and can easily be provided within the general housing stock (figs. 9.10, 9.11).

Table 9.1

OPTIMAL PROXIMITIES			
Support Space	**Adjacent**	**On the Block**	**Walking Distance**
Convenience store			X
Performance space			X
Coffee shop			X
Grocery store			X
Café			X
Restaurant			X
Meeting space			X
Multipurpose space			X
Wellness center			X
Senior center			X
Outpatient rehab center			
Geriatric clinic			
Home health delivery hub			X

A.2 PERMANENT HOUSING TYPE: INDEPENDENT LIVING

Figure 9.12
Example of building
type.

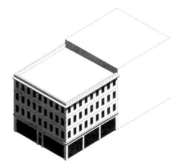

Figure 9.13
Disposition in a neighborhood
unit.

Form	Some single-family same types—mostly apartments—units are sized as general market housing; should support single-level living, multi-floor buildings need elevators.
Typical increment	Fifty units.
Description	The housing is similar to active-adult, but it is coupled with adjacent services, the most critical of which is food service. Independent living (IL) typically includes one meal a day. The provision of food service and other amenities leads to issues of critical mass (having enough users to make provision of the services economically efficient).
Purpose	Provides housing for people who are beginning to feel the effects of aging who are also looking for a living situation that will allow them to be independent for as long as possible. This includes easy access to essential services and some monitoring of their situation. Minor cognitive problems are an issue for some IL residents.
Community alternative	The independent-living housing unit varies little from the units supplied in the general market and can easily be provided within the general housing stock (figs. 9.12, 9.13, 9.14).

Table 9.2

OPTIMAL PROXIMITIES			
Support Space	**Adjacent**	**On the Block**	**Walking Distance**
Convenience store		X	
Performance space			X
Coffee shop		X	
Grocery store			X
Café			X
Restaurant			X
Meeting space			X
Multipurpose space	X		
Wellness center	X		
Senior center			X
Outpatient rehab center			
Geriatric clinic			
Home health delivery hub		X	

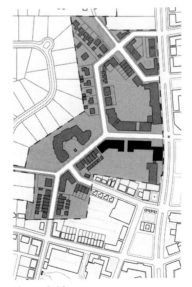

Figure 9.14
Disposition in Barnes Square.

A.3 PERMANENT HOUSING TYPE: ASSISTED LIVING

Figure 9.15
Example of building type.

Figure 9.16
Disposition in a neighborhood unit.

Form Traditional care building or small houses assisted.

Typical increment 25,000 square feet; thirty residents per floor.

Description This housing generally consists of moderately sized single-bedroom apartments grouped with public and service spaces into either small houses or small wards in a larger building. Staff is present twenty-four hours a day and three meals are served daily. Staffing and food service create issues of critical mass.

Purpose Provides living accommodations for people who need help with certain day-to-day life activities, possibly including mobility, taking medication, bathing, and so on. Minor cognitive issues are quite common among residents.

Community alternative The assisted-living housing units create a specialized form of apartment building. This type is not something that can be readily dispersed into a neighborhood environment, but rather should be better integrated into the wider community fabric (figs. 9.15, 9.16, 9.17). A movement known as senior co-housing, pioneered by architect Chuck Durrett, is developing a model a collective living that provides many benefits similar to those found in assisted living, but in a noninstitutional setting.

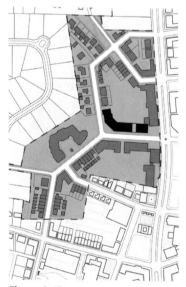

Figure 9.17
Disposition in Barnes Square.

Table 9.3

OPTIMAL PROXIMITIES			
Support Space	**Adjacent**	**On the Block**	**Walking Distance**
Convenience store	X		
Performance space		X	
Coffee shop		X	
Grocery store			X
Café		X	
Restaurant	X		
Meeting space	X		
Multipurpose space	X		
Wellness center	X		
Senior center		X	
Outpatient rehab center			X
Geriatric clinic			X
Home health delivery hub	X		

A.4 PERMANENT HOUSING TYPE: MEMORY SUPPORT

Figure 9.18
Example of
building type.

Figure 9.19
Disposition in a
neighborhood unit.

Form   Traditional care building or small houses.

Typical increment   10,000 square feet; fourteen residents.

Description   This type of housing generally consists of small single-room living accommodations with private baths that are grouped with public and service spaces into either small houses or wards in a larger building. Staff is present twenty-four hours a day and three meals a day are served within the ward or small house. The ward or small house is secured to prevent wandering and adjacent secure exterior space is required. Staffing and food service create issues of critical mass.

Purpose   Provides living accommodations for people with significant cognitive impairments but with little or minor physical impairments. All living spaces are designed to provide the most supportive environment possible for the residents. Memory support units can be incorporated into large assisted living or skilled nursing homes, which, in some cases, are located on separate floors.

Community alternative   Memory support housing units create a specialized form of apartment building. This type is not something that can be readily dispersed into a neighborhood environment, but rather should be kept whole and integratedv into the wider community fabric (figs. 9.18, 9.19, 9.20).

Table 9.4

OPTIMAL PROXIMITIES			
Support Space	**Adjacent**	**On the Block**	**Walking Distance**
Convenience store	X		
Performance space		X	
Coffee shop		X	
Grocery store			X
Café		X	
Restaurant	X		
Meeting space	X		
Multipurpose space	X		
Wellness center	X		
Senior center		X	
Outpatient rehab center			X
Geriatric clinic			X
Home health delivery hub		X	

Figure 9.20
Disposition in Barnes Square.

A.5 PERMANENT HOUSING TYPE: NURSING CARE

Figure 9.21
Example of building type.

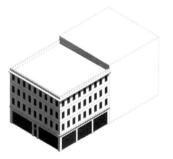

Figure 9.22
Disposition in a neighborhood unit.

Form Traditional care building or small houses.

Typical increment 10,000 square feet; fourteen residents.

Description This type of housing generally consists of small single-room living accommodations with private baths that are grouped with public and service spaces into either small houses or wards in a larger building. Staff is present twenty-four hours a day and three meals a day are served within the ward or small house. Adjacent secure exterior space is highly desirable; strict local regulations dictate staffing requirements and affect building layout. Staffing and food service create issues of critical mass.

Purpose Provides living accommodations for people with significant physical needs. Residents usually have very poor mobility. Cognitive issues often present as well.

Community alternative Nursing care housing units are most commonly a specialized form of large apartment building that would be compatible in town centers, although small-house versions that are more neighborhood compatible are becoming more common (figs. 9.21, 9.22, 9.23).

Figure 9.23
Disposition in Barnes Square.

Table 9.5

OPTIMAL PROXIMITIES			
Support Space	**Adjacent**	**On the Block**	**Walking Distance**
Convenience store	X		
Performance space			
Coffee shop			
Grocery store			
Café			
Restaurant	X		
Meeting space			
Multipurpose space	X		
Wellness center			
Senior center			
Outpatient rehab center	X		
Geriatric clinic			
Home health delivery hub	X		

B.1 TRANSIENT HOUSING TYPE: HOSPICE

Figure 9.24
Example of
building type.

Figure 9.25
Disposition in a
neighborhood unit.

Form Traditional care building or small houses.

Typical increment 10,000 square feet; fourteen residents.

Description This type of housing generally consists of small single-room living accommodations with private baths that are grouped with public and service spaces into either small houses or wards in a larger building. Staff is present twenty-four hours a day and three meals a day are served within the ward or small house. Adjacent secure exterior space is highly desirable; strict local regulations dictate staffing requirements and affect building layout. Staffing and food service create issues of critical mass.

Purpose Provides living accommodations for people with significant physical needs who are expected to live less than six months. Residents usually have very poor mobility. Cognitive issues are often present as well. Hospice units can be incorporated into large assisted living or skilled nursing homes, and in some cases they are separated by floor.

Community alternative Hospice units are most commonly a specialized form of large apartment building that would be compatible in town centers, although small-house versions that are more neighborhood-compatible are becoming more common (figs. 9.24, 9.25, 9.26).

Table 9.6

OPTIMAL PROXIMITIES			
Support Space	**Adjacent**	**On the Block**	**Walking Distance**
Convenience store	X		
Performance space			
Coffee shop			
Grocery store			
Café			
Restaurant	X		
Meeting space			
Multipurpose space	X		
Wellness center			
Senior center			
Outpatient rehab center	X		
Geriatric clinic			
Home health delivery hub	X		

Figure 9.26
Disposition in Barnes Square.

B.2 TRANSIENT HOUSING TYPE: RESPITE CARE

Figure 9.27
Example of
building type.

Figure 9.28
Disposition in a
neighborhood unit.

Form Small houses or area within a traditional care building.

Typical increment 10,000 square feet; 14 residents or can be accommodated within another care facility type at any scale.

Description housing generally consists of small single-room living accommodations with private baths grouped with public and service spaces into either small houses or wards in a larger building. Staff is present twenty-four hours a day and three meals a day are served within the ward or small house. Adjacent secure exterior space is highly desirable. Strict local regulations dictate staffing requirements and affect building layout. Staffing and food service create issues of critical mass.

Purpose Provides living accommodations for people with significant physical needs who are expected to live less than six months. Residents usually have very poor mobility. Cognitive issues are often present as well. Respite units can be incorporated into large assisted living or skilled nursing homes, in some cases separated on their own floor. In other cases, small hospice houses will also accept residents for respite stays.

Community alternative Respite Care housing units are most commonly a specialized form of large apartment building that would be compatible in town centers, although small house versions that are more neighborhood-compatible are becoming more common (figs. 9.27, 9.28, 9.29).

Figure 9.29
Disposition in Barnes Square.

Table 9.7

OPTIMAL PROXIMITIES			
Support Space	**Adjacent**	**On the Block**	**Walking Distance**
Convenience store	X		
Performance space			
Coffee shop			
Grocery store			
Café			
Restaurant	X		
Meeting space			
Multipurpose space	X		
Wellness center			
Senior center			
Outpatient rehab center	X		
Geriatric clinic			
Home health delivery hub	X		

B.3 TRANSIENT HOUSING TYPE: REHAB CARE

Figure 9.30
Example of
building type.

Figure 9.31
Disposition in a
neighborhood unit.

Form Small houses or area within a traditional care building.

Typical increment 10,000 square feet; fourteen residents.

Description Housing generally consists of small single-room living accommodations with private baths grouped with public and service spaces into either small houses or wards in a larger building. Staff is present twenty-four hours a day and three meals a day are served within the ward or small house. Adjacent secure exterior space is highly desirable. Strict local regulations dictate staffing requirements and affect building layout. Staffing and food service create issues of critical mass.

Purpose Provides living accommodations for people with significant physical needs, but expected to recover after physical therapy. Residents usually have very poor mobility. Cognitive issues often are present as well.

Community alternative Rehab Care housing units are most commonly a specialized form of large apartment building that would be compatible in town centers, although small house versions that are more neighborhood-compatible are becoming more common (figs. 9.30, 9.31, 9.32).

Table 9.8

OPTIMAL PROXIMITIES			
Support Space	**Adjacent**	**On the Block**	**Walking Distance**
Convenience store	X		
Performance space			
Coffee shop			
Grocery store			
Café			
Restaurant	X		
Meeting space			
Multipurpose space	X		
Wellness center			
Senior center			
Outpatient rehab center	X		
Geriatric clinic			
Home health delivery hub	X		

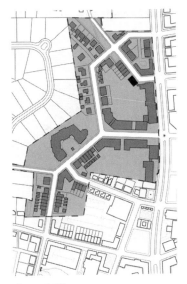

Figure 9.32
Disposition in Barnes Square.

C.1 SERVICE BUILDING TYPE: HOME HEALTH

Figure 9.33
Disposition in a
neighborhood
unit.

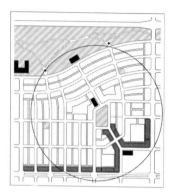

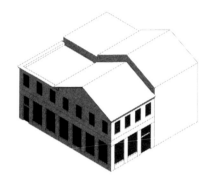

Figure 9.34
Example of
building type.

Delivery-hub home healthcare is delivered to the individual's home, but a neighborhood would benefit from having a collective staging area.

Form	Office building or storefront.
Increment	500 square feet; fifty seniors.
Catchment	Local.
Flexibility	Seniors only as programmed, but office space could be shared.
Community alternative	Home health hubs are usually housed in office parks or strip mall locations. Since they are a staging area for mobile services, they do not generally need to be in main street locations. However, hubs in a main street storefront setting can provide a beneficial community presence for hospital systems. The Beacon Hill Villages model discussed in Chapter 11 can also be a form of community-based alternative to a remotely located office hub (figs. 9.33, 9.34).

Table 9.9

OPTIMAL PROXIMITIES			
Senior Housing Facility	**Adjacent**	**On the Block**	**Walking Distance**
Active adult			X
Independent living			X
Assisted living	X		
Memory support			
Nursing care			
Hospice			
Respite care			
Outpatient rehab center			
Rehab care			
Home health delivery hub			

C.2 SERVICE BUILDING TYPE: GERIATRIC CLINIC INCLUDING VISION AND DENTAL CARE SERVICES

Figure 9.35
Example of building type.

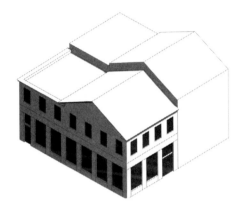

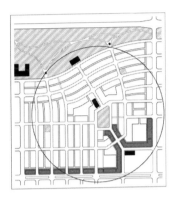

Figure 9.36
Disposition in a neighborhood unit.

Form	Office building or storefront.
Increment	2,100 square feet; 800 seniors.
Catchment	Regional.
Flexibility	Seniors only as programmed; could be shared.
Community Alternative	Geriatric clinics are usually housed in medical office building complexes. However, a simple exam room with an accompanying small office can be integrated into many types of storefront operations and these can be used for weekly or biweekly visits by geriatricians. Such community-based time-shared clinic operations have been successfully integrated into boutique massage businesses for instance, as a massage room can easily double as an examination room (figs. 9.35, 9.36).

Table 9.10

OPTIMAL PROXIMITIES			
Senior Housing Facility	**Adjacent**	**On the Block**	**Walking Distance**
Active adult			X
Independent living			X
Assisted living	X		
Memory support			
Nursing care			
Hospice			
Respite care			
Outpatient rehab center			
Rehab care			
Home health delivery hub			

C.3 SERVICE BUILDING TYPE: REHAB, PHYSICAL THERAPY

Figure 9.37
Example of
building type.

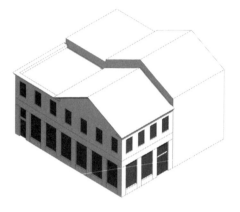

Figure 9.38
Disposition in a
neighborhood
unit.

Form Office building or storefront.

Increment 2,250 square feet; 800 seniors.

Catchment Regional.

Flexibility Seniors only as programmed, could be shared.

Community alternative Rehab facilities are best packaged with assisted living or skilled nursing operations where they can serve the residents of the care home as well as the surrounding community (figs. 9.37, 9.38, 9.39).

Figure 9.39
Disposition in Barnes Square.

Table 9.11

OPTIMAL PROXIMITIES			
Senior Housing Facility	**Adjacent**	**On the Block**	**Walking distance**
Active adult			X
Independent living			X
Assisted living		X	
Memory support			
Nursing care			
Hospice			
Respite care			
Outpatient rehab center			
Rehab care			
Home health delivery hub			

C.4 SERVICE BUILDING TYPE: ADULT DAYCARE

Figure 9.40
Example of
building type.

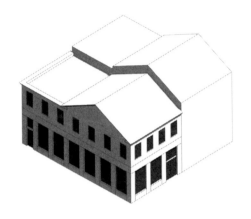

Figure 9.41
Disposition in
a neighborhood
unit.

Form Community building or storefront.

Increment 4,000 square feet; forty-five seniors.

Catchment Regional.

Flexibility Seniors only.

Optimal proximities Often best associated with work centers where caregivers can drop off and pick up easily at beginning and end of work day (figs. 9.40, 9.41, 9.42).

Table 9.12

OPTIMAL PROXIMITIES			
Senior Housing Facility	**Adjacent**	**On the Block**	**Walking Distance**
Active adult			
Independent living			
Assisted living			
Memory support			
Nursing care			
Hospice			
Respite care			
Outpatient rehab center			
Rehab care			
Home health delivery hub	X		

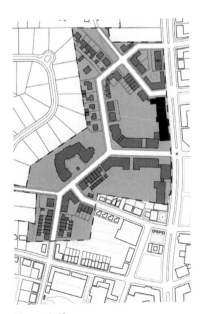

Figure 9.42
Disposition in Barnes Square.

C.5 SERVICE BUILDING TYPE: SENIOR CENTER

Figure 9.43
Example of
building type.

Figure 9.44
Disposition in a
neighborhood
unit.

Form Community building or storefront (figs. 9.43, 9.44, 9.45).

Increment 5,000 square feet.

Catchment Local.

Flexibility This is for seniors-only programming, but it could be time-shared with other uses.

Figure 9.45
Disposition in Barnes Square.

Table 9.13

OPTIMAL PROXIMITIES

Senior Housing Facility	Adjacent	On the Block	Walking Distance
Active adult			X
Independent living		X	
Assisted living		X	
Memory support			
Nursing care			
Hospice			
Respite care			
Outpatient rehab center			
Rehab care			
Home health delivery hub			

C.6 SERVICE BUILDING TYPE: GERIATRIC HEALTH CLUB AND WELLNESS CENTER WITH POOL

Figure 9.46
Example of
building type.

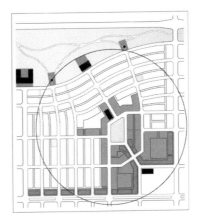

Figure 9.47
Disposition in a
neighborhood
unit.

Form Office building or storefront (figs. 9.46, 9.47, 9.48).

Increment 5,000 square feet; 800 seniors.

Catchment Regional.

Flexibility Seniors-only as programmed; could be shared.

Table 9.14

OPTIMAL PROXIMITIES			
Senior Housing Facility	**Adjacent**	**On the Block**	**Walking Distance**
Active adult			X
Independent living	X	X	
Assisted living	X	X	
Memory support			
Nursing care			
Hospice			
Respite care			
Outpatient rehab center			
Rehab care			
Home health delivery hub			

Figure 9.48
Disposition in Barnes Square.

D.1 SENIORS DEVELOPMENT COMPONENT PIECE: MULTIPURPOSE SPACE INCLUDING RESTROOMS, STORAGE, AND SERVICE SPACE

Figure 9.49
Disposition in Barnes Square.

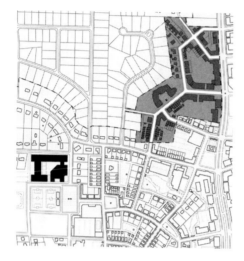

Figure 9.50
Location in a town-center-in-a-box elevation.

Area	3,000 square feet.
Capacity	165 occupants.
Catchment	Regional.
Flexibility	Shared.
Community alternative	Multipurpose spaces can be easily integrated into the neighborhood and co-programmed with any number of community center functions (figs. 9.49. 9.50, 9.51).

Table 9.15

OPTIMAL PROXIMITIES			
Senior Housing Facility	**Adjacent**	**On the Block**	**Walking Distance**
Active adult			X
Independent living		X	
Assisted living		X	
Memory support			
Nursing care			
Hospice			
Respite care			
Outpatient rehab center			
Rehab care			
Home health delivery hub			

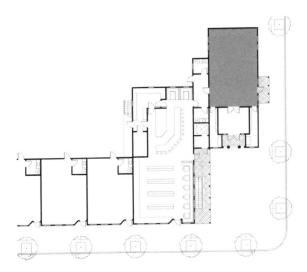

Figure 9.51
Location in a town-center-in-a-box plan.

D.1A SENIORS DEVELOPMENT COMPONENT PIECE: MEETING SPACE, RESTROOMS, AND STORAGE

Area 500 square feet.

Capacity 30 occupants.

Catchment Local.

Flexibility Shared by schedule.

Community alternative Meeting spaces can be easily integrated into the neighborhood and co-programmed with any number of other public and private functions.

Table 9.16

OPTIMAL PROXIMITIES			
Senior Housing Facility	**Adjacent**	**On the Block**	**Walking Distance**
Active adult			X
Independent living	X	X	
Assisted living	X		
Memory support			
Nursing care			
Hospice			
Respite care			
Outpatient rehab center			
Rehab care			
Home health delivery hub			

D.1B SENIORS DEVELOPMENT COMPONENT PIECE: GROCERY STORE

Figure 9.52
Grocery store
in relation to
Barnes Square.

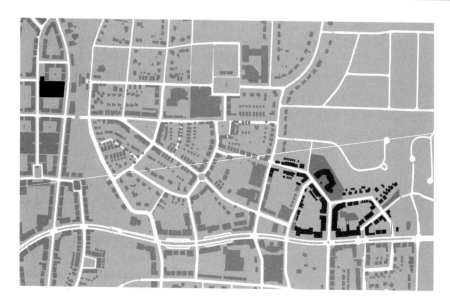

Area 30,000 to 45,000 square feet.

Catchment Regional.

Flexibility Shared.

Community alternative Grocery stores depend on volume, and thus those serving the whole community are likely to provide better quality, selection, and prices than those serving only a single housing facility. In addition, several of the pioneering NORC organizations have successfully negotiated with local grocery stores to provide scheduled delivery services to community spaces within the neighborhood or seniors development (figs. 9.52, 9.53, 9.54).

Table 9.17

OPTIMAL PROXIMITIES			
Senior Housing Facility	**Adjacent**	**On the Block**	**Walking Distance**
Active adult			X
Independent living			X
Assisted living			
Memory support			
Nursing care			
Hospice			
Respite care			
Outpatient rehab center			
Rehab care			
Home health delivery hub			

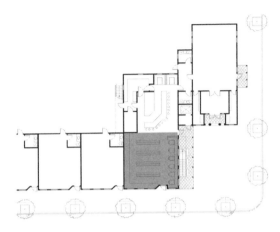

Figure 9.53
Location in a town-center-in-a-box plan.

D.2A SENIORS DEVELOPMENT COMPONENT PIECE: CONVENIENCE STORE

Area 2,500 to 5,000 square feet.

Catchment Local.

Flexibility Shared.

Community alternative A convenience store in some form is a typical element of any seniors housing development. There is no reason that this service cannot be supplied through a nearby store, or alternatively, there is no reason why the internal one could not be positioned to face outward and be open to the general public.

Table 9.18

OPTIMAL PROXIMITIES			
Senior Housing Facility	**Adjacent**	**On the Block**	**Walking Distance**
Active adult			X
Independent living		X	X
Assisted living	X		
Memory support			
Nursing care			
Hospice			
Respite care			
Outpatient rehab center			
Rehab care			
Home health delivery hub			

D.3 SENIORS DEVELOPMENT COMPONENT PIECE: RESTAURANT/CAFÉ

Figure 9.54
Location in a town-center-in-a-box plan.

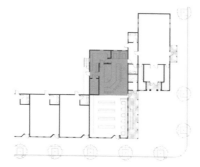

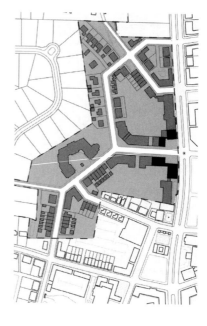

Figure 9.55
Disposition in Barnes Square.

Area 4,000 to 10,000 square feet.

Catchment Regional.

Community alternative Increasingly, seniors housing developments are moving away from large, singular cafeteria food service to a varied collection of smaller restaurant-style operations. For the very frail, there will probably always be a preference for segregated dining opportunities within the facility, but for many residents the opportunity to dine regularly in cafés along a main street would be a welcome amenity and their regular patronage would help support the businesses. Because the main expense in a restaurant is the food service equipment, a hybrid model might be possible wherein a single kitchen supplies both a segregated, internally oriented dining space as well as a public, outwardly facing dining space.

Table 9.19

OPTIMAL PROXIMITIES			
Senior Housing Facility	**Adjacent**	**On the Block**	**Walking Distance**
Active adult			X
Independent living		X	X
Assisted living	X		
Memory support			
Nursing care			
Hospice			
Respite care			
Outpatient rehab center			
Rehab care			
Home health delivery hub			

Figure 9.56
Location in a town-center-in-a-box elevation.

D.3B SENIORS DEVELOPMENT COMPONENT PIECE: COFFEE SHOP/DINE-IN BAKERY

Area 2,500 to 5,000 square feet.

Catchment Local.

Flexibility Shared.

Community alternative The coffee shop/bakery serves as an important third place for informal gathering and socializing. These spaces play an important role within a senior housing development and perhaps function even more effectively when positioned in a nearby main street setting. The Mather Café is a highly successful related movement to reposition typical senior center programs in a coffee shop environment.

Table 9.20

OPTIMAL PROXIMITIES			
Senior Housing Facility	**Adjacent**	**On the block**	**Walking Distance**
Active adult			X
Independent living		X	X
Assisted living		X	X
Memory support			
Nursing care			
Hospice			
Respite care			
Outpatient rehab center			
Rehab care			
Home health delivery hub			

Service Policy Components

As seniors housing developments open up and integrate into neighborhoods, communities should also encourage a broad enough range of private pay and public services to address the full spectrum of needs across the lifetimes of a diverse population. This includes services for home-based older adults including meal programs, transportation services, and referral services for healthcare and other services, some of which can be provided out of a seniors housing development with outreach capacity. The resources available to support these types of services vary greatly by community, particularly when comparing dense urban communities to rural ones. A good first stop to begin to assess the existing service environment is the local area agency on aging (AAA). Most AAAs methodically track what programs and resources are currently available. The local YMCA and Jewish community centers, local parks, recreation departments, and a range of local businesses can also be valuable partners and collaborators in developing lifelong neighborhood. WalkScore.org is a valuable online resource that can help gauge how pedestrian friendly an area is, what resources are nearby, and the website's Street Smart tool can provide an initial analysis of the connectivity and block structure of the surrounding neighborhood. The goals of the initial community survey and meetings are to establish the condition of the existing urban form, the built and programmatic assets that exist within the community, and any local needs that can be served by a new development.

In most areas there is a deficit of geriatric medical facilities that are specialized in the treatment of disease and injury among seniors. Seniors housing developments can support this effort by opening up services provided for residents to the surrounding community on an outpatient basis. Many new technologies are coming onto the market that facilitate remote monitoring and support of older adults living in their homes. There are many possibilities opened up by the technologies for seniors housing facilities to extend their service and support coverage further into the surrounding community and draw on the surrounding community in supporting their own residents. Several national organizations that have formed around the Culture of Change movement in skill nursing that can be consulted regarding the current regulatory, funding, and policy opportunities and challenges within a particular state. Of special importance is a review of the utilization of Home and Community Based Services Waivers (HCBSW), which are an important source of funding for in-home supportive services for low-income seniors.

Local outreach efforts to seniors and seniors housing providers should educate on eligibility and application processes. Ideally, service resources like HCBSW can be increasingly directed toward prevention-oriented wellness programs that can effectively minimize the costs associated with medical care while also supporting a higher quality of life. Wellness programs can encompass a broad array of services to help insure that citizens maintain healthy and independent lifestyles but should include: health education, exercise and fitness classes, recreational activities, and cultural awareness programs. Civic participation programs can also be considered part of a wellness strategy, supporting the mental well-being of local seniors, keeping them engaged and free from suffering loneliness or isolation. Civic participation programs are also an enormous resource for the community and when well organized and well supported, they can produce a wide range of public benefits for all members of the community.

Built-Environment Policy Components

As seniors housing developments open up and integrate into neighborhoods, communities can reciprocate by upgrading the policies that shape their general built environment. As a first step in venturing with private seniors housing developers to establish lifelong neighborhoods, regulatory barriers to the construction of desirable senior housing development should be lifted to the greatest extent possible, and clear paths to entitlement, protected from unpredictable NIMBY battles, should be created.

Beyond making it more predictable for seniors housing and care facility developers to obtain necessary entitlements, local governments and service providers can meet progressive developers halfway by working to upgrade the general built environment. These upgrades serve to make neighborhood locations more desirable for seniors housing residents, allowing them to move more freely between the development and the surrounding community and resulting in cost-efficient resource sharing between private and public care providers. A greater diversity of buildings and uses in each neighborhood can be encouraged simply by removing regulatory barriers to new construction that introduces use diversity, as well as proactive programs to maintain and adapt the existing building stock. The following list details specific regulatory avenues that can be explored for their potential to affect upgrades to the local built environment.

1. **Zoning ordinances and livability**—Zoning ordinances often are responsible for enabling or preventing the development of livable, lifelong neighborhoods. Lifelong neighborhoods are sufficiently flexible—in physical infrastructure and service and social resources—to accommodate the changing needs of all residents as they age and move from one part of their lifecycle to the next. The primary measure of the livability of a neighborhood is its walkability. A multitude of social, economic, and health benefits will accrue for residents if streets can be easily walked and are designed so that they are pleasant to walk along and have destinations that are near enough to walk to.

   a. Allow mixed uses, types, densities, and costs

      i. Change zoning to encourage diverse uses, housing types, and densities

      ii. Encourage form-based zoning as an alternative to use-based zoning

      iii. Allow integration of commercial and residential properties in close proximity or on the same site

      iv. Allow integration of high-, medium-, and low-density housing types within the same residential district

      v. To preclude NIMBY sentiments, educate citizens about the advantages of legalizing building diversity

      vi. Zoning should allow neighborhood retail establishments without special-use permission at regular intervals of no more than a half mile apart, preferably one-quarter mile apart

  b. Allow diversification of existing housing stock

      i. Allow certain types of multifamily residences, like shared housing, on single-family lots

      ii. Allow subletting in single-family residential neighborhoods as to provide additional income streams, security, and companionship, as well as to preclude over-housing

      iii. Allow "family of choice" option, which would allow unrelated people to be recognized as a family and thus be exempted from zoning restrictions that limit the number of unrelated people living in a single-family home.

      iv. Encourage shared housing

         (1) Legalize free-market shared housing options (e.g., renting out extra bedrooms)

         (2) Allow agency-assisted shared housing (allow nonprofits, churches, schools, and so on to play "matchmaker")

         (3) Establish special code definitions to differentiate shared housing from "rooming houses" or "boarding houses" in case of NIMBY sentiments toward housing perceived as "transient housing"

  c. Walkability

      i. Discourage neighborhood dependency on cars and encourage pedestrian friendly designs

         (1) Services and resources must be located in close proximity to residences, either within a five-minute walk from residential neighborhoods, or within a five-minute walk from public transportation options

         (2) Construct sidewalks on both sides of all streets, with buffers between sidewalks and curb cuts and count-down crosswalks

         (3) Create bicycle lanes or another bicycle integration strategy

         (4) Plant grassy, tree-planted medians in multilane streets (to the exclusion of dedicated turning lanes)

         (5) Reduce the required width and turning radius of neighborhood streets to dissuade speeding

         (6) Plant trees along roadside (trees provide shade for pedestrians, protection from errant vehicles, and also tend to slow traffic)

         (7) Allow on-street parking to decrease the need for on-site parking and to create a protective physical barrier between travel lanes and sidewalks

    ii. Construct safer street crossings

        (1) Ensure curb cuts are manageable at crosswalks

        (2) Provide clear signage at crosswalks for both pedestrians and motorists

        (3) Construct pedestrian islands in the medians of multilane streets

        (4) Extend times of crossing signals to ensure adequate time for elderly, disabled, and slow-moving pedestrians to cross streets safely

        (5) Locate crosswalks at all intersections and crossing-lights at all intersections with traffic lights

        (6) Smaller curb radii at intersections slow traffic and allow pedestrians to cross more easily and safely

d. Accessibility

e. Lifelong residency

    i. Require or encourage housing diversity across jurisdictions. The Fair Share Housing Plan is a citywide or regional approach to the provision of affordable or other social purpose housing. The rationale behind a fair share housing plan is that all areas should provide a proportionate amount of affordable or supportive housing. Because gentrification reduces the amount of affordable housing, additional means to provide affordable housing are needed. Legislation at the municipal and/or state level would be required.

    ii. Require or encourage housing diversity within individual developments. Inclusionary zoning is defined as either a mandatory requirement or a voluntary goal to reserve a specific percentage of housing units for low and moderate income, or special needs households in new residential developments. Municipal legislation would be required.

    iii. Allow construction and subleasing of accessory apartments on single-family home lots

    iv. Allow implementation of ECHO (Elderly Cottage Housing Opportunity) homes: small, portable "cottages" that can be placed in the back or side yard of a single family home

    v. Encourage homebuilders to construct housing that facilitates retrofitting or conversion to multi-tenant housing (e.g., duplexes, etc.), and change zoning to allow such conversion

    vi. Zone lands for congregate living. At a time when the growth of group homes, nursing homes, skilled nursing facilities, and hospices has increased, the resistance to proposed projects in many communities has also grown. Care homes provide important services and benefits to the community as a whole, but nonetheless are confronted by NIMBY sentiments

vii. Educate the public as to the benefits of senior congregate living facilities as well as greater sensitivity towards community concerns regarding development issues

2. **Housing affordability and quality, both internal and external to seniors housing developments**—Affordability is perhaps the single most difficult housing issue for many seniors. Retired citizens who live on fixed incomes often struggle to keep up with the surge in rents and property taxes, particularly in areas that have experienced gentrification in the past decade. The following items offer opportunities for localities to support older adults as they stay in their homes, and ways of combating the displacement associated with gentrification.

  a. Changes to tax code: Many states and municipalities have instituted tax exemptions, caps, or deferment options to protect homeowners from losing their homes due to in ability to pay property taxes.

   i. Tax Deferrals: Property tax deferrals allow certain homeowners to opt to pay all of their accumulated property taxes in one lump sum, usually at the time of resale.

   ii. Tax Postponement: Property tax postponements allow the state to pay all or part of the annual property tax bill. This deferred payment is a lien on the property and becomes due upon sale, change of residence, or death. A lien secures the right to take and hold or sell the property of a debtor as security or payment for a debt or duty.

   iii. Property Tax Assistance: Rather than change the tax code itself, some localities have simply developed tax assistance programs to provide grants to assist members of low-income households who cannot pay property taxes. In a property tax assistance program, the state provides cash reimbursement to pay the property taxes for an individual whose annual income falls below a set limit. Filing for the program should not reduce the amount of taxes owed, nor should it result in a lien being placed on a homeowner's property.

   iv. Property Tax Caps: Property tax caps limit or freeze the growth of the assessed value of a person's property, thus preventing increases in the amount he or she will have to pay in the future. They also protect homeowners from escalating taxes due to circumstances like gentrification, when increases in the value of a person's property result from the property's location and not improvements in its condition. Seven states have adopted property tax caps that may offer model legislation: Maryland, California, Iowa, Arizona, Florida, Washington, and Texas.

   v. Limiting Assessed Values: Local governments can also adopt limitations on growth in assessed value but those limitations apply only to local taxes. The assessed value of such property can be increased only if the property ownership changes (other than between spouses), there is an addition to or renovation of the property, or if there had been an error in a previous assessment.

vi. Homestead Exemptions: Property tax exemptions free homeowners who fit certain criteria from having to pay some or all of their property taxes. Elderly Homestead Exemptions may be added to standard Homestead Exemptions and create further Homestead Exemptions to aid low-income senior homeowners. A locality has the option to exempt all or part of the assessed value of a senior homeowner's property from school taxes and or exempt all or part of the assessed value of a senior homeowner's property from state and county taxes.

vii. Property Tax Credits: Property tax credits reduce an individual's property tax liability dollar-for-dollar. Additional tax credits to senior homeowners may be added to standard Homeowner's Tax Relief Credits. It is important to ensure that procedures for obtaining tax credits are easy for builders and homeowners to navigate and that tax credits are granted quickly and efficiently.

b. Finance tools to protect affordability

i. Deferred Payment Loan Programs: Deferred payment loans can provide a valuable asset for seniors currently without resources to pay for home modifications. Deferred payment loan programs require lump-sum repayment at a certain interest rate at the end of the loan's term instead of gradual monthly repayments.

ii. Predatory Lending Protections: Predatory lenders offer clients subprime mortgages or loans and take advantage of them through the inclusion of abusive terms and hidden fees. Often these lenders prey on elderly homeowners who own their homes outright or have a considerable amount of equity in their house. State and local governments should educate citizens, particularly elderly and low-income homeowners, so they are better prepared to recognize and resist the solicitations of predatory lenders. States have the jurisdiction to enact legislation to protect homeowners' equity in subprime mortgage transactions, by regulating practices such as deceptive marketing, incomplete loan disclosure, and outright fraud.

iii. Reverse Mortgages: In a reverse mortgage transaction the client receives money from a lender in a lump sum paid at closing, as a line of credit, in monthly payments, or in a combination of any of these options. The client must repay the money at a certain interest rate in one lump sum at the sale of the property in question. Governments and developers can educate citizens about reverse mortgage programs and distinguish them from predatory lending scams. Public policy can be created to change intangible taxes to exclude reverse mortgages and ensure that proceeds from reverse mortgages do not affect the homeowners' eligibility for state means-tested programs nor be considered income for tax purposes.

c. Home maintenance, repair, and modification—internal and external—to seniors housing developments: The quality of a community's housing stock must be renewed periodically through maintenance, modification, and/or reconstruction. Many homes will require remodeling or retrofitting to accommodate changes in people's mobility. Programs should be available to provide service assistance and/or grants to maintain homes, redesign single-family homes to meet needs of senior occupants, or to make them barrier-free and handicapped accessible. The elderly may have more difficulty with the general upkeep of their home, as well as with paying for and accessing maintenance services. Very poor owners and renters, particularly those living alone are even more likely to occupy physically deficient dwellings. Problems can include faulty electricity, plumbing and kitchen inadequacies, leaks, heating and cooling deficiencies, and various upkeep concerns.

i. Maintenance contracts can be developed for homes much like property management contracts that are used for beach homes and other rental property

ii. Independent advisory/contractor broker services can be developed to help homeowners select remodelers, draw up contracts, and check for quality of work before making payments. Service could be a public entity or a private nonprofit that charges a small fee to participating contractors for each referral. Contractors would be screened and monitored through customer feedback.

iii. Weatherization programs can be required or encouraged for public utility companies to dedicate a portion of their earnings to a weatherization fund that would offer grants and deferred payment loans to elderly low- and moderate-income homeowners.

iv. Funding subsidies in the form of grants, no-interest loans, and low-interest loans could be issued

3. Transportation

a. Roads: There are many existing resources for adapting roads to better serve lifelong neighborhoods and communities. The following are the four most critical resources to consider:

i. Integrate the Federal Highway Administration's guidelines for older driver road design into state Department of Transportation standards

ii. Adopt and utilize Complete and Connected Streets standards

iii. Adopt and utilize the Institute of Transportation Engineers' Context Sensitive Approach Design Manual

iv. Adopt anti-cul-de-sac laws similar to those adopted by the State of Virginia

b. Public transportation: A community's transportation network must provide easy, safe, and efficient access for all persons to every neighborhood. Although public transportation is readily available in some areas, many seniors have difficulty using the system for a variety of reasons. In some neighborhoods, seniors may fear walking to bus stops and waiting for the bus in desolate or unsupervised areas.

   i. Reorient public transit to balance the goal of regional congestion mitigation with a goal for supporting local individual mobility

     (1) Integrate local circulator buses and trams with regional transit lines, increasing mobility within the community while making the regional lines more efficient by reducing the need for closely spaced local stops

   ii. Make transit more user-friendly

     (1) Locate transit stops and stations in well-supervised, easily accessible areas—preferably surrounded by civic and retail buildings

     (2) Educate older adults on how to take better advantage of the transit system

     (3) Consider individual mobility vouchers as an alternative to paratransit provision. Vouchers can be utilized to purchase rides from friends, relatives, neighbors, or taxicabs at a much lower cost per trip than public provision of that service

COLOR PLATES: LIFELONG REGIONS, NEIGHBORHOODS, BLOCKS, AND DEVELOPMENTS

Regional Development: Scenario Analysis

The most effective way to incorporate health impact considerations into planning the built environment is through regional development scenario analysis. At this scale, the choices made about where to concentrate development have significant implications for the health of the population, and the relationships documented in the outcomes tables can be directly correlated with population-wide health outcomes. The following scenario and outcome diagrams are from a Duany Plater-Zyberk & Company regional study of Hertfordshire, England.

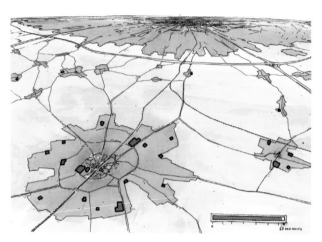

C.1. Scenario 1

Continue existing trends. This scenario continues the status quo, allowing new development to go wherever opportunity arises.

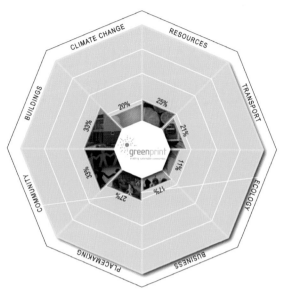

C.2. Scenario 1

Outcomes.

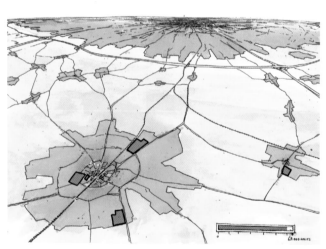

C.3. Scenario 2

Brownfield and greyfield sites. This scenario concentrates new development on industrial brownfield sites and commercial parking sites, or greyfields.

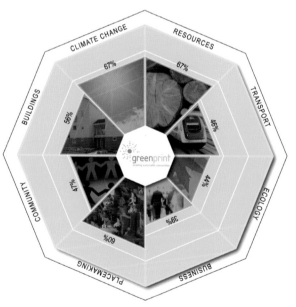

C.4. Scenario 2

Outcomes.

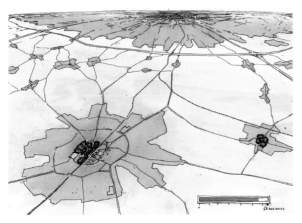

C.5. Scenario 3
Transit-oriented development. This scenario concentrates
new development within walking distance to existing rail and
bus stations.

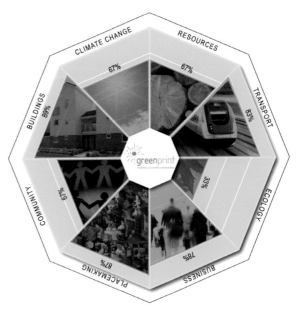

C.6. Scenario 3
Outcomes.

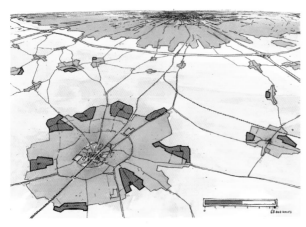

C.7. Scenario 4
Existing settlement extensions. This scenario concentrates new
development on the boundaries of existing communities.

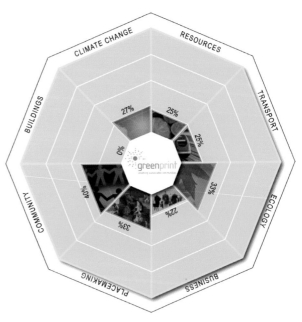

C.8. Scenario 4
Outcomes.

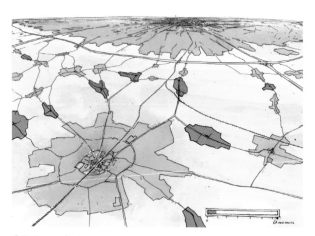

C.9. Scenario 5
Satellite villages. This scenario concentrates new development beyond the existing boundaries of developed communities.

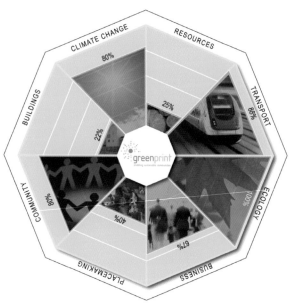

C.10. Scenario 5
Outcomes.

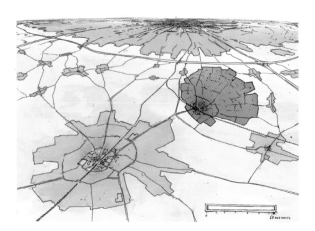

C.11. Scenario 6
Stand-alone cities. This scenario concentrates new development in an entirely new city built along the existing rail network.

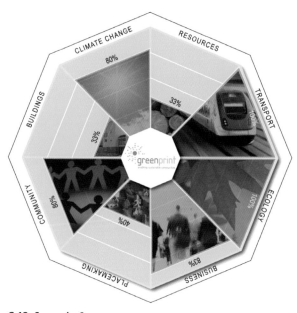

C.12. Scenario 6
Outcomes.

Neighborhood: Scenario Analysis

Jim Chapman and Lawrence Frank of Urban Design 4 Health, Inc. were commissioned by the Georgia Regional Transportation Authority in 2004 to evaluate the potential impacts of redevelopment plans produced as part of the Atlanta Regional Commission's Livable Centers Initiative. The following three scenarios were compared:

1) Base—the existing conditions

2) Livable centers initiative (LCI)—the projected conditions of the study area in v2030 after implementation of an LCI plan

3) Status quo—the projected build-out of the study area in 2030 if developed using current development trends and standards instead of following an LCI plan

Shown here are examples of scenario comparisons for the West End Historic District in Atlanta, Georgia, including:

Park proximity—the average walking distance from the center of each residential parcel to the closest park

Transit-oriented residential density—the average number of dwelling units per gross residential acre within a half mile of bus and rail transit stops.

This scenario analysis provides the base data needed to then estimate the relative health impacts of either maintaining the status quo or following the LCI plan. For more information, see the full report "Before and After Studies: Livable Centers Initiative Report," which can be downloaded from the SMARTRAQ website (www.act-trans.ubc.ca/smartraq/).

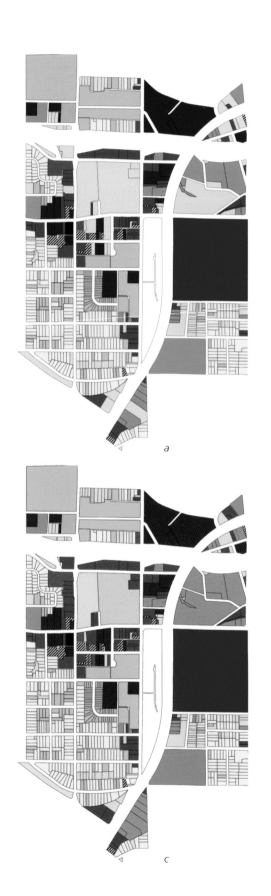

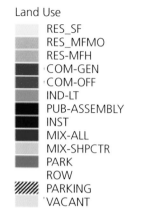

Land Use

- RES_SF
- RES_MFMO
- RES-MFH
- COM-GEN
- COM-OFF
- IND-LT
- PUB-ASSEMBLY
- INST
- MIX-ALL
- MIX-SHPCTR
- PARK
- ROW
- PARKING
- VACANT

C.13

Land use: (*a*) base; (*b*) LCI; (*c*) status quo.

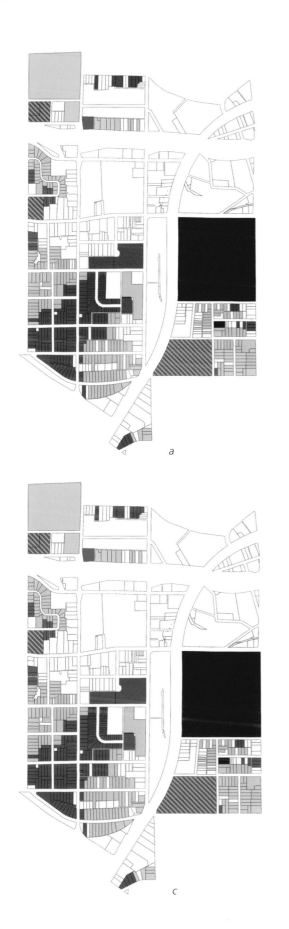

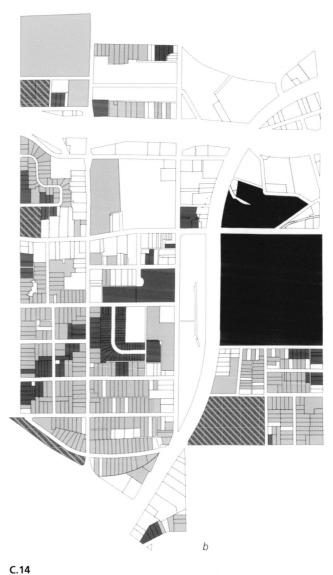

parcels
parks and school yards
park proximity
0-660 feet
660-1,320
1,320-1,980
1,980-2,640
2,640+

C.14
Park proximity: (a) base; (b) LCI;
(c) status quo.

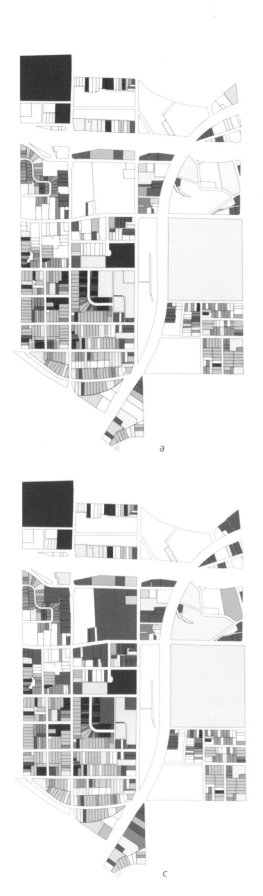

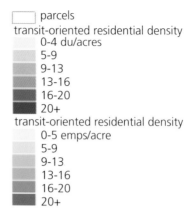

parcels
transit-oriented residential density
0-4 du/acres
5-9
9-13
13-16
16-20
20+
transit-oriented residential density
0-5 emps/acre
5-9
9-13
13-16
16-20
20+

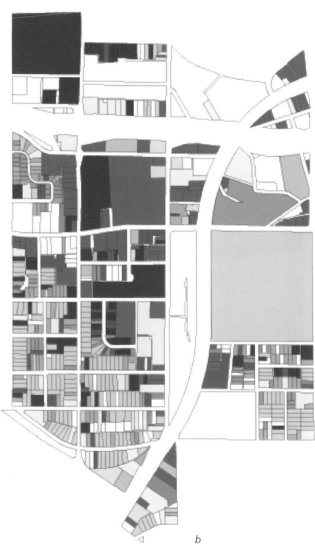

a

c

b

C.15

Transit proximity: (*a*) base; (*b*) LCI; (*c*) status quo.

Block Strategies
Block Subdivision
There are a number of approaches to block subdivisions that help support lifelong dwelling arrangements. Documented here are block subdivision strategies developed by Duany Plater-Zyberk & Company that support grow houses, family compounds, townhomes, apartment villas, and common open space.

Houses That Grow   Because single-family houses typically occupy only a portion of their lots, additional small buildings may be added. These back buildings and outbuildings can serve to house younger or older family members or to provide housing for care assistants. There are two types additions: One is called a "back building" when it is attached to the existing house, and the other is called an "outbuilding" when detached from the house. Both may be placed over parking.

Family Compounds   Clustered, compound dwellings used to be common in America and are currently being rediscovered for their symbiosis of intergenerational care and richness of social life. These clusters can be seen from the historic houses of Williamsburg, Virginia, to the Spanish haciendas throughout the southwest. A compound is a grouping of buildings within a single lot comprising a larger nuclear house with host of additional dwellings and specialized outbuildings. This building type supports both family-based assisted care and cohousing living arrangements.

Townhomes and Apartment Villas   Higher density building types may be seamlessly integrated into existing neighborhoods to overcome their age and socioeconomic monoculture. Townhouses can yield 16 to 20 units to the acre and apartment villas of 4 to 6 units can yield 24 to 30 units to the acre. Both building forms blend easily into a typical lower-density neighborhood.

Common Open Space   Common open spaces within blocks are particularly helpful in creating communal, supportive environments that encourage seniors to integrate into the communal life of the neighborhood. Community gardens, playgrounds, and school playing fields with cottages along their edges provide safe, secure, and well-supervised gathering areas. These areas are particularly supportive of intergenerational activities involving the very young and very old.

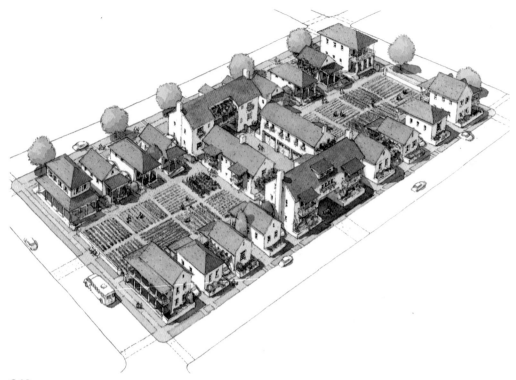

C.16
Initial condition.

C.17
Addition of side and back
buildings.

C.18
Initial condition.

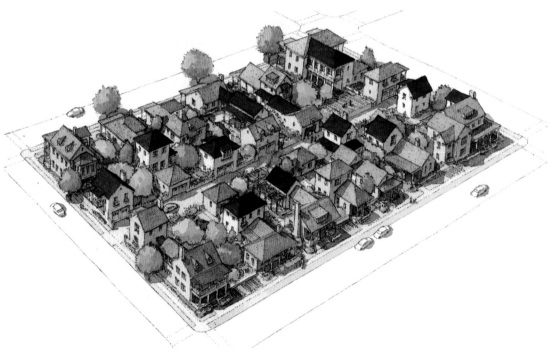

C.19
Growth of family
  compounds.

C.20
Block of mansion apartments.

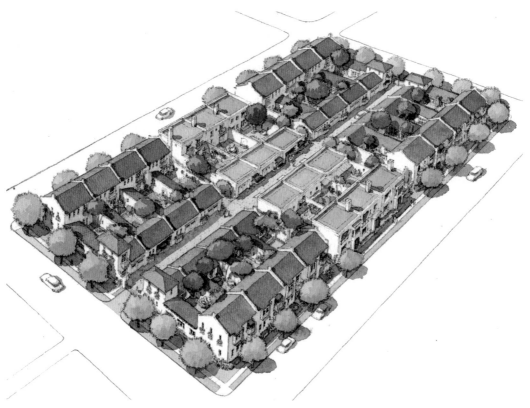

C.21
Block of townhouses.

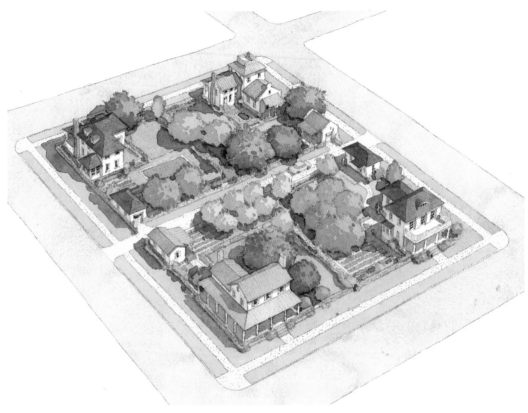

C.22
Block with internal park.

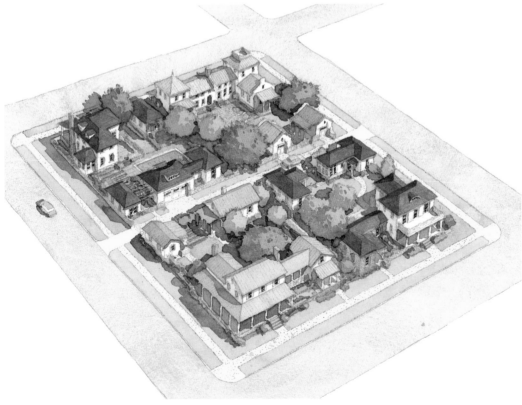

C.23
Block with community
gardens.

Developments: Community Integrated CCRCs

Barnes Square: A Community Integrated CCRC

Barnes Square, planned by Duany Plater-Zyberk & Company with Brown Craig and Turner, gathers all of the components of a typical CCRC and lays them out along a main street open to the public and connected to the surrounding community. The development borrows from and contributes to the main street and neighborhood. Independent living apartments (1) on the east side of the street mix with general market apartments, lofts, and townhomes; (2) on the west side of the street an entire block is wrapped by an assisted-living facility; (3) a small-house memory support facility; (4) a small house-care facility; (5) a rehab clinic; (6) independent living town-homes; and (7) a nursing home. A single kitchen serves all facilities as well as a café and restaurant that line the square at the entry. Also in the square is a home-based care hub that is integrated into the management and staffing of the care facilities. Through this hub, the supports provided within the facility are extended to the surrounding community, breaking down the distinction between independent-living units integrated into the block and general population housing within the larger community. The rehab clinic provides services to temporary and permanent residents of the nursing facility and serves as an outpatient service as well. Through these various facilities and services, the CCRC becomes a contributor to the larger neighborhood and a beneficiary of its community relationships.

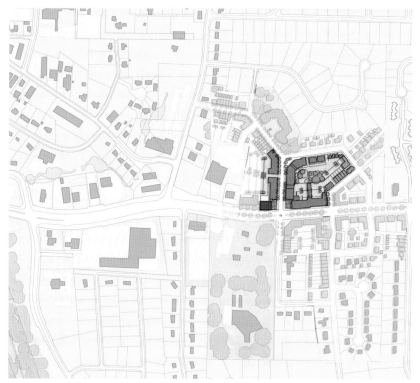

C.24
Barnes Square care facilities in context.

C.25
Detail of Barnes Square with care facilities labeled (see opposite page).

PART IV

URBAN AND RURAL CASE STUDIES

P ART IV IS A COLLECTION OF FOUR CASE STUDIES THAT EXAMPLE HOW THE ELEMENTS of a lifelong neighborhood can come together in wide range of urban-to-rural contexts. The first two case studies—Penn South co-op in New York City and Beacon Hill in Boston, Massachusetts—were chosen because they have become landmarks in the field of community-based care. Penn South has been a pioneering force in the Naturally Occurring Retirement Community (NORC) movement and Beacon Hill has pioneered the Villages approach to community-based concierge service provision. However, for the most part, both landmarks have been studied in the past only for the organizational and service structures they have developed, and little mention has been made of the actual urban environments in which these innovations were fostered. The tendency to solely export lessons learned about organizational and service structures undermines critical lessons that urban context provides in facilitating successful aging. The urban contexts of both communities are critical to the success of their programmatic offerings. Chapters 10 and 11 review some of the innovations alongside a discussion of their urban contexts. The case studies are not meant to establish direct causal relationships between the urban form and the innovations that have ensued, but rather to highlight the innovations as unique responses in uniquely local places. Both Penn South and Beacon Hill provide urban contexts as unique and interesting as the service programs for which they have become famous.

The second two case studies, Mableton, Georgia, and Indiana's Elder-Centric Villages, relate urban form and service provision in a more direct and causal manner than the first two studies. Both studies examine redevelopment initiatives that place emphasis on creating urban form that will facilitate healthier living across the entire lifecycle, while particularly focusing on older adult populations. In Chapter 12, Mableton's redevelopment planning is reviewed as an example of how aging issues can be garnered to forward a general upgrading of the urban environment. Additionally, Mableton provides an example for how seniors housing development can define a public realm that stimulates transformation of the surrounding community. The Continuing Care Retirement Community designed for Barnes Square in Mableton orients outward to the main street and contributes a sense of place and vitality to the surrounding community.

At the beginning of each case study is a short evaluation of the community in terms of context, connectivity, building diversity, completeness of care services, presence of wellness services, and quality of community building spaces. Rating

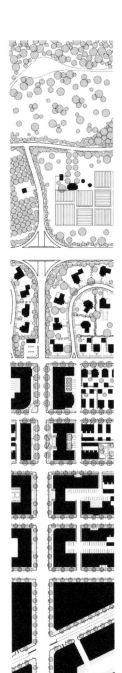

This transect image diagrams the changes in form from rural to urban in Washington, DC.

scores and a short discussion are given for each evaluation criterion. Ratings are the author's subjective "judging" scores and are not derived through empirical quantitative analysis. However, a Walk Score is also listed and that score was derived by entering an address at the website walkscore.com. Walk Score generates its walkability scores using an algorithm based on walking distances from an address to a diverse set of nearby amenities.

PENN SOUTH NORC CASE STUDY OF AGING A DENSE URBAN CORE

CHAPTER 10

Should this development, built by union and public funds and dedicated to working people, be destroyed as a middle-income cooperative, where only the well-to-do can live? The concept behind Penn South was that working people, small-business owners, teachers, and the like could walk to work. The people coming in will want amenities—carpeting in the hallways, microwave ovens, maybe even gold-plated urinals.[1]

—David Smith, Chairman of the Penn South board, imploring residents in 1986 to remain a nonprofit, affordable cooperative rather than disband and sell of units at market rate. He was successful in his campaign.

Lifelong Summary

An urban core community is surrounded by all the amenities and services that a big city has to offer. The Penn South co-op (fig. 10.1) has organized its critical mass of older adults to collectively negotiate with the city's economic, healthcare, and political systems and to maximize its lifelong community attribute ratings.

Context: 10

Penn South is a highly organized and close-knit community. It is a small city unto itself nestled within Chelsea in Manhattan and is connected by rail to a wide surrounding region. It has easy access to all that New York City offers while preserving a close neighborhood community within the development.

Connectivity and Transit: 10

Penn South is directly connected to Manhattan's bus, subway, and taxi networks and is located right next to Penn Station. It is one of the most transportation-networked places in the nation and possibly the world.

Dwellings and Retail: 8

The range of dwelling types within the development is limited to apartments, which range in size but were all built as economy units. Because the development is a limited equity co-op, it provides a level of affordability that is unavailable elsewhere

---

[1] D. W. Dunlap, "Remembering David Smith, Housing Advocate," *New York Times,* March 17, 2009.

Figure 10.1

Penn South is a high-rise co-op development in Manhattan in the heart of Chelsea.

in Chelsea. What it lacks in diversity of dwelling, it makes up for in diversity of nearby retail. Within a tenth of a mile there are a wide range of restaurants, stores, galleries, and other retail and entertainment venues.

Community Building Spaces: 9

Penn South has a good collection of common spaces within the development—particularly by New York City standards. The co-op structure gives a common sense of purpose and the common spaces are well supervised and well cared for. However, the Intergenerational Garden could definitely be expanded.

Health and Wellness: 10

There is a large athletic club just across the street from Penn South and many health and wellness programs are managed within the development, especially for older adults.

Walk Score:[2] **98**

Context

Penn South is a study in the interaction between 1960s communitarian approaches to both social organizing and planning. It is a 2,820-unit, 6,200-person cooperative housing development in the densely urban Chelsea area of Manhattan in New York City.

---

[2]http://www.walkscore.com/.

The spectacularly well-located cooperative provides moderate income, nonprofit, limited-equity housing in ten high-rise apartment buildings between Eighth and Ninth Avenues and Twenty-third and Twenty-eighth Streets—a short distance from Penn Station and Madison Square Garden. Penn South is surrounded by all the retail and services one would expect to find in a thriving portion of Manhattan.

Constructed by the International Ladies' Garment Workers' Union in 1962 (fig. 10.2), Penn South has always been a place where a sense of common purpose could flourish. Many of its original residents came from union labor and union organizing backgrounds. The ethos of co-op living, where property is jointly held and democratically managed, was easily adopted by the workers and organizers. Collective endeavor is a highly valued aspect of community life for these early founders. The co-op structure thrived at Penn South, not only providing a basis for collectively owning and managing property, but also for serving as a vehicle for collective entrepreneurial endeavors.

Perhaps one of the most striking collective ventures undertaken by Penn South was the construction of its own electrical generating facility. The entire collection of residential high-rises is off of the Con Edison power grid. Through a sophisticated collection of technologies, Penn South's plant has generating capacities fueled by both natural gas and crude oil. As the prices of natural gas and oil fluctuate, the plant switches between generators to utilize the cheaper of the two fuels. The generator's cooling systems are integrated into a massive boiler that recaptures waste heat and pumps it out to keep the residences warm in the winter. Through these innovative and energy-efficient techniques, the co-op has been able to cut its utility costs by a third since removing itself from the city's power grid—even after figuring in the amortized cost of constructing the facility.

Figure 10.2
Penn South was built in 1962 by one of the oldest unions, the International Ladies' Garment Workers' Union, shown here in 1909 in New York City.

Penn South has developed a long track record of innovative endeavors to support collective living since it opened in 1962. An emphasis on cooperative, egalitarian endeavor can be seen in the plan and architecture of the complex as well as the legal and management structures. It is not surprising that as Penn South's community began to reach its retirement years, the co-op board began to brainstorm on how the struggles inherent to aging could be met collectively.

Innovations in Health and Wellness Programming: Penn South Discovers the NORC Concept

By 1985, more than 75 percent of Penn South's population was over the age of 60, and the co-op board began to investigate possible ventures that would help support the senior residents. As part of these investigations, the board came across the research of Michael Hunt and Gail Gunther-Hunt in which they coined the term "NORC," or Naturally Occurring Retirement Community.

NORCs are buildings, apartment complexes, or neighborhoods not originally planned for older people, wherein over time, the majority of residents have become elderly. Michael Hunt and Gail Gunther-Hunt recognized in a 1985 study that NORCs differ from the stereotypical retirement community, and "yet are the most common form of retirement community in the USA." An AARP study conducted in 1989 found that 27 percent of all older Americans lived in NORCs, compared to 5 percent in planned senior housing or retirement communities. The study concluded that "naturally occurring retirement communities are the [nation's] most dominant and overlooked form of senior housing."

Penn South co-op found something in the Hunts' work that resonated with its sense of collective purpose. The NORC concept provided a model for thinking of their aging population as a specific community based in a place. According to the Hunts' study, Penn South did not need to transform itself to become some form of senior housing complex, rather they were already a senior housing complex—a NORC—and simply needed to be recognized as one. Once that determination had been made by a group of long-time union organizers and political activists, it would not be long before Penn South would be officially recognized as a NORC, and NORCs would begin to shed their distinction as the nation's most overlooked form of senior housing.

Upon organizing itself as a NORC, the co-op board set up a special committee charged with the responsibility of organizing and finding funds for a comprehensive service program, the Penn South Program for Seniors (PSPS). This committee sought to carry out two tasks: find independent sources of funds to implement a comprehensive program of social work, nursing, recreation, mental health, education, and cultural enrichment; and enlist social and health agencies already established in the community to provide programs and services on-site. The primary charge of the PSPS committee was to forestall nursing home placement and encourage the elderly to remain in their own homes among family, friends, and caring neighbors.

After interviewing several service providers, PSPS selected three primary agencies to provide the programs and services to the NORC: Selfhelp Community Services, Inc.; Jewish Home & Hospital for the Aged, Inc.; and The Educational Alliance, Inc. UJA-Federation of New York, a major private philanthropic organization, helped bring this together with much enthusiasm and added its own funds to assist the program. Many social and health agencies in the community also agreed to bring their services to the co-op.

Within a few years of operation, PSPS had achieved a strong level of organizational maturity, acceptance within the co-op community, and recognition within the field. A new nonprofit corporation, Penn South Social Services, Inc. (PSSS), was organized to assume the fiscal responsibility for and policy determination over PSPS. PSSS enabled the NORC to formally contract with social and health agencies and receive direct government and foundation grants. PSPS was now mobilized, sheltered within its own 501(c)(3) umbrella organization, and gaining momentum. Soon the acronyms NORC and N-SSP (NORC Supportive Service Program) would both be written into state legislation.

PSPS realized early on that they had many valuable political commodities to work with. The difficulties associated with aging are universally experienced and thus serve as a firm foundation for a widespread coalition. In addition, seniors typically devote more time to keeping abreast of politics and are more likely to vote than the general population. In 1994, after a campaign spearheaded by PSPS, New York State passed legislation providing support for NORC Supportive Service Programs. This N-SSP legislation established a channel to fund housing and social services in a coordinated manner. The program sought to prevent costly housing problems common to senior residents and to strengthen intergenerational ties in the housing complex. It was endorsed by both political parties in the legislature and was approved by two governors of opposing political parties. As the result of the program's early successes, New York City also took an interest in NORC programs (and their highly organized blocks of voting constituents) and created its own local N-SSP legislation to supplement the state program.

Within a decade, fourteen N-SSPs were operating in New York State under the N-SSP legislation and funding. The programs were quickly found to save public dollars by requiring each housing entity that requests state funds to match the grant with their own funds, as well as philanthropic dollars. Each N-SSP was designed as a collaborative venture between New York State, a housing company, and social service and health agencies. The N-SSPs often received collateral benefits by providing attractive sites for private medical providers, home-care agencies, and others to offer services. These private providers came to take advantage of the efficient service delivery produced by concentrated populations of seniors. As a result of partnerships with private providers, New York State dollars have successfully leveraged almost four times as many dollars in private investment—above and beyond the required philanthropic match. According to the New York State legislature, N-SSPs saved New York State an estimated $11 million over three years by forestalling 460 hospital stays and 317 nursing home placements.

The inspiration of Penn South's sense of collective purpose and entrepreneurship is easy to recognize in the state legislation. The New York State–funded programs are all constructed as private/public partnerships, reflecting the belief that each N-SSP needs to have an entrepreneurial stake in its own program. Self-ownership and self-determination have been important parts of PSPS's success. Penn South residents feel that they have earned the help that they receive, and, therefore, the usual barriers to accepting social services among many moderate-income people do not exist. This notion of ownership and entitlement has been encapsulated within the very fabric of the entire N-SSP and has become the unwritten policy underpinning the program. The residents do not think of their program as a form of charity—rather they will relay with great pride the multiple ways in which their entrepreneurship has both saved tax dollars and contributed to the community.

Connectivity and Access

It is easy to locate Penn South on a map. When the multi-block site was cleared in 1960, Twenty-fourth and Twenty-eighth Streets were both bent to form curves across the site. These two curves stand out on a map—unique inflections in the otherwise rigidly rectilinear grid of Chelsea (fig. 10.3). Also unusual within the Chelsea urban fabric are the high-rise condo buildings that orient to open space

Figure 10.3

Right in the middle of Manhattan's street grid and transit systems, and just a few blocks from Penn Station, Penn South is one of the most street- and transit-connected places on earth.

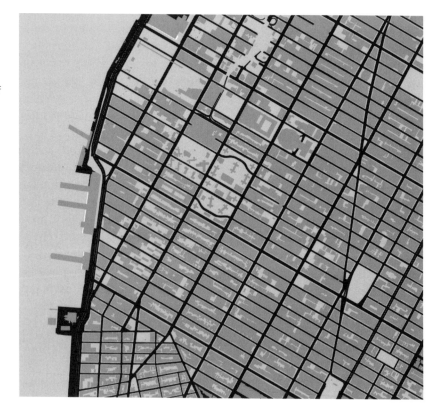

in the middle of the block rather than to the space of the street. Both the curved streets and internally oriented buildings are characteristic of the modernist "mega block" housing developments favored in the 1950s and 1960s for inner-city redevelopment. These large-scale residential projects were intended to create enclaves within the larger fabric of the city, pulled back from the street grid in both urban and architectural gestures. In its best examples, the mega-block approach was able to provide access to the services, vitality, and energy of the surrounding city, yet it provided a distinct and tranquil setting to help foster stronger community bonds. In its worst examples, the mega-block approach did just the opposite: It became disconnected and isolated from the rest of the city and was dehumanizing and hostile to the formation of community. The 1954 Pruitt-Igoe housing project in St. Louis, Missouri, is the most infamous of the failed mega-block projects; it consolidated more than thirty city blocks into a separate island within the city (fig. 10.4).

While Penn South has mega-block characteristics, it is not a pure mega-block type. While its planners succeeded in bending Twenty-fourth and Twenty-eighth Streets, they only managed to entirely disconnect Twenty-seventh Street from the grid. The flow and energy of the surrounding city is thus able to continue through the development. It is also much smaller than a fully realized mega block like Pruitt-Igoe, and the smaller scale provides a degree of intimacy instead of dehumanization. The compromise reached between the Penn South planners and the insistent continuity of the NYC grid produced an environment that has proven to be very good for lifelong residency.

Transit access at Penn South is excellent, even by New York City standards. Immediately in front at Twenty-third Street and Eighth Avenue is a subway stop, buses run uptown along Eighth Avenue, downtown along Ninth Avenue, and crosstown along Twenty-third Street. Just a few blocks immediately to the north, Penn Station offers both regional and national transit options.

Figure 10.4
Like the ill-fated Pruitt-Igoe housing project in St. Louis, Penn South is a 1960s-style mega-block redevelopment. However, Pruitt-Igoe was set apart from the surrounding city, whereas Penn South is nestled within it.

Dwellings and Retail

The Chelsea neighborhood is a dense mixed-use environment typical of Manhattan. Over the past two decades Chelsea has become known as a cultural center with hundreds of art galleries concentrated between Tenth and Eleventh Avenues and Nineteenth and Twenty-seventh Streets. The blocks that comprise Penn South support diverse buildings including entertainment, grocery, school, church, and medical office facilities. These retail and service uses ensure that the blocks contribute to the commerce and vitality of the surrounding city and provide residents ready access to daily needs. Unlike much of Chelsea, however, the Penn South blocks segregate use by building. Commercial buildings pull up close to the street and are only one-story tall. Residential buildings are set back, with landscaped frontages and fences that separate the ground floor from the sidewalk. The co-op developed several on-site commercial properties and an 800-car parking facility. These business ventures help support the co-op's $22 million annual operating budget and keep the cost of housing low for its residents.

From its inception, Penn South has operated as an affordable housing, limited-equity cooperative: Each member has an equity investment in the complex and a vote in its governance structure. Several forms of public subsidy have been invested in the co-op, the largest of which is a renewable, twenty-five-year tax abatement. This affordable cooperative financing and governance structure makes the development uniquely affordable in the high-rent Chelsea neighborhood. On the one hand, by providing affordable housing in this area, Penn South diversifies the neighborhood. On the other hand, it concentrates the affordable units all within one area and creates a homogenous condition within the complex.

The primary generating element of the co-op's urban plan is the cruciform plan of the buildings (fig. 10.5). A single cruciform building footprint is replicated fifteen times: five times as a single footprint and five times joined to form double cruciform buildings (fig. 10.6). The cruciform plan was a core element of an urban reform agenda that had roots in early twentieth-century European social housing movements. Modernist architects such as Le Corbusier and Mies van der Rohe viewed the traditional city plan as an environmentally and socially unhealthy pattern. The traditional urban structure of blocks lined with continuous buildings surrounding interior courts was too closed to allow the flow of fresh air and sunlight through the buildings and city as a whole. Additionally, the traditional division of grand public street faces and informal private interior faces of buildings was believed to have reinforced inequitable social hierarchies: Aristocracy typically claimed building spaces that faced the street, and servant/proletariat classes were relegated to the building spaces that faced the interior court. The cruciform plan form was used by modernists of this era to break up these urban patterns of the traditional city. Because the cruciform does not create a front and back of the building, and does not privilege any one public face, it was considered more egalitarian in its distribution of space. The use of the cruciform plan in Penn South follows this modernist, egalitarian, nonhierarchical approach to space distribution along facades that avoid front/back distinctions.

In terms of actual building and unit types, Penn South does not provide much diversity. Units range from one to three bedrooms in a small collection of types, each of which is repeated without much adjustment throughout the entire complex.

Figure 10.5
Penn South's towers are all built on the single and double cruciform footprints shown here.

Figure 10.6
The Penn South
Campus.

As stated earlier, an emphasis on egalitarian distribution of space guided the development of the co-op, and this translated into a mechanical replication of a few unit types many times across the entire 2,820-unit complex. More variety of building and unit type would have created greater variation in the character and feel of public and private spaces alike. It was common for social housing advocates of that era to mistake sameness of unit and building type with egalitarianism. A more diverse approach would have been to allow spaces to take on a variety of characteristics (public/private, open/closed, dark/well lighted, etc.) so that a wide variety of programs and personality types could be accommodated in appropriate, unique settings.

Health and Wellness

As a very dense urban core, the Chelsea neighborhood provides easy access to nearly every form of health and wellness service with just a short walk or transit ride (fig. 10.7). The New York Sports Club on Eighth Avenue, immediately across from Penn South, is a particularly notable facility with a full range of pool, fitness, group exercise, and racquet court spaces.

However, the dense urban core also creates many entrepreneurial opportunities to invert the relationship and utilize a concentration of customers to bring services to residents rather than residents to services. This is a significant advantage to aging in an urban core: Density supplies the critical mass necessary to generate robust home-based and neighborhood-based care systems.

Penn South Program for Seniors utilized its critical mass of older adults to bring providers to their co-op. Beth Israel Hospital and St. Vincent's Hospital both opened offices at Penn South as they realized that the co-op supplied many new potential patients. In addition to providing an opportunity for improved and coordinated care, the offices provided free services in exchange for assistance in marketing to residents. Penn South worked with St. Vincent's psychiatry program to have their fellows rotate through the co-op as part of a geropsychiatry training program. It gave the psychiatrists much-needed experience in the field, while providing free care to Penn South seniors. Nursing service was the most expensive staff line of the budget for Penn South co-op. The co-op was able to form a partnership with the Visiting Nurse Service of New York, which saw an opportunity to find reimbursable cases for

Figure 10.7
Penn South has a host of health and wellness services within the development and in the surrounding community.

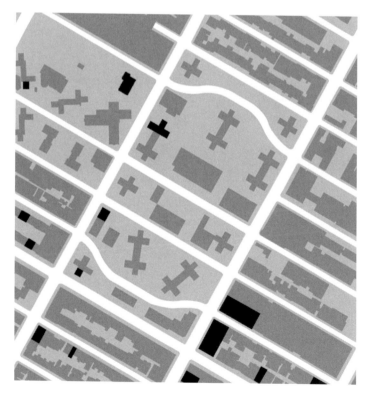

the agency, while providing free nursing care to co-op residents. As a result of the Visiting Nurse Service and the hospital offices and programs on-site, Penn South now receives free screenings, lectures, flu shots, and so on for its senior residents.[3] The dense urban core thus provides both easy access to nearby health and wellness facilities, and also provides a critical mass of customers that can be organized to collectively negotiate with providers for on-site service provision.

Community Building Spaces

As stated previously, the cruciform plan was believed by European social housing advocates to be socially and environmentally healthier than traditional urban building types. Because the cruciform did not create a continuous building mass-perimeter of the block, it was thought to be healthier in allowing light and breezes to flow through the block interior. The paved street and sidewalk surfaces were deemphasized as public gathering spots, and, instead, landscaped block interiors were emphasized as the primary public spaces for social interaction and recreation. These verdant, park-like interior block spaces were believed to be healthier and more conducive to social interaction than the street.

Penn South's plan is based on this interior public space approach (figs. 10.8, 10.9). Meticulously maintained greens work through the complex creating a park-like

Figure 10.8
The parks surrounding Penn South are smaller neighborhood parks. Central Park is thirty-five blocks to the north, and the new Highline conversion of Chelsea's elevated rail to a linear park is located nearby.

---

[3] N. Yalowitz, and K. Bassuk, "An Intergenerational Community With Supportive Services: The NORC Model at Penn South Program For Seniors," Paper presented at the American Society on Aging, San Francisco, March 1998.

Figure 10.9
Jeff Dullea Intergenerational
Garden is shown in black.

setting. The cruciform's emphasis on egalitarian distribution of space is echoed in the fact that a small number of unit types are replicated on all twenty-one floors in each of the ten buildings. The same egalitarian emphasis can be seen in the one voter per household legal structure of the co-op: A percentage of equity in the complex is allocated to each of the households based on the size of their unit, but voting rights are provided one per unit, regardless of unit size. Sixty-five percent of the Penn South property is open space and includes gardens, paths, play spaces for children, and sitting areas for adults.

Jeff Dullea Intergenerational Garden

Penn South proactively encourages and plans for positive interactions between its older and younger residents. The co-op grounds have been intentionally arranged to make it possible for older residents to have their walking and sitting spaces close to playgrounds and outdoor play spaces for children of all ages. Interior and exterior spaces, where children's play is readily visible to seniors, are provided throughout the development. One area of the grounds was fenced off and designated the Jeff Dullea Intergenerational Garden (fig. 10.10). Beds were laid and assigned to teams of young and old, with one 8-year-old to every 80-year-old as the goal for generational mixing. Demand for beds has been substantial and there are multiyear waiting lists for them. In an effort to accommodate more resident participants, many of the beds were subdivided, and for some of the older participants who did not need as much produce and did not want the pressure of keeping up with a whole bed, the beds were subdivided yet again. Residents look out for each other's gardens and work collectively, but a committee maintains oversight of the garden and if a resident is not utilizing or adequately maintaining his bed, the committee will ask him to turn it over to the next resident on the waiting list. This garden has become

Figure 10.10
Jeff Dullea Intergenerational
Garden is a verdant and well-
maintained community space
that stresses intergenerational
activities.

a leading intergenerational activity for the residents and has been so well received
that it is often used for weddings and other special celebrations. Originally the garden was laid out in "plots" but many seniors who had had to make arrangements for
grave plots preferred the term "beds"; the change was a source of amusement for the
elderly residents of the development. There are many other planned shared experiences as well: A quilting group that involves seniors and children meets regularly;
a program arranges for senior residents to volunteer time reading to children in a
local public school; and another volunteer group involves seniors who encourage
and support teenagers to form their own groups within the co-op structure.[4]

[4]Ibid.

BEACON HILL CASE STUDY OF AGING AND TOWN CENTERS

For wee must consider that wee shall be as a citty upon a hill. The eies of all people are uppon us. Soe that if wee shall deale falsely with our God in this worke wee haue undertaken, and soe cause him to with drawe his present help from us, wee shall be made a story and a by-word through the world.[1]

—From John Winthrop's 1630 sermon "A Modell of Christian Charity" given aboard the ship Arbella in the Atlantic Ocean on the way to settle the Massachusetts Bay colony.

Lifelong Summary

Context: 10
An upscale historic community positioned to provide immediate access to all that downtown Boston has to offer while retaining a close, intimate neighborhood environment.

Connectivity and Access: 7
Excellent street and transit networks. Inaccessibility of streetscape and buildings would be a substantial challenge for any frail or impaired person.

Dwellings and Retail: 8
Excellent, except for the lack of accessible homes.

Health and Wellness: 10
Best-in-class hospital and complete range of neighborhood-based continuing care services.

Community Building Spaces: 8
Very few exterior community spaces for unplanned encounters. Community building relies heavily on structured events and relationships.

Walk Score: 97

---

[1]John Winthrop, "A Modell of Christian Charity," in *Collections of the Massachusetts Historical Society* (Boston, 1838), 3rd series, 7:31–48.

Context

Beacon Hill is the kind of urban place residents would fight to remain in as they grow old (fig. 11.1). A unique mixture of enclave and open network, it has both a distinct identity as a separate community while also integrating with and extending to the surrounding city of Boston (fig. 11.2). This moderated relationship, both expansive and contained, provides an ideal setting for fostering a strong sense of place and collective identity among residents.

Figure 11.1
Beacon Hill is a distinct and cozy neighborhood with access to all the cultural, civic, and retail opportunities that Boston has to offer.

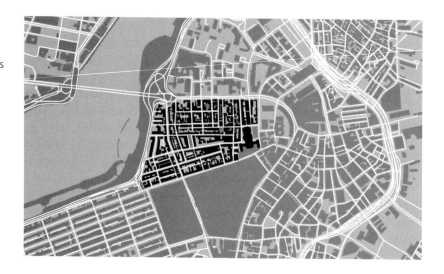

Figure 11.2
The Bullfinch-designed state capital building presides over Beacon Hill.

Beacon Hill is situated in a deeply historical context, defined by some of the most dramatic and storied boundaries ever to demarcate an American neighborhood. After flowing eighty miles through twenty-two cities, the Charles River takes one last bend at the western edge of Beacon Hill before emptying a short distance beyond into the Atlantic Ocean. Puritan settlers formed the southern boundary of the neighborhood in 1634 with the creation of the fifty-acre Boston Common. Many pivotal events in the nation's history have occurred in Boston Common, from witch hangings to protests and riots. Charles Bulfinch's Palladian-inspired Massachusetts State house has presided grandly over the eastern edge of the neighborhood since 1798. It was in the state house in 1961 that John F. Kennedy rekindled John Winthrop's City on a Hill sermon as the theme for his new presidential administration. The northern edge of the neighborhood is anchored by Harvard's Massachusetts General Hospital. Founded in 1811, it is the third-oldest hospital in the United States and is consistently ranked as one of the nation's best. The Beacon Hill neighborhood was originally founded in 1634 as an intentional community of Puritan settlers. It was the original seat of the American exceptionalism worldview: the Puritan belief that they had been chosen by God to lead the nations of the world.

Nestled within this auspicious government, health, recreation, and natural context, the neighborhood itself is as idyllic as it is historic. A little less than a half-mile long and a quarter-mile wide, the ninety acres that make up the neighborhood form a single pedestrian shed that bundles natural environments of park and river to the south and east, with the dense urban core to the north and east. The streets are tight and buildings are pulled close to narrow sidewalks. The architecture and streetscape detailing is a comprehensive catalog of every imaginable way stone and brick masonry can be negotiated into hilly terrain. Mature deciduous trees line the streets and yet miraculously the sidewalks are reasonably flat, rather than broken up by tree roots. With such an ideal setting, it is no surprise that residents fight to remain in the community as they grow old.

Innovations in Health and Wellness Programming

Beacon Hill in Boston, Massachusetts, has become widely known as the original "Village" model of older adult community-based support. A close cousin to the Naturally Occurring Retirement Community pioneered by Penn South, the Village model is a grassroots, entrepreneurial endeavor. Founded in 2001 by a small group of older residents, the Village model is a cooperative structure for organizing a wide variety of services useful to older adults such as transportation, home care, house maintenance, and medical and care-management services. Over a single decade, the Beacon Hill Village has proliferated, attracting hundreds of resident members who are better able to age in their own homes rather than move to institutional care settings.

A Village is initiated as an organizing effort to establish a community-based non-profit organization. Residents over 50 years old within the Village community are invited to become members of the nonprofit by paying an annual fee ($500 to

$1,000, typically). The nonprofit organization serves as concierge for its members providing on-demand assistance with a wide range of daily functions including acquiring tickets to an evening show or arranging home care, house maintenance, medical care, or care-management services. By serving as a single clearinghouse for general assistance, the concierge organization has a view into the unique needs of that specific community and can tailor services and programs to suit. Because these programs are developed organically over time in response to local needs, they incorporate qualities of place: the cultural, environmental, social, and economic nuances of the community.

While the concierge assistance is a membership benefit, the services themselves are provided on a fee basis by independent providers, usually at a reduced rate negotiated for Village members. Village staff screen service providers and organize the collective purchasing power of its members to get quality service with member discounts. In addition to concierge services, Villages typically organize a number of social networks and events including newsletters, outings and excursions, parties, and affinity groups focused on shared interests.

All aspects of the Villages model are managed cooperatively, blending staff and contractor services with volunteer work from the members themselves. The volunteer component helps keep costs down and members engaged with each other.[2]

Connectivity and Access

Beacon Hill manages to tap into to the vibrancy and excitement of downtown Boston while also providing an intimate neighborhood setting removed from the immediate hustle and bustle. Connection to the surrounding city is modulated to provide balance of networked and cloistered spaces (fig. 11.3).

Figure 11.3 Beacon Hill is a well-connected enclave. Its unique street grid provides ample connection to the surrounding city and region, but provides little access for through traffic.

---

[2]For more information on the Villages Network see http://www.vtvnetwork.org/.

The neighborhood fabric has a wood-like grain. Streets running east to west are long and provide open vistas out across the river below. Most streets running north to south terminate after less than three blocks, capping the space of the street and creating a sense of interiority. Joy Street, which runs north to south uninterrupted across the entire neighborhood, does not allow through traffic. Joy Street reverses its one-way direction mid-neighborhood to allow only outbound traffic at either end. The play between openness and extension in the outbound direction and close interiority in the inbound creates both a variety of spatial experiences for the pedestrian and serves to regulate the flow of traffic. The "grain" of the internal network runs against pass through traffic and with local circulation. The blocks are very small for the most part, although they elongate in the east to west direction due to topography.

It is easy to access the region and world from Beacon Hill. South Boston train station is less than a mile away where a wide range of national and regional train lines can be accessed. Logan International Airport is fifteen minutes to the north by car or by train. This proximity to regional, national, and international travel opportunities is particularly ideal for older executives who may choose second careers as consultants and who need to travel frequently.

Beacon Hill is well supplied with transit. With ADA-compliant subway stops at its northwest and southeast corners, both red line and green line routes can be easily reached. Subway is the primary form of transit within the city, but two bus lines also run along the southern edge of the neighborhood.

Dwellings and Retail

Although Beacon Hill has more than 120 businesses scattered throughout the neighborhood, the western base of the hill on Charles Street serves as a main street and retail center (fig. 11.4). Charles Street is the one place where through traffic is

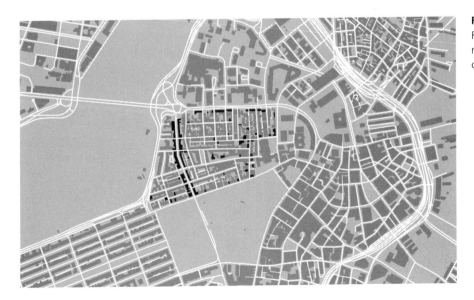

Figure 11.4
Retail is scattered throughout the neighborhood but is concentrated on Charles Street.

allowed to penetrate the core of the neighborhood, even if it is only in one direction. The three lanes of through traffic provide a sufficient customer base to develop a robust retail district. Regional retail along Charles Street is oriented toward boutiques, including thirteen apparel shops and twelve art and antique galleries. Local amenities are scattered throughout the neighborhood and include four beauty shops, two computer service shops, two dry cleaners, eleven grocery and liquor stores, and an impressive four different hardware stores. Most daily needs can be met in the neighborhood with a surprising variety of choices (figs. 11.5, 11.6).

Figure 11.5
The historic storefronts along Charles Street attract many high-end boutique businesses.

Chris Ritter

Figure 11.6
Beacon Capitol Market is in the center of the neighborhood and mixes convenience groceries with social gatherings.

Chris Ritter

While there is much about the urban form of Beacon Hill that fosters a desire to stay-in-place as one grows old, the built environment of the neighborhood also presents several accessibility barriers. Housing is expensive and would present financial challenges for those on limited or fixed incomes. The historic building types that make up the neighborhood provide few zero-step entries or one-floor living opportunities. Many of the buildings predate indoor plumbing, and small bathrooms have been squeezed into spaces already tight by modern standards. Outside, many of the sidewalks are short of 32 inches clear width, and the historic brick, river stone, and cobblestone paving presents challenges for anyone at risk for falls. As the name implies, Beacon Hill is a hill, and the grade is steep enough to make walking or wheeling difficult for frail or impaired persons. Large trees regularly choke the clear width of the sidewalk down to less than 20 inches. Parking is tight and mostly on the street, making it difficult to predictably find spaces close by and unlikely that any would have accessibility features. The climate is known for extremes, both hot and cold, and weather intensifies the accessibility challenges of the streetscape (fig. 11.7).

Figure 11.7
This street is typical of Beacon Hill. Steep slopes, narrow sidewalks, stoops, and river stone gullies all present enormous challenges to an unsteady or wheelchair-bound person. Long, cold winters and hot summers exacerbate these difficulties.

Chris Ritter

Health and Wellness

As an aging-in-place alternative environment to institutional care, Beacon Hill could not be better endowed with modern medical facilities (fig. 11.8). The proximity to Massachusetts General Hospital (MGH, or Mass General), one of the nations highest-ranked medical facilities, is a case study in itself. The proximity is ideal—it is close enough to walk, but far enough to not hear ambulances and medivac helicopters, or experience the general deadening effect of a massive, internally oriented, high-traffic regional hospital. In addition, Mass General is not your typical hospital. As Harvard's teaching facility, Mass General offers a wide array of outpatient services including optometry, dental care, and other nonemergency health-maintenance services (fig. 11.9). Routine and emergency services alike are staffed by the best and brightest of Harvard Medical School.

With a best-in-class acute and outpatient care institution a stone's throw away, the Beacon Hill Village completes the range of health and wellness services with an array of programs nearly as complete as a Continuing Care Retirement Community. Cooperative purchasing results in discounts for Villages members. Grants and private contributions have provided an endowment that keeps membership dues low and offsets costs for low-income members. Services offered or arranged by the Village include the following:[3]

Wellness:

Exercise classes

Discounts at local health and fitness clubs

Personal trainers

Dieticians

Massage

Expert-led wellness seminars

Figure 11.8

Beacon Hill could not be in a better spot for medical care. Massachusetts General Hospital is near enough to be accessed easily and quickly, but it is far enough as not to impinge on the quiet and intimate neighborhood setting.

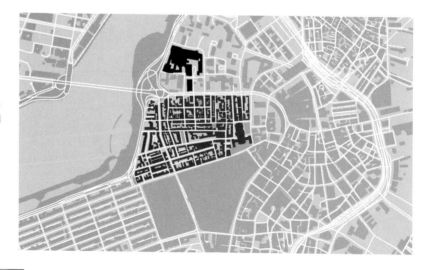

[3]From the Beacon Hill Village website: http://www.beaconhillvillage.org/.

Chris Ritter

Figure 11.9
Massachusetts General Hospital is a typical institutional medical campus. It is good to have nearby, but it is not compatible with the neighborhood form.

Home Maintenance:

    Home repairs and adaptation

    Computer assistance

    Gardening and plant care

    Pet care

Household Assistance:

    Chores such as cleaning, cooking, and organizing

    Errands such as grocery shopping

    Transportation services

    Home office, bill-paying, and financial organizing assistance

    Companionship

    Memory-loss home technologies

    Health insurance and Medicare assistance

Medical Support:

    Medication reminders

    Home care aides/home health aides

    Speech-language pathologists

    Registered nurses and licensed practical nurses

    MGH Executive Registry, which allows access to international healthcare

Geriatric care management

Occupational therapists

Physical therapists

Social workers

Hospice services

Community Building Spaces

The entire Beacon Hill neighborhood is a well-crafted community building space. The neighborhood boundaries are clearly defined: demarcated by a river, park, government center, and arterial (fig. 11.10). These clear boundaries help establish a distinct identity for the community. Additionally, several factors lend the neighborhood an unusually close character. The streets narrow significantly from those of the surrounding city, making the environment comparatively intimate. Block sizes are also smaller in the neighborhood than in the surrounding city, reinforcing the close feel of the environment. The grade slopes up the hill, creating another noticeable shift from the surrounding flat land. All these characteristics help shape Beacon Hill as a distinctly intimate place and encourage community bonds.

There is a lack of exterior community space within Beacon Hill. In the middle of the neighborhood is Louisburg Square (fig. 11.11), which, oddly, has never functioned as a social space. It is a private, ornamental green encased by a wrought iron fence with entry provided mostly for maintenance. The function of the square has always been to emphasize the status of the surrounding grand townhomes, which today range in value from $6 million to $26 million. There are small, hardscape vest-pocket parks at Myrtle and Philip Streets, and these are programmed primarily for children's use.

Figure 11.10
Beacon Hill is surrounded by regional park spaces, but it has relatively few parks and greens that are internal to the neighborhood. There are more interior than exterior community spaces.

Chris Ritter

Figure 11.11
Louisburg Square is primarily an ornamental green, rather than a functional community space.

The paucity of parks and the uninhabitable square within such a dense neighborhood can be explained in part by the tremendous regional park spaces that bound the neighborhood and by a culture that collects mostly in interior spaces. Along Beacon Hill's western edge, Esplanade Park fronts the river and is home to a network of foot and bike trails, as well as Community Boating, Inc., the nation's longest-running community sailing program. To the south is the world famous, 50-acre Boston Common, which supports organized activities ranging from concerts to protests to softball games. However, neither of these regional park spaces fosters the regular informal and unplanned encounters among neighbors in the way that neighborhood greens and squares do. Interior "third place" spaces in the neighborhood pick up much of the role of informal community building typically provided by greens and squares. There are nineteen bars and restaurants scattered throughout the neighborhood, including the pub that was the setting of the 1980s television series "Cheers."

Some of the deficiency in exterior community space may be explained by the culture of the neighborhood: It is a formal community that places much greater emphasis on civic engagement than chance encounters and gatherings as a basis for socializing. For a small neighborhood, Beacon Hill has an impressive list of formal neighborhood associations. In addition to the Village cooperative that supports older adult residents, there are associations for neighborhood business, civics, dog owners, young professionals, gardeners, friends of the parks, hikers, and seminargoers. In total, Beacon Hill is home to one public library, five schools, one university, four museums, four places of worship, twenty community-based nonprofit organizations, and the state capitol building. There is also a weekly neighborhood newspaper. This is an impressive civic inventory for a 90-acre neighborhood, so it is reasonable to conclude that what it lacks in exterior community spaces, it makes up for in interior gathering spots and civic institutions.

Volunteerism is also highly valued in Beacon Hill both as a civic contribution and as a form of social engagement. The Village structures volunteer opportunities that include at-home visits, errands and assistance for other members, as well as community service at the Commonwealth Children's Center, Beacon Hill Nursery School, MIT AgeLab, Generations Incorporated, and pediatric division of Mass General. The Village structures a wide array of social events for older adults including a luncheon club that tours local restaurants, special social events, private tours to museums and art shows, evening conversations with Boston notables, educational seminars, travel clubs, film groups, and singles occasions.

A nice example of how the neighborhood's strong sense of community can be mobilized to support older adults is exampled by a scene described in a 2006 *New York Times* article on aging at home in Beacon Hill:

> Mr. Sears said everybody at Beacon Hill Village was concerned about him being alone. It helps that the "cane brigade," as some of the women call themselves, escort him to "little functions," Mr. Sears said. On this bitter night, Erin Lehman, Beacon Hill's 29-year-old program coordinator, not only brought dinner but also kept him company while he ate. So did Cynthia Scott, 65, a member who said she should have been at home with her husband, who had a cold, but was enjoying Mr. Sears's charming patter.
>
> "Just look at the rough-looking mob here this evening," Mr. Sears said, with an exaggerated sweep of the hand toward his helpers. "There's always somebody around if I need them. This is a marvelous aid to older people, especially those of us who live alone."[4]

---

[4] J. Gross, "Aging at Home: For a Lucky Few, a Wish Come True," *New York Times,* February 9, 2006.

MABLETON CASE STUDY OF AGING AND NEIGHBORHOOD CENTER

The only viable way to accept the gift and meet the challenge of longevity is to match the dramatic transformation of the twentieth century that made it possible to grow old, with an equally dramatic and fundamentally new way of being old. In the same tradition as Social Security, Medicare, Medicaid, and the Older Americans Act, any new effort cannot be small-minded or small in scope. Rather than simply focus on new funding or changes in regulations, the next significant response to the growing older-adult population must look at ALL funding. We must reconsider the way roads are designed, sidewalks are poured, houses are constructed, stores and clinics are located, parks are planned and the way opportunities for recreation and entertainment are programmed. Cholesterol scores, blood pressure, and glucose levels are often measured, but the true determinants of successful aging must assess addresses, zip codes, zoning codes, and transportation policy.[1]

—Kathryn Lawler's welcome speech to the Lifelong
Communities Charrette Team, February 2009

Lifelong Summary

Mableton is a historic suburban community that has declined over the years as it was bypassed by rail and highway traffic (figs. 12.1, 12.2).

Context: Existing, 3; Proposed, 6

Redevelopment will create a critical mass of residents, and retail will help solidify Mableton's position as a bedroom community to nearby Atlanta and Marietta. Even though it is near to both cities, Mableton will continue to be isolated by the long stretches of outdated and rundown commercial corridor of the now underutilized Bank Head Highway that connects the community to I-285 and downtown Atlanta.

---

[1]Kathryn Lawler's welcome speech to the Lifelong Communities Charrette Team, As transcribed by author, February 2009.

Figure 12.1
Mableton originally developed as railroad terminal surrounded, for the most part, by a few homesteads and woods. Today it is a small, low-density suburb of Atlanta.

Figure 12.2
Mableton functions as a town center for the surrounding southern section of Cobb County. The master plan upgrades the urbanism to a quality and form more appropriate to a town center.

Connectivity and Access: Existing, 7; Proposed, 9

Mableton's historic grid remains intact and with a few strategic road additions and pedestrian improvements it could be well connected. Currently, transit is limited to regional routes. An internal circulator bus route is proposed.

Dwellings and Retail: Existing, 4; Proposed, 8

Dwellings are currently limited to single-family homes on large lots. Retail is present, but mostly in the form of auto-oriented strip malls along the major arterials.

Community Building Spaces: Existing, 5; Proposed, 10

Mableton has many existing community building spaces, but lacks a quality pedestrian realm to connect them. Because they are disconnected, they do not foster informal use and integration into the daily lives of residents.

Health and Wellness: Existing, 3; Proposed, 10

Currently, there are few health and wellness services and facilities in the neighborhood. The lifelong redevelopment concept proposes many additions to this category.

Walk Score: Existing, 62; Proposed, 80+

Overview

Mableton is a small suburban community just outside of the City of Atlanta that is seeking to reposition itself in the region as an attractive, livable community for people of all ages. It is reviewed in this chapter as an example of a community readying to redevelop, not as a community that has arrived at a mature state like Beacon Hill or Penn South. Since 2009, Mableton has been the focus of an intense Lifelong Communities Initiative led by the Atlanta Regional Commission (ARC), the regional planning and intergovernmental coordination agency for the ten-county metropolitan area. The Lifelong Communities Initiative is intended to develop policy and programs that will better integrate aging issues into regional planning processes.

ARC developed the Lifelong Communities Initiative in 2007 as a comprehensive effort to help communities in the metro area respond to a changing population and its diverse needs. The Initiative is a set of interdisciplinary regional programs and policies intended to support people to remain in their homes and communities. The program grew out of the Commission's Aging Division, the region's Area Agency on Aging, but it has since grown to involve disciplines from other of the commission's divisions including transportation, land use, and government services. In May 2008, the ARC board underscored the interdisciplinary approach of the initiative by adopting the three Lifelong Community goals as agency-wide policy. The work is based on the premise that it is not possible to meet the needs of the growing older adult population with supportive programs or innovations in healthcare alone, but rather it requires rethinking plans and regulations for the built environment.

ARC resolution adopted May 2008:

> Now therefore, be it resolved that the Atlanta Regional Commission Board as representatives of the communities that make up the ten county metropolitan area, *adopts*

as agency policy its goal to transform the Atlanta Region into a Lifelong Community by: promoting housing and transportation options, encouraging healthy lifestyles, and expanding information and access services.[2]

By 2009, cities and counties in the region had successfully implemented a wide range of programs and policies to support the goals of a Lifelong Community. Still, a number of specific challenges prevented the Initiative from actualizing its goals:

- Local officials, planners, and developers did not have concrete examples of what lifelong communities look like and how design principles can shape them. The region needs practical ideas to better integrate housing and transportation alternatives and retail and health services into neighborhoods.

- Lifelong Communities challenge existing development patterns and regulations. While many community groups and professionals acknowledge that change is needed, accepting and approving plans that reflect new ways of organizing communities is hard to do. ARC needs to build momentum in the region to imagine how the different goals of a Lifelong Community can be realized on the ground.

- Even after consensus is achieved, critical decisions about development are often made in late-night planning and zoning meetings. Local officials need simple and direct guidelines for deciding which developments can support the goals of a Lifelong Community and which do not.

In February of 2009, ARC hosted a nine-day lifelong communities charrette in partnership with Duany Plater-Zyberk & Company. The charrette brought together experts from around the region and across the country to examine how Atlanta area communities could become places where people of all ages and abilities can live as long as they would like. Healthcare, aging, mobility, transportation, accessibility, architecture, planning, and design experts were convened to explore the challenges of creating lifelong communities in the largely suburban landscape where most baby boomers live. The charrette developed:

- Five conceptual master plans that incorporate mixed-use, mixed-income, multi-generational designs and promote physical activity and healthy living;

- Model Lifelong Community standards and zoning codes; and

- Regional development principles to meet the needs of the growing older adult population.

Context

Mableton was one of the five communities planned as part of the lifelong communities charrette. It is one of Cobb County's oldest identified areas, although it has remained unincorporated for all but two years of its history. As a result of its

---

[2]Atlanta Regional Commission, Directors' Board Agenda, Notes, and Resolutions 2008 (Atlanta, 2008), 64. http://www.atlantaregional .com/File%20Library/About%20Us/committee%20agendas/archive/dr_board_agendas_notes_resolutions_2008.pdf

unincorporated standing, the name "Mableton" can refer to a wide geographic area and residents from all over South Cobb may refer to their community as Mableton. With a post office, regional library, and arts center all grouped at its major intersection, the historic area of Mableton has today begun to function as a town center for the entire southern section of Cobb County. The community is in flux as the county gears up to implement some of the first phases of its recently completed redevelopment master plan and new form-based zoning code for the area. With more than 30 percent of its population above the age of 65, the community is considered to be a Naturally Occurring Retirement Community (NORC) like Penn South in New York. Originally included as one of the five study sites chosen as part of the Atlanta Regional Commission's Lifelong Communities Regional Guide to Aging, Mableton has kept issues of aging and community design at the forefront of its redevelopment strategy.

Mableton is typical of towns that have been bypassed when modern interstates drew away automobile traffic and with it the stream of passing retail customers. The town has actually been twice stranded in its century and a half history. Initially developed as a watering and fueling stop for steam-driven locomotives, it had to reinvent itself when the railroad moved to long-haul diesel locomotives that no longer needed a watering hole in that location. Without the need to refuel, the train no longer stopped in Mableton. Even though Mableton lies only twelve miles to the west of downtown Atlanta, Georgia, and nine miles south of Marietta, Georgia, it has become physically and economically isolated from the region.

Isolation from the explosive and often unplanned growth in the Atlanta region over the past three decades may in the long term prove to be a blessing in disguise. Much of the urban expansion of that period was auto dependent and sprawling and will be difficult to sustain over time. The town did not experience the major investments and subsequent busts of the housing boom, thus it still waits ready for redevelopment guided by the less auto-dependent principles of lifelong design. Today, Mableton is well suited to become a compact, sustainable bedroom community for both Marietta and downtown Atlanta, and is the home to major employers like Coca-Cola, whose headquarters are only a seven-minute drive down the now underutilized Bank Head Highway (today renamed Veterans Memorial Highway). Recently, development pressures have begun returning to the area, spilling over from the heavy investment that North Cobb experienced during the past decade, and the town is poised for a comeback once again. The community has actively sought to ensure that future development will be carried out in a manner to include existing residents and to create a healthy, walkable environment for people of all ages.

Redeveloping as a Lifelong Community
Step One: Establishing Neighborhood Nodes

A common characteristic of sprawling development is a lack of identifiable neighborhood centers and edges: one neighborhood tends to spill into another with no change in character. Mableton is too large to function as a single pedestrian-oriented neighborhood, and thus initial investigation looked into how it could be best subdivided into a series of distinct, walkable neighborhoods. Four neighborhood nodes were identified:

Old Town Center   The original town center formed around the railroad depot by the tracks along the south. This old town center anchored the original main street for the town and could once again be an important transit-oriented center if a proposed regional passenger rail station is realized there. Transit-Oriented Development would provide regional access to those who are not able to drive or do not wish to do so and provide sufficient regional retail market opportunities to support the compact, mixed-use developments that are excellent environments for the aging.

The Barnes Site   The Barnes homestead is a 23.5-acre parcel that is currently the largest private development site in Mableton and an opportunity to integrate some Lifelong Communities facilities into Mableton.

John Mable House Area   The John Mable House was not the original town center, but with its collection of post office, library, arts center, amphitheater, and other civic functions immediately surrounding, it currently functions as the town center for the South Cobb area. The John Mable House has all the ingredients necessary to establish a clear center and place-identity for the area. Developing a sense of arrival and place, this site is absolutely critical to its regional role as a town center. It is easy to slip by Mableton while traveling on Floyd without ever noticing the community. The redevelopment will need to shape an entire environment that reflects the place and character of Mableton as an important South Cobb regional destination.

Mableton Elementary School Site   The school anchors the northern end of Church Street, which was the original main street for the town. The school site holds promise as a neighborhood center for health, recreation, and education programs. If Floyd Road redevelopment is critical to Mableton's regional role, Mableton Elementary School is the most significant opportunity to improve the community's internal core. The trend in Cobb County, as in most of the nation, is to view an elementary school as a regional facility whose immediate surrounding neighborhood is incidental to its function. However, Mableton Elementary is not off by itself in a field at the edge of town: It is in the heart of Mableton and perched at its highest point. As the heart of the community, the school has rare opportunities to weave its program into its surroundings for the benefit of students, older adults, and all other neighborhood residents.

No single public or private entity will be emerging to assemble all property in Mableton, to then carry out in lock step a perfectly logical and sequential redevelopment process. Instead, the county's master plan and form-based code will work incrementally over time to coordinate the independent timing and decision-making of all of Mableton's individual property owners. The absence of a master development entity places a greater burden on the larger initial public and private interventions to set a direction and example for the look and feel of future redevelopment. If implemented well, these initial actions can anchor the overall framework of the master plan and help establish the momentum and credibility necessary to influence the actions of the surrounding individual owners as they work on their properties over time.

Step Two: Enhancing Connectivity and Access

As discussed in Chapter 5, connectivity and access are absolutely necessary for lifelong neighborhoods: A well-networked street and transit system is the enabling prerequisite requirement for many of the other urban features covered in this chapter.

In historic Mableton, the existing street network is reasonably well connected and is a mix of rectilinear grids in the area that was originally subdivided in the 1890s with more organic sections to the east that probably evolved over time from footpaths and dirt drives (fig. 12.3). The original blocks are scaled well and subdivide the neighborhood into comfortable walking routes. Outside of the historic area the urban fabric is more recently developed and does not cohesively mesh with the original street network: Streets do not form blocks and result in long distances between intersections. This latter development is much more oriented to automobile traffic than foot traffic and concentrates the automobiles onto a few arterials rather than dispersing it across multiple local roads. A rail corridor to the south is bridged at only three points in the immediate vicinity and thus it forms a strong southern boundary for the area.

The thoroughfare network adjustments proposed in the master plan enhance connections within the community while taking advantage of every possible opportunity to extend connection opportunities to some of the more recently development surrounding the historic area (fig. 12.4).

The master plan prioritizes a collection of small road extensions to better connect the interior of the community and significant redesigns of the major arterials to create more pedestrian friendly frontages. The master plan builds upon existing

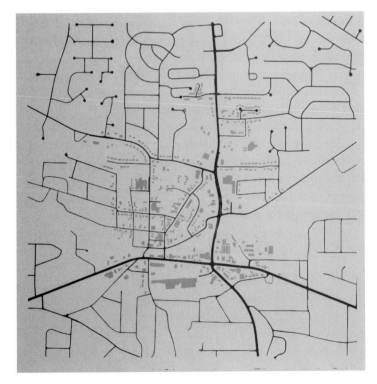

Figure 12.3
The original street grid is a mix of rectangular and organic sections, beyond which most of the more recent development is in a cul-de-sac and loop-road form.

Figure 12.4
The proposed thoroughfare network introduces patches to better weave the urban fabric. The patches are carefully woven to follow property lines and vacant lots in order to avoid displacement.

sidewalk installation programs and proposes a wide range of streetscape improvements to better integrate traffic into a pedestrian scaled environment. These include reduced or reclaimed front setbacks, planted medians, and a civic square. Most notable among these improvements is that the major north to south arterial, Floyd Road, will be transformed from a high-speed suburban road into a true boulevard, with a median and slip roads accommodating parallel parking, one-way lanes, and well-protected sidewalks. Though the proposed design requires some acquisition and reorganization to reach its fullest potential, it demonstrates how a cohesive and welcoming pedestrian environment could evolve over time.

Mableton's transit stops would provide much more local mobility if a local circulating bus was added as shown (fig. 12.5). The circulator bus would better connect the four neighborhood nodes with regional bus and train routes resulting in better transit access and enhanced customer catchment areas for local retail. This coordinated assemblage of transit options would serve the full range of transit needs throughout a lifetime: bus routes for school age children, regional commuting to employment centers for working adults, and circulation throughout the community for the daily-need errands of people of all ages.

Step Three: Enhancing Dwellings and Retail

Mableton area is currently composed of single-family detached housing. Redevelopment as a Lifelong Community would need to introduce the wide variety of housing types proposed in the plan. These range from apartments and townhomes to single-family homes. Live-work units are a particularly attractive type for older adults that continue to work but no longer commute to an office.

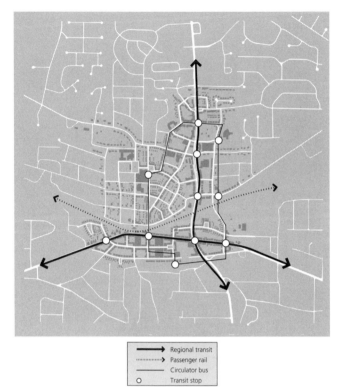

Figure 12.5
A circulator bus route is proposed that will help integrate the regional transit line with local retail centers.

→	Regional transit
⇢	Passenger rail
—	Circulator bus
O	Transit stop

Mableton does not yet have the critical mass of retail enterprises necessary for achieving its full potential as a retail and service center for the area. To better support this potential, the master plan structures three distinct neighborhood units connected by a circulating shuttle bus. There is probably not a sufficient market catchment area to support retail for all daily needs in each neighborhood, but between the three, most necessities could be provided in neighborhood settings (fig. 12.6). However, a critical piece of the design strategy is to capture the strip mall to the south within a neighborhood structure and redevelop it as a mixed-use development. Infilling the site with dense housing and retail units could provide the critical mass of residents to support retail in the area.

At the initiation of its master planning process for the area, Cobb County's zoning of Mableton prevented the diversification of the housing stock and the integration of retail into neighborhood centers. The existing zoning code was a conventional suburban development approach that divides a community into several separate zones, each of which permit only a single building use and a single type of building type. In order to create conditions more conducive to the development of cohesive buildings of diverse types capable of supporting a wide range of uses, the county created a new overlay zoning code to accompany the new master plan (fig. 12.7; see also fig. 6.3).

Critical to creating a more diverse, mixed-use environment is greater attention to the shape of the public realm through regulating the placement, massing, and frontage detailing of the lining buildings. It is the coordination of a cohesive public realm that allows the private buildings to be more diverse in type and use without appearing to be out of place with each other (fig. 12.8).

Figure 12.6
The master plan shapes main street settings that move retail from its current strip forms to more neighborhood-compatible storefront forms.

Figure 12.7
The community is divided into designated transect zones. These zones are used to structure regulations by the desired urban form rather than by restricting uses.

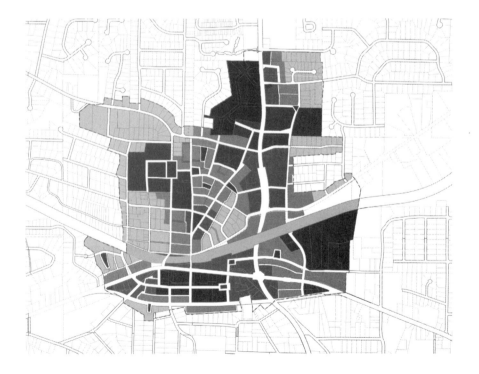

SMARTCODE 134.286.5. TRADITIONAL NEIGHBORHOOD DEVELOPMENT STANDARDS
Mableton, Georgia

TABLE 5C - PRIVATE FRONTAGES

		SECTION		PLAN	
		PRIVATE ▶ FRONTAGE	◀ PUBLIC FRONTAGE	PRIVATE ▶ FRONTAGE	◀ PUBLIC FRONTAGE
T2 T3	**a. Common Yard:** A planted *frontage* wherein the *facade* is set back substantially from the *frontage line*. The front yard created remains unfenced and may be visually continuous with adjacent yards, supporting a common landscape. The deep *setback* provides a buffer from the higher speed *thoroughfares*.				
T3 T4	**b. Porch & Fence:** A planted *frontage* wherein the *facade* is set back from the *frontage line* with an attached porch permitted to *encroach*. A fence at the *frontage line* maintains street spatial definition.				
T4 T5	**c. Terrace or Lightwell:** A *frontage* wherein the *facade* is set back from the *frontage line* by an elevated terrace or a sunken Lightwell. This type buffers *residential* use from urban *sidewalks* and removes the private yard from public *encroachment*.				
T4 T5	**d. Forecourt:** A *frontage* wherein a portion of the *facade* is close to the *frontage line* and the central portion is set back. The *forecourt* created is suitable for vehicular drop-offs. This type should be allocated in conjunction with other *frontage types*.				
T4 T5	**e. Stoop:** A *frontage* wherein the *facade* is aligned close to the *frontage line* with the first *story* elevated from the *sidewalk* sufficiently to secure privacy for the windows. The entrance is usually an exterior stair and landing but may be recessed into the volume of the building in where *setbacks* are shallow.				
T4 T5	**f. Shopfront:** A *frontage* wherein the *facade* is aligned close to the *frontage line* with the building entrance at *sidewalk* grade. This type is conventional for *retail* use. It has a substantial glazing on the *sidewalk* level and an awning that may overlap the *sidewalk*.				
T4 T5	**g. Gallery:** A *frontage* wherein the *facade* is aligned close to the *frontage line* with an attached cantilevered shed or a lightweight colonnade overlapping the *sidewalk*.				
	h. Arcade: N/A				

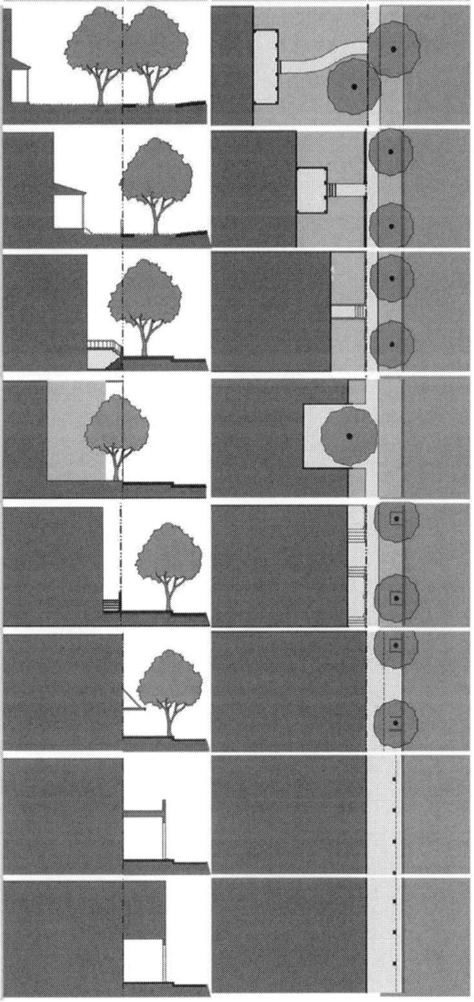

Figure 12.8
These tables from the Mableton SmartCode show how building form is regulated to produce a cohesive public realm out of the spaces of the street.

As an example of what could be accomplished under the form-based code, the proposed town square is envisioned as the civic focus for the community with a few specialty retail opportunities provided to enliven the area. Because the existing shopping centers to the south and north were better suited to be the primary regional retail cores, the town square was designed to target specialty and "third place" venues. The mix of these three retail types in close proximity could improve the market prospects of each (figs. 12.9, 12.10).

Figure 12.9
The intersection of Floyd and Clay Roads is home to a public library, a post office, a community art center, and a history museum. In spite of this abundance of civic assets, the intersection has little civic realm to bring them together.

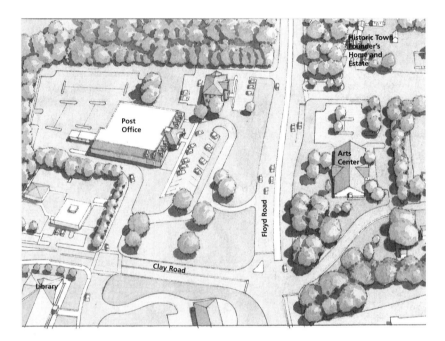

Figure 12.10
The master plan proposes taking advantage of the abundance of underutilized right-of-way to redevelop the intersection as a civic square.

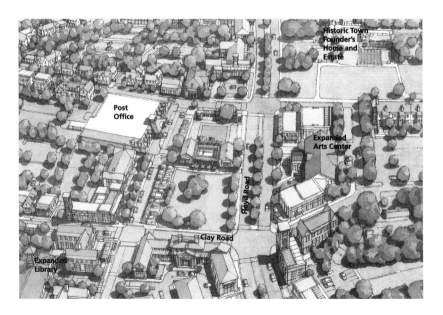

Figure 12.11
Neighborhood squares and greens are proposed throughout Mableton are shown in black. These public spaces encourage social interaction and recreation and can help keep older adult residents engaged and active. They include greens, parks, squares, and linear greens along road ways.

Step Four: Community Building Spaces

Currently in Mableton, there are significant existing or easy-to-realize opportunities for social interaction spaces throughout the community, although they could be immediately improved by better pedestrian connection. For example, in the town center site it is nearly impossible to imagine an older adult or child walking to the library and then stopping by the post office before heading to the arts center. The facilities are all within a few hundred feet of each other, but they somehow manage to exist in complete isolation from one another. There is no urbanism to connect them.

This isolation within close proximity represents a significant lost opportunity for community building. Without the interstitial urbanism, these facilities all serve as intentional destinations for focused social exchange, but the important opportunity for chance encounters that occur between destinations is lost. Residents will not bump into their neighbors and say hello while walking from the post office to the arts center. When driving past the library on the way to the post office a resident will probably not see that his favorite local author is giving a reading inside, or that the book he has been waiting for is now available. These chance encounters with neighbors and events are very important to the high percentage of older adults prone to depression and withdrawal. Chance encounters are more likely to keep an older adult engaged.

The master plan proposes a relatively easy way to meaningfully insert some urbanism between existing civic and cultural institutions (fig. 12.12). A civic square cobbled together out of a collection of parking lots, vacant property, and existing street right-of-way also resolves the awkward and dangerous traffic situation in this area. With this square in place, an entirely new realm of social interaction is created

Figure 12.12
Proposed greenway corridors support recreation, environmental quality, and biodiversity.

that would encourage residents to be more effortlessly engaged with other people and interesting events even during the times when their motivation to do so wanes.

The proposed design for redevelopment of this area organizes a collection of civic, cultural, and open spaces all within close proximity, but each with its own character and purpose. The inserted square has a formal, civic character: the Mable property maintains the rural history and culture of the area; the surrounding neighborhood retail districts would provide rich opportunities for third-places like coffee houses and cafés. Weaving together these types of socially fertile spaces provides the opportunities for social engagement that are critical to a lifelong neighborhood.

Proposed Greenway Corridors   Figure 12.12 depicts the proposed open-space network for the study area. Parks, squares, plazas, and greenways are all featured, with many of the greenways enhancing the connection to the Silver Comet Trail, which is a half mile north of the site. Public civic space, including pocket parks and small plazas, will be accessible within a less than five-minute walk of every residence, and will serve as community gathering places for neighborhood residents and visitors.

Walking Loops and Signage   Figure 12.13 highlights street and path "loops" to designate as walking and running routes. For those who walk or run on a regular basis, the routes they take significantly influence their neighborhood perception. Walking and running routes help establish a more intimate familiarity with neighbors and the neighborhood along the route and can contribute to a greater sense of ownership and safety. Many inexpensive amenities are available to enhance this experience ranging from tree species labels to resting and gathering area furniture. A little extra attention along these routes would go a long way in increasing the health, well-being, and sense of stewardship among residents.

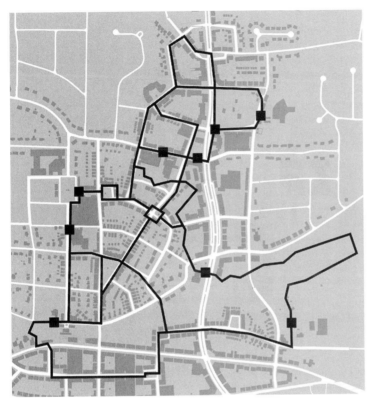

Figure 12.13
Walking loops are inexpensive to develop but can provide many lifelong benefits. Walking in groups or individually helps residents to monitor their community and develop more comfort and familiarity with its spaces. This walking loop plan proposes point-of-interest nodes where street furniture and informative signage would enhance recreational uses.

The master plan features a variety of options for pedestrians, including sidewalks along the streets, some cross-block passages, as well as a robust greenway system. These connections encourage walking for both transportation and recreation, and they can be important elements in community building.

Civic Buildings   Existing civic buildings include the Mableton Elementary School, a history center, amphitheater, public library, arts center, and post office (fig. 12.14). Civic buildings proposed for new construction include an expansion of the arts center, a YMCA, an urban campus for the elementary school, and a new rail station along Floyd Road to support the future passenger rail service. For a lifelong approach to community design, it is not only important that these types of civic facilities exist nearby, but also that they are integrated into the surrounding neighborhood. Too often civic buildings are planned in a way that ignores their local context and does not contribute to a main street or civic square context.

Intergenerational Gardens   The master plan proposes the integration of gardens in central locations rather than residual spaces left over after development is finished (fig. 12.15). Prominent locations increase the likelihood that the gardens will support social gathering and interaction as well as the more practical food production functions.

Figure 12.14
Civic buildings line both the new town square and the new elementary school campus.

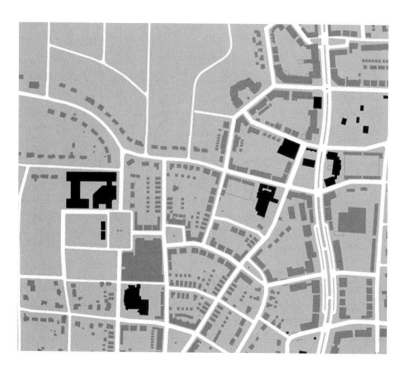

Figure 12.15
The master plan proposes designating some public spaces for community garden programs.

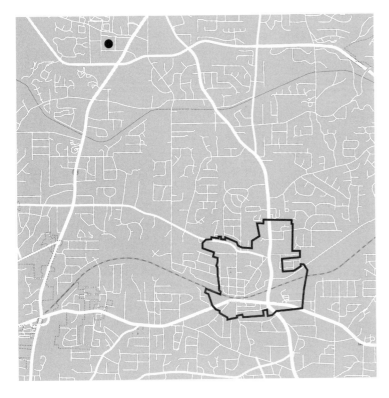

Figure 12.16
A large regional hospital is two miles away to the north.

Step Five: Health and Wellness Supports

The traditional, comprehensive, market-tested solution to supplying senior housing, service, and care needs has been the Continuing Care Retirement Community (CCRC), which provides the full range of independent living apartments and homes, assisted-living apartments, and guaranteed access to various forms of more intensive care such as rehab and long-term care nursing, memory support, and even hospice. The CCRC also provides a wide array of lifestyle enhancing services and amenities, from multiple dining venues to holistic programs, supportive of all aspects of wellness, including physical, medical, emotional, social, intellectual, spiritual, and creative dimensions of life. The diversity of physical spaces in which these various programs occur takes place in one or more facilities that collectively are known as the community center or commons. These buildings can often rival the finest country club or resort hotel in their design and accoutrements.

Like cruise ships, the vast majority of CCRCs are completely self-contained: Every amenity and service, multiple dining settings, and a range of accommodations are made available to residents. Like a cruise ship, a CCRC can feel like a world onto itself, separate from the environment that surrounds it. Most CCRCs are in isolated suburban settings and do not have any relationship with the very community they serve. Also like a cruise ship, the typical CCRC provides luxurious settings for luxury pricing. The CCRC is nearly always privately financed and paid for by the residents through entry fees and monthly service charges.

Figure 12.17
The proposed Barnes Square development, highlighted in gray, contains all the components of a CCRC clustered together but integrated into the wider community fabric. CCRC components include (1) independent living apartments; (2) an assisted-living home and home-based care hub serving the surrounding community; (3) a memory support small house; (4) a skilled nursing small house; (5) a rehab clinic serving residents and outpatient clients; (6) independent living cottages, town homes, and mansion apartments; and (7) a skilled nursing home.

The Proposed Barnes Square Model

The proposed Barnes Square expands the cruise ship model of senior housing development and opens it to a neighborhood center available to the old and young alike. There will be no fence or gate around the development; rather, it will face a public street and engage the public realm of the community. The proposed concept anticipates that at this site a small array of neighborhood retailers will provide some of the services that are typically incorporated into a CCRC: possibly a bistro, coffee shop, convenience store, pharmacy, or home-care outreach storefront. However, rather than the cost of providing such facilities being borne on the shoulders of the relatively few CCRC residents, the entire retail market will share those facilities, yielding greater affordability to all, and further breaking down the cruise ship model (see fig. 6.3).

In addition to opening up the physical form of the senior housing development, the district serviced by the provider will also expand beyond the development's boundaries. An outpatient rehabilitation facility is planned that will serve both residents and the larger public. Care services will also be provided beyond the development's property boundaries. Wireless technological innovations will allow in-home monitoring of seniors in varying degrees. When care delivery is no longer efficient or appropriate through in-home care, a small assisted living apartment facility in the heart of the neighborhood is proposed for those who need more assistance with activities of daily living. Ideally, the housing facility will serve as a hub, providing medical offices, rehab facilities or perhaps adult daycare services for the whole surrounding community and not just its own residents. As discussed in Chapter 7, many forward thinking sponsors and operators of CCRCs and other senior services are seeing this new model as a way of expanding their reach to serve a larger market. As the tremendous growth of aging baby boomers impacts our society, this new form of community-integrated senior housing and home care services will likely become more commonplace.

Barnes Square plays a formative role in shaping a distinct community with a center and an edge and a strong emphasis on public spaces. The combination of a geographic focus and a defined limit help create a sense of place: a social and cultural identity that includes people of all ages. In this case, the geographic focus is positioned at the outer edge of the senior development at the main neighborhood intersection and entry, but the center may in other cases be any square, green, neighborhood retail center, or important street intersection that provides a primary public gathering space for the community. Civic buildings and spaces as well as shops and workplaces that serve the community are concentrated in the center, optimally including senior services. Senior developments integrate into this general community mix rather than tuck into a distinct senior housing pod with its own separate and isolated center. The lifelong neighborhood gives priority to the creation of public space and to the appropriate location of civic buildings and senior facilities.

Lifelong Mableton

Lifelong Mableton is a three-year effort to reenvision Mableton as a healthy place for all ages to live. It is a partnership between the Atlanta Regional Commission, a committee of technical advisors, and a stakeholders steering committee composed of Mableton residents. The initiative operates out of an office in the greater Mableton area with a full-time project manager. It is funded by one of only thirteen federal grants awarded nationwide by the Administration on Aging. The goals of Lifelong Mableton are to advance the lifelong principles of housing and transportation options, healthy living, and expanded access to services. Some of the early projects of the initiative have been a walkability assessment, the organization of a Farmers' Market, the creation of a Historic Community Garden, and the creation of a Walking Club.

Mableton Elementary School Redeveloped as a Civic Center

While the development of a town square is critical to Mableton's regional role, Mableton Elementary School is the most significant opportunity to improve the neighborhood's core. A critical aspect of the potential elementary school site is to recast the public school as a lifelong facility capable of supporting the needs of a wide range of residents. Reimagining schools to perform more extensive ranges of community service will be critical in the future as the population skews increasingly to older demographics. Currently, older adult constituents often vote against school bonds and referendums simply because they can see no personal stake in those facilities. It would take very little adjustment to schools to change that impression by benefiting a larger segment of the public.

The trend in Cobb County, as in most of the nation, is to view an elementary school as a regional facility, serving the needs of a limited range of age groups (some subset of school age children), whose immediate surrounding neighborhood is incidental to its function.

The image of a recently completed Cobb school is an example of this detachment (fig. 12.18). Developed as an isolated pod, the school sits in the middle of its property surrounded by fields and parking lots. The building does not contribute to forming a street wall with neighboring buildings and it taps into the arterial it fronts at two points rather than weaving into a network of local streets.

Mableton Elementary is a good counterpoint to this typical approach. It is not off by itself in a field at the edge of town: It is the heart of Mableton, perched at the highest geographic point, and nestled within a network of local streets. As the heart of the community, the school has opportunities to weave its program into the surroundings for the benefit of both students and neighborhood residents. The school is well located to function as a neighborhood center and to draw on the Mable House, arts center, library, and Barnes Amphitheater, as well as a proposed YMCA—all as an expansive community campus (fig. 12.19).

Two critical elements are necessary to achieving these campus/community integration goals. First, the school building must pull up close to the street so that it can be part of the surrounding street wall and integrate into the pedestrian-oriented environment. Second, playing fields, parking lots, and all other open spaces must integrate into a larger open-space network, preferably open to a variety of community uses outside school hours. A third, nonessential but advantageous element is the coordination of the school redevelopment with the development of an adjoining YMCA. The school board is considering a proposal in which the new school would be developed without a gymnasium and would instead enter into a cooperative endeavor agreement with the YMCA for use of their gymnasium during the necessary school hours. This cooperative agreement would help the YMCA fund its development and would also extend the benefits of the gymnasium to a

Figure 12.18

The school building type being built across Cobb County exists as an autonomous program that is accessed entirely by vehicle and has no relationship to the surrounding urban fabric.

Smith Aerial Photos

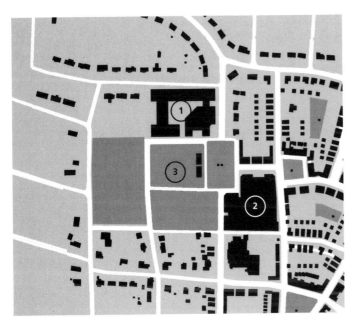
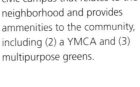

Figure 12.19
The master plan repositions the school (1) as an element of a civic campus that relates to the neighborhood and provides ammenities to the community, including (2) a YMCA and (3) multipurpose greens.

Figure 12.20
The proposed school is detailed to contribute to the neighborhood's style and setting.

wide range of residents, young and old alike. Additionally the association with the YMCA would serve to extend to the students a wide range of after-school programs regularly provided by the Y. All three of these elements help move the school from a self-contained, segregated operation, into a form more appropriate to the large public investment it represents: an integrated community center that contributes to the civic realm of its community (fig. 12.20). In addition to enhancing the learning environment and providing multiple values to the neighborhood, the configuration also makes use of the street network to efficiently stack busses and provide parallel parking alternatives to expansive parking lots.

ELDER-CENTRIC VILLAGES: EXPLORING HOW SENIOR HOUSING CAN INCENTIVIZE URBAN RENEWAL IN RURAL AMERICA

CHAPTER 13

Contributed by Dodd Kattman, AIA, LEED AP,
and Zachary Benedict, Assoc. AIA, LEED AP

Lifelong Summary

Next we discuss a program working in rural areas of Indiana (fig. 13.1), encouraging the adaptive reuse of small, historic town centers as seniors housing, and discouraging continued development of green field seniors housing developments. Scoring of urban conditions is not applicable to this consulting practice.

In analyzing the dynamics of rural cities within Indiana, every city within the state with populations between 10,000 and 25,000 people[1] were examined in an effort to explore the feasibility of utilizing seniors to stimulate and temporarily stabilize the localized economy of existing downtowns. As the data were collected for these cities, two statistics continually surfaced as critical components to this thinking: (1) the percentage of the population age 65 and older and (2) the percentage of the population with a bachelors degree or higher (fig. 13.2). The target cities were

Photo by Morrison Kattman Menze, Inc. (2009)

Figure 13.1
Downtown Kendallville.

---

[1] The thirty-one cities explored by this research effort included (from largest to smallest): Crown Point, Franklin, La Porte, Logansport, Seymour, New Castle, Vincennes, Shelbyville, Huntington, Greenfield, Frankfort, Crawfordsville, Lebanon, Connersville, Beech Grove, Jasper, New Haven, Lake Station, Bedford, Warsaw, Peru, Auburn, Madison, Martinsville, Washington, Wabash, Plymouth, Greensburg, Princeton, Greencastle, and Kendallville.

Figure 13.2
Community demographic comparisons, December 2009.

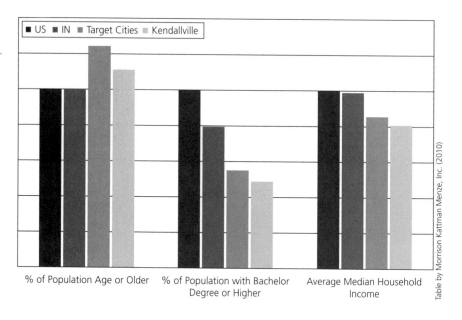

Table by Morrison Kattman Menze, Inc. (2010)

found to be exposed to 24.2 percent more residents 65 and older and 45.1 percent fewer individuals with a bachelor's degree or higher, when compared to the national average. This further highlights the challenges many rural communities face in the coming decades. Therefore, as "Brain Drain" haunts many rustbelt communities, this escalating presence of aging baby boomers will only further shift the cultural identity of many small cities and towns throughout the Midwest. While these trends were further considered, the theories outlined to respond to this phenomenon were tested in Kendallville, Indiana, the smallest of the target cities.[2]

As the physical organization of each of these target cities is still suited to accommodate a vibrant walkable neighborhood, the sidewalks are often empty, leaving downtown business owners nervously waiting for a renewed pedestrian activity to increase their sales and in some cases save their businesses. What if the growing senior population was the catalyst needed to renew this main street activity?

To outline the impact older adult residents could grant rural communities, special attention should be given to the activity patterns of seniors. In a survey of Indiana residents age 60 or older,[3] participants indicated that within the last week they engaged in the following activities:

■ 61 percent socialized with friends or neighbors

■ 57 percent attended church, temple, or another religious event

■ 67 percent attended movies, sporting events, or group events

[2]Kendallville is a city of 10,018 residents (per 2005 census data) located in northeast Indiana (Noble County). Median age = 32.2; percentage of population age 65 or older = 13.8; percentage of population with bachelor's degree or higher = 11.9; and median household income (1999 USD) = 33,899.

[3]AdvantAge Initiative Community Survey in Indiana, *AdvantAge Initiative: Improving Communities for an Aging Society* (Centers for Home Care Policy & Research, 2008) http://www.agingindiana.org/files/survey%20reports/state/Indiana_CHARTS.pdf.

- 88 percent engaged in at least one social, religious, or cultural activity

- 39 percent participated in volunteer work

Surprisingly, this study also revealed that 85 percent of this demographic voted in their local elections in the last three years, highlighting the growing political power this population will undoubtedly have on the identity and market habits of the local civic policy trends within these smaller communities—most notably the reprioritization of a pedestrian lifestyle.

Evaluating Small-Town Living and Walkability

With the demand for these walkable urban neighborhoods increasing, so too has an interest grown in providing metrics to gauge the actual walkability of specific areas. In a study facilitated by *CEO for Cities* that analyzed data from 94,000 real estate transactions, the worth of walkable neighborhoods was demonstrated by increased property values in locations where key "destinations" were within walking distance. Calculated through a Walk Score algorithm,[4] properties were awarded points based on the distance to amenities in various categories within a one-mile proximity (e.g., grocery stores, restaurants, coffee shops, bars, movie theaters, schools, parks, libraries, bookstores, fitness, drug stores, hardware stores, clothing stores, and music stores). The scores are then summed and normalized to yield a score from 0 to 100 with the following scorecard:[5]

- 90–100: Walker's Paradise—daily errands do not require access to a car

- 70–89: Very Walkable—most errands can be accomplished on foot

- 50–69: Somewhat Walkable—some amenities within walking distance

- 25–49: Car-Dependent—a few amenities within walking distance

- 0–24: Car-Dependent—almost all errands require a car

Ultimately, the study established that a one-point increase in a Walk Score resulted in an increase of property value ranging from $700 to $3,000.[6]

Additionally, when discussing the future of an aging population, the concept of walkable environments becomes even more critical. As these individuals age, their mobility and endurance decreases, often resulting in an inability to drive or walk long distances (commonly walking no more than 900 feet or three city blocks). By stripping them of their freedom and independence, these limitations can be devastating for seniors. However, the walkable environments so common in downtown rural communities offer the elderly the ability to live near the everyday goods and

---

[4]While the Walk Score algorithm calculates the diversity and proximity of goods and services within a predetermined "walkable" distance, it does not calculate other challenges that should be addressed when considering environments for the elderly. Special attention should be given to specific elements within an area's infrastructure (e.g., frequent curb cuts, delayed crosswalk signalization, outdoor seating and areas of respite).

[5]For more information see Walk Score's website at www.walkscore.com.

[6]J. Cortright, "Walking the Walk: How Walkability Raises Home Values in U.S. Cities," *CEO for Cities* (August 2009).

Figure 13.3
Downtown Kendallville's urban core overlaid with the footprint of a regional CCRC.

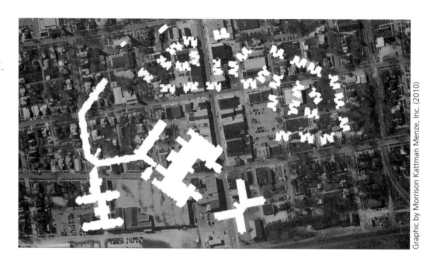

Graphic by Morrison Kattman Menze, Inc. (2010)

services needed to age-in-place,[7] often with walking distances comparable to or less than conventional senior living campuses (fig. 13.3). In understanding the marketability of these walkable environments, existing rural communities can position themselves as ideal locations in response to the preference of intergenerational living.

In the pursuit to better connect elderly populations with rural communities as a response to the market demand introduced by retiring baby boomers, a quick and effective way to quantify the available amenities within the immediate area can be found by exploring the Walk Scores of existing neighborhoods. As the demand for these areas grow, the ability to market the walkability of existing rural cities will become a valuable commodity for communities, especially as a resource for amenity-seeking seniors.

By compiling a listing of the 166 senior care providers affiliated with the Indiana Association of Homes and Services for the Aging (IAHSA), this case study evaluated the walkability of existing senior living environments throughout Indiana. The geographic disconnects between these facilities and their neighboring downtowns were clearly evident. While the average Walk Score for an Indiana senior care provider was 42.85, the average score for their respective community's local downtown area was 76.23. More notably, sixteen senior living campuses received a score of less than 10, with eight facilities receiving a score of 0 (table 13.1).

While the walkability of these campuses becomes a vital concern for the residents, it also offers a unique opportunity regarding the financial burden assumed by the more isolated campuses. As the Walk Score increases, so does the senior care provider's ability to fundamentally rely on the local community's private sector to provide independent residents with cultural and social amenities (e.g., movie theaters, ice cream parlors, beauty salons). Inversely, the lower scores assume the responsibility of the care providers creating, operating, and maintaining these more internalized on-site amenities.

---

[7]For more information on age-friendly mobility infrastructure reference the World Health Organization's report, "Global Age-Friendly Cities," 2007.

Table 13.1

WALK SCORE COMPARISON, DECEMBER 2009			
Description	Walk Score Range	Senior Living Campuses (%)	Adjacent Downtowns (%)
Car-Dependent	0–24	25.7	3.0
Car-Dependent	25–49	33.5	9.0
Somewhat Walkable	50–69	28.1	15.6
Very Walkable	70–89	10.8	47.9
Walker's Paradise	90–100	1.8	24.6

To explore the monetary savings assumed by allowing independent living residents to access their daily goods and services through the private sector, closer consideration was given to the specific conditions found in Kendallville, Indiana. Within this strategy, care providers would be granted the ability to (a) remove the construction and/or maintenance costs from the campus's operational budget, and (b) allow seniors the ability to experience these activities as an inclusive member of an intergenerational community. In working with an existing CCRC located along the outskirts of the city (referred to throughout this case study as Provider ABC), this scenario was explored in greater detail.

Located within a campus isolated from the historic downtown Kendallville (the CCRC and downtown area had Walk Scores of 18 and 72, respectively), Provider ABC was preparing to increase their independent living offering by thirty-two units.[8] In addition to these residential apartments, the proposed project scope also included a series of services within an internalized mall (e.g., salon, café, etc.). The research explored how removing these support and social amenities from the project scope would affect the overall construction budget and, if within the predetermined walking distance of 900 or so feet, how the reintroduction of these services within the private sector would affect the vitality of the existing downtown area.

Although the square footage for the proposed residential units remained identical within the two scenarios, the reduced need for support and activity space decreased the construction total from $6,420,975 ($200,665 per unit) to $3,341,250 ($104,414 per unit)—a savings that resulted in an approximate reduction of 48 percent in the overall estimated costs (table 13.2).

The ability to rely on these walkable areas to provide social services and support spaces dramatically increases as rural cities increasingly pursue downtown realization efforts. Furthermore, as care providers prepare for the influx in resident census, this strategy can become an attractive method in offering unique intergenerational living options for future residents while granting providers a product that could be offered as market-rate housing as post-boomer censuses decline. More specifically, this approach becomes a unique strategy for rural communities to compete

---

[8]These additional thirty-two independent living units were validated by two separate third-party market studies commissioned by Provider ABC indicating that the local economic climate could support these proposed units.

Table 13.2

COST COMPARISON OF SUBURBAN AND URBAN MODELS, MARCH 2010*		
Building Element	**Cost, Suburban ($)[†]**	**Cost, Urban ($)[‡]**
Site Development**		
General earthwork	100,000	75,000
Storm-water detention	75,000	35,000
Parking, roads, etc.	150,000	50,000
Lawns, landscapes, etc.	75,000	60,000
Site lighting	50,000	25,000
Furniture, Fixtures, and Equipment (FF&E)[††]		
Food-service equipment	160,000	—
Dining furniture	12,000	—
Misc. furniture and equipment	40,000	40,000
Low-voltage systems	25,000	25,000
Project subtotal	*5,837,250*	*3,037,500*
Soft costs	583,725	303,750
TOTAL[‡‡]	6,420,975	3,341,250

*Both the Suburban and Urban models assume 32 independent living apartments—12 one-bedroom units at 650 sq. ft. each, 12 one-bedroom deluxe units at 775 sq. ft. each, 6 two-bedroom units at 900 sq. ft. each, and 2 two-bedroom deluxe units at 1,100 sq. ft. each.

[†]Estimated costs include 5,220 sq. ft. of common space (e.g., lobby, lounge, activity room, etc.) and 4,415 sq. ft. of support spaces (e.g., kitchen, dining area, storage, etc.)—all based on best practices for conventional independent living facilities.

[‡]Estimated costs include a reduced allocation of commons space of 800 sq. ft. of common space (specifically, the removal of the conference and activity areas) and 1,775 sq. ft. of support spaces (specifically, the removal of the kitchen and dining areas)—all assuming these functions are to be absorbed within the local private sector.

**The Urban model assumes a denser footprint for the living units, resulting in a reduced site development scope.

[††]The Urban model assumes dining is to be absorbed within local restaurants and eateries within walking distance of the residents.

[‡‡]Neither model has estimated costs for project financing, debt service, interest, insurance, or construction contingency associated with the overall totals.

for migrating baby boomers as they age, in an attempt to introduce new resident income and spending habits into the community.

The success of this urbanized strategy, especially as it relates to the economic growth of local businesses, is contingent on a community's willingness to understand and appreciate a collaborative pursuit for an intergenerational existence. As Jeb Brugmann emphasizes in his book *Welcome to the Urban Revolution: How Cities Are Changing the World,* this strategy "begins with the belief that progressive transformation in our cities is possible. We often perceive cities to be tethered to their problematic legacies and fixed development patterns. We tend to define them by their entrenched politics, social divisions, sunk capital investments, and gridlock. But cities are engines of self-transformation, more powerful than any established development pattern."[9]

As popular culture begins to demand walkable neighborhoods and as growing elderly populations rely on accessible services and amenities to age-in-place, rural communities will find themselves perfectly positioned to offer a vibrant intergenerational experience within their existing downtown that will redefine modern communities.

Providing an Elder-Centric Village

Assuming that this urban model would be pursued by Provider ABC, this case study concluded its research by exploring the ability to offer an Elder-Centric Village (ECV) service network through existing communal services and civic offerings. Even though many rural communities currently possess the infrastructure to offer walkable intergenerational neighborhoods that are able to accommodate an aging demographic, the success of this strategy is reliant on civic coordination and collaboration. If the economic development initiatives within struggling cities and towns can appreciate the importance of stabilizing their urban cores through an ECV, these relationships can be designed to incentivize smart growth and urban renewal.

During the fall of 2009 a focus group[10] was established to explore the potential of creating a network within the downtown areas to stabilize and increase economic activity for local businesses. The initial discussions centered on mapping the current assets within Kendallville and exploring what existing amenities could be utilized as focal points for the proposed downtown network.

Throughout these discussions it was evident that even within a city the size of Kendallville there was an exceptional variety of cultural and wellness offerings that could be utilized in the pursuit of offering an elder-friendly service network (fig. 13.4).

Graphic by Morrison Kattman Menze, Inc. (2010)

Figure 13.4
An aerial map of Kendallville, Indiana: (1) public golf course, (2) lake, (3) downtown retail district, (4) Veterans of Foreign Wars hall, (5) youth center and recreation hall, (6) elementary and middle school, (7) YMCA, (8) high school and sporting fields, (9) public park and beach, (10) library, (11) County Council on Aging, (12) county fairgrounds.

[9]J. Brugmann, *Welcome to the Urban Revolution: How Cities are Changing the World* (New York: Bloomsbury, 2009), 202–3.

[10]The focus group consisted of local elected officials from the Chamber of Commerce, the County Convention and Visitors Bureau, a local CCRC, the Aging and In-Home Services Agency, as well as various civic and community leaders and regional economic development official(s).

Following this analysis, the project established a concept of offering an age-qualified "menu of services" for residents within a defined geographic area for a monthly fee. This service would not only provide access to clinical support services, but also intended to incentivize the support of local business and downtown activities. Inspired by a recent study that found 73 percent of Indiana residents age 60 and over found appeal in a membership cooperative,[11] this network was designed to offer members a sliding scale of services through a monthly fee structure with the ability to accommodate various levels of personal need. While the discussion covered a wide variety of considerations, they primarily focused on the following six categories:

1. *In-home care:* By partnering with local care providers (e.g., CCRC, Council on Aging, YMCA, local area churches), members will have access to an inclusive offering of various care services ranging in all levels of need. Available services would include assistance with activities of daily living (ADLs), personal care and wellness, licensed home health, cooking, cleaning, light housekeeping, and select errands.

2. *Café and community center:* In addition to the various businesses located throughout the downtown area, economic development efforts would prioritize the realization of a community/senior center located at the heart of the downtown area. Designed after a similar model established by Mather Lifeways, "Mather's—More Than A Café," these facilities function as a senior center, offering social services and activities while disguised as a trendy coffee shop or café. The success of these centers is largely reliant on the adjacent community and its ability to provide affordable, quality food for all ages without being perceived as a destination designated specifically for seniors. With the surrounding neighborhood offering a critical mass of customers to support the café, these locations can be accessed by a variety of older, local residents.[12]

3. *Voucher program:* Through a partnership with the local chamber of commerce, a voucher program was designed to guarantee participants and local businesses a minimum amount of services within the monthly rate (e.g., four tickets to a local movie theater per month). By allowing these participants to exist within a series of intergenerational relationships, they serve as a critical mass for local businesses and offer a series of cultural amenities to future residents.

4. *Senior housing:* In partnership with local developers and funding support from rental housing tax credits through the state housing authority,[13] various housing options were prioritized as potential offerings within the downtown area

[11]P. Stafford, *Elderburbia: Aging with a Sense of Place in America* (Santa Barbara, CA: ABC-CLIO, 2009), 132.

[12]M. S. Rosenbaum, J. Sweeney, and C. Windhorts, "The Restorative Qualities of an Activity-Based, Third Place Café for Seniors: Restoration, Social Support, and Place Attachment at Mather's—More Than a Café," *Seniors Housing & Care Journal* 17, no.1 (2009), 39–54.

[13]For more information on Indiana's financing support for Rental Housing Tax Credits see their "Qualified Allocation Plan"; *2011 QAP* (Indiana Housing & Community Development Authority, 2011).

for local and migrating seniors. While available land was recommended by the market study for the construction of the thirty-two independent-living apartments, additional coordination was explored to offer home maintenance and technical support for additional residents throughout the area in an attempt to allow residents to remain in their existing homes.

5. *Co-working:* Despite the fact that over 45 percent of Indiana residents age 60 and over are or would like to work full or part time for pay, current economic conditions indicate that seniors will continue to work as they age.[14] While retirement planners suggest that an individual's income upon retirement should be approximately 70 percent of what their annual income was during their working years, a recent survey indicated that Kendallville area residents (those in Noble County) were at approximately 53 percent.[15] By partnering with a regional business incubator, a downtown co-working suite would be offered to promote startup businesses. Within the suite, seniors would be offered leasable space to work in exchange for donated consultation to emerging professionals in an effort to encourage intergenerational relationships.

6. *Transportation:* Although many counties or regions offer transportation for aging populations, few do so through an intergenerational offering. Inspired by the success of the transportation efforts of a neighboring county that saw their senior ridership quadruple when services were offered to residents beyond the elderly,[16] this service would allow all individuals with the inability to drive the freedom to maneuver throughout the city.

As these concepts were finalized with the community, it became critical to the discussion to explore how these services could be packaged and marketed as (a) lifestyle options for regional amenity-seeking elderly migrants approaching retirement and (b) an increased quality of life for Kendallville as entrepreneurial growth and economic stability are pursued within the downtown area.

---

[14]*AdvantAge Initiative Community Survey in Indiana,* 2008.

[15]R. Shawgo, "Census Numbers," *Journal Gazette* (Fort Wayne, IN), December 31, 2010.

[16]For more information see the Wells County Council on Aging website: www.councilonaginginc.com

INDEX